Sapporo

Sendai

o

PAN

*Pacific
Ocean*

Cabanatuan

LUZON

*Philippine
Sea*

San Fernando

ubic Bay

Polillo
islands

**Bataan
Peninsula**
Mariveles

Manila

*Manila
Bay*

Corregidor
Caballo island

Cavite

*Lamon
Bay*

Batangas

*Tayabus
Bay*

Atimonan

Marinduque
island

MINDORO

CAGED DRAGONS

CAGED DRAGONS

An American P.O.W. in WW II Japan

by Robert E. Haney

Sabre Press
A Division of Momentum Books Ltd.
Ann Arbor, Michigan

Manufactured in the United States of America

1994   1993   1992   1991   5   4   3   2   1

Published and Distributed by Sabre Press
A Division of Momentum Books Ltd.
210 Collingwood, Suite 106
Ann Arbor, Michigan 48103
USA

ISBN 1-879094-06-1

Selected lines from the poem "I Have a Rendezvous with Death" by Alan Seeger, used in the introduction to "Part One: A Disputed Barricade," reprinted with the permission of Charles Scribner's Sons, an imprint of Macmillan Publishing Company, from *Poems* by Alan Seeger. Copyright 1916 by Charles Scribner's Sons, renewed 1944 by Elsie Adams Seeger.

Dedication

To Sue, wife and friend; and to my children and my children's children and all those descendants who—in the marvelous chain that is a part of the human condition—may be affected in some small way by events that already seem so distant to most.

Author's Note

All of the events and conditions recorded here were experienced
or witnessed by myself. Except for totaling the numbers of
planes involved in bombing raids, and checking a few historic
dates, I have not conducted any secondary research that is reflected in the text. Memory can be fallible after half a century;
but the events I have included remain so vivid as to defy egre-
gious error. A few names have been disguised to avoid purpose-
less embarrassment or unwanted attention.

Contents

From the Publisher ix
Foreword xi
Preface xiii

Part I: A DISPUTED BARRICADE 1

1 From Michigan to the Corps 3
2 Fools' Paradise in China 11
3 A Tragedy of Errors 23
4 Retreat Toward the Enemy 39
5 Besieged in the Bay 47

Part II: KORAH!!! 73

6 The Degradation Begins 75
7 A War of Nutrition 89
8 Hell Below Deck 99
9 A Slave in Japan 109
10 Signs in the Sky 121
11 "You Will be Killed" 131
12 Never Again, Never Again 141
13 Roaming a Vanquished Land 163
14 Free and Bewildered 185
15 "I'm Not the Same" 195
16 Stateside at Last 209

Part III: AFTERMATH   219

17   An Uneasy Truce   221
18   The Silence Begins   235
19   Finding a Niche   241
20   An Island in the Hills   247
21   Pain and Progress   257

UNFINISHED BUSINESS   263

Acknowledgments   267

From the Publisher

This is the story of a brother I almost never knew. It is the story of one marine. It is also the story of countless young men who left home to serve their country. On the beaches of the Pacific and the battlegrounds of Europe. In Korea and in Vietnam. In the deserts of the Persian Gulf. Of some who came back. Of those who did not. It is the story of many who would never be the same again and who would spend a lifetime wondering what had happened to them, and forever wondering why.

Bill Haney
July 1991

Foreword

Nearly half a century has passed since Bob Haney and his compatriots began an ordeal that would rank among the cruelest captivities ever endured by American fighting men. Now, Haney has written an account of their suffering and their courage that will remind us again why Corregidor and Bataan are such hallowed names in the memories of so many Americans.

His painful retelling of the hopelessness, the deprivation and the cruelty that he suffered from the siege of Corregidor until his liberation helps us to better appreciate how dear a condition is freedom. The price to preserve that condition for a nation was never higher than when Bob Haney was called to pay it.

During his captivity, he became better acquainted than most not only with the depths of human depravity, but also with the formidable resiliency of the human spirit. To his great credit, Bob Haney exemplified the latter condition so as not to succumb to the former. In this story are the lessons of his salvation, as compelling today as they were when a 20-year-old Marine corporal dutifully obeyed his orders to buy his country a little time.

John S. McCain, III
United States Senator from Arizona
June 1991

Editor's note: Senator McCain, Captain (Ret.), U.S. Navy, was a P.O.W. during the Vietnam War.

Preface

Dragons conjured from past experience haunt us all. Most are mere nuisance beasts, intruding no more frequently or ferociously than an uncomfortable moment at a class reunion. But for some of us, unimaginable events have left terrible creatures lurking forever just beyond the campfires of mind and memory. Their shadowy outlines emerge far more often than the sun sets. Sometimes they dart forward in full view, taunting with flame-thrown bursts of too-familiar uncertainty and pain.

The psychiatrists expend huge amounts of time and patients' money seeking to identify dragons—even nuisance dragons—so they can be expunged. Give the dragons a name, it is said, and they will go away.

I never wanted or needed such detective work. I've always known my dragons. They were born under siege in the Philippines and nurtured through 41 months of slavery to the Japanese.

For four decades after the war I held the dragons at bay by caging them. I did not speak about them, even to my own family. I avoided the thousands of former soldiers, sailors and marines, American and Filipino, who had acquired their own dragons in the same time and place. If I did encounter a compatriot, we said nothing of the war. I did not even read about it, though reading is one of life's major gifts and I have always sought through books to expand my knowledge about all manner of things.

It was I, of course—not the dragons in the cage—who was held captive 40 long years in a secret desert. That realization, and this book, took shape together. I began writing at age 66. It took four years of trepidation and hurt to produce a manuscript. Now the dragons are loosed to maraud, and I am wary of them, but I am the one who is freed.

Halfway through the writing of "Moby Dick," Herman Melville worried that his whale would become a "hideous and intolerable allegory." Not to worry here. I will not use the word "dragons" again. This is simply one old corporal's war story, told straight, for whatever interest it may bear.

It is a story not of symbols and allegories but of gut-wrenchingly literal instances of valor and cowardice, ingeniousness and incompetence, human degradation and proof that the human spirit—even when pummeled beyond recognition—is a thing of incredible resiliency and strength.

I did think you should know, however, about the fire-breathing creatures that came home with all who survived.

R.E.H
July 1991

Part I

A DISPUTED BARRICADE

I have a rendezvous with Death
At some disputed Barricade
When Spring comes round with rustling shade
And apple blossoms fill the air . . .
When Spring brings back blue days and fair

* * *

And I to my pledged word am true,
I shall not fail that rendezvous
   —Alan Seeger, from "I Have a Rendezvous with Death"

1

From Michigan to the Corps

I can remember Bessie, our cow, and Teddie, our pony, and I can remember watching from a neighbor's window as our house burned level to the ground. We lived on 2½ acres about eight miles north of Detroit. We were poor. The cliche would say that we didn't notice because everyone else was poor, too. It was the Depression. The cliche was true.

Early images etched in memory—a pink-eyed rabbit and a cat that played together, the "chore" of searching for eggs in a straw-covered and spider-filled cow shed, putting Bessie out to graze, my mother reading aloud by a kerosene lamp while my father read want ads to himself—are clearer than the view from the office towers that now rise above the same real estate. Upscale shopping malls and clogged surface roads have obliterated fields that once were a good place to bag a pheasant. Nearby homes sell for more than anyone we knew made in two dozen lifetimes working two jobs. What passes for progress has made it easy to buy an expensive suit without walking too far from the car phone. The tradeoffs are enormous. Whatever values a youngster learns in the modern consumerist society would not have served me well. I doubt I would have survived the Philippines. I am certain I would not have survived Japan.

This is not to say that some kind of bucolic peace settled over our little home every evening like lights-out at the end of a "Waltons" episode. In fact, when I was 16 I fled west looking for something better, or at least something more exciting. So in a sense my childhood led me into harm's way sooner rather than later, in the earliest days of World War II. But my childhood also contributed greatly to my coming back alive.

I was the one who awakened my father in the middle of the night, after the barking of our bull terrier had awakened me. The kitchen was on fire. We all got outside to the frozen ground before the rest of the house was aflame. I remember the arson investigators questioning me closely. They went away after finding a money changer half-full of melted coins and the charred remains of the currency that was to have paid for the next load of Sinclair gasoline my father would pump at his service station.

We moved into "town," the village of Big Beaver, three short streets well-populated with small houses. Soon we matched off with neighbor children our own ages instead of associating almost exclusively within our own family. It was the first we realized how insular we had been on our acreage a mile away across cornfields and pastures. A year or so later, my parents bought one of the village houses with $600 of the fire insurance money. It was a tiny place, just one house away from the school where I was in sixth grade.

Few Detroiters today are aware that our rural village ever existed, though Big Beaver Road is now a main east-west artery in the affluent northern suburbs. Amazingly, just beyond the shadow of the office towers, our $600 home was still standing in 1991.

My parents, three sons and a daughter had lived in the burned-out farmhouse. Another brother and sister were born, after a gap of 14 years, in the glazed-brick house in Big Beaver. It was a house where the boys all slept in a 10-foot by 10-foot bedroom, where we pumped water in the kitchen, where the well went dry some summers and the basement flooded some springtimes. It was a home where I learned and practiced my religion, where we shared books with each other, where we skirmished and bedeviled and teased and took our turns at dishes, sweeping, oiling the linoleum and carrying out the slop bucket.

It was a place where I learned the difference between wants and needs.

My elder brother and I remained somewhat private in our social adjustment after moving to the village, while my younger brother, two years my junior, and my sister, two years younger still, took immediately to the "urban" life. We stayed close as a family, largely centered around my mother.

In the summer of 1936, at age 15, I was able to get a three-week taste of the hobo life, picking spinach along the Saginaw River and searching for work in the fruit-growing district farther north around Traverse City. The next summer, at 16, I managed to land two "driveaway" assignments, getting paid to drive new cars from the nearby Motor City to buyers in New Orleans and in Hartford, Connecticut. Those trips gave me great confidence in my ability to range afar and still find—and pay—my way back. The trips also helped set the stage for my departure, permanently, the next year.

Relations between my father and myself had taken a turn for the worse when I reached high school, for reasons I did not understand. He took no interest in my academic status, though I was a good student. I earned a letter in football, made all-league in basketball, and was assured by my baseball coach that my bat would win a scholarship to Michigan State College—though in those days that did not mean anything like a "full ride." Sports were important to me, and I was proud that I had some successes; but my father did not attend a single game, or even ask me about the results.

He seemed embarrassed at having to ask me to take a semester off from school to work at the gas station, which I did—later taking extra classes so I would not fall behind. That he was unable or unwilling to pay me built a barrier that I never succeeded in removing, nor did he try.

In March 1938, amid undeclared hostilities at home and a hopeless automobile-dominated economy in southeastern Michigan, I quit high school in my junior year and hit the road. The plan was vague, but it pointed to Alaska.

A youthful imagination had left me susceptible to Jack London adventure books, to several books about the fisheries of Sitka and Ketchikan, to tales of Matanuska Valley strawberries that would each fill a teacup, and to the abundance of game and fish in the Yukon. I sold the idea to my friend Jack Maddock, relying on his three-year-older wisdom for feedback. Jack was relying on what he thought was my erudition. We were a dangerous pair.

Before leaving school and home, I accumulated as much cash as I could by washing and painting houses, doing yard work, cleaning up trash, cutting lawns and gardening. The pay was about 20 cents an hour, seldom more than a dollar a day. I reclaimed returnable bottles at dump sites, and I recovered and repaired electric motors and sold them for 25 or 50 cents or whatever the traffic would bear. I put together a stake of $55. Some $10 or $15 of the total was derived from my competence as a pool player.

I had delivered two new Hudson Terraplanes intact and on time in the summer of '37, and the driveaway agent welcomed me to try again, so we had a means west. That the cars Jack and I were assigned in '38 were to be delivered to Los Angeles rather than Seattle, gateway to Alaska, bothered us not at all. It gave us a chance to see California.

I drove a Cadillac Sixty Special in the caravan. Delivery was due by Easter, to a Hollywood western personality whose name I recall as William (Wild Bill) Hall. Jack drove a Buick. A Polish mechanic from Hamtramck seeking a better job in California drove another Buick. The caravan leader drove his own car with another in tow.

When I arrived at the Cadillac's destination on West Pico Boulevard in Los Angeles, the caravan financier told me to return the next day for my pay of $5 plus a dollar a day. I told him I would, and would bring the keys with me. He paid on the spot.

Jack and I spent that night in a hotel on Pico Boulevard. It cost a dollar, double occupancy. I took a hand towel and felt guilty about it for weeks. We left the next morning for the freight yards, walking the four or five miles to downtown Los

Angeles. We found the railroad tracks and followed them northward for about a mile to the freight makeup station. Hoboes were everywhere and we easily learned which train was headed north. When it moved, we crossed a dozen sets of tracks and swung aboard. We were on our way, we thought, to Alaska.

On a siding near San Bernardino, we discovered that the train was taking us back to the Midwest. We abandoned our false start, hitchhiked back to Los Angeles and caught a bus to Santa Monica. Five days later found us in San Jose, where, on better advice, we caught a train going north.

It was a difficult trip, mostly because we were poorly prepared. We had little food, no water, and we had selected a through freight. The few stops were on sidings miles from anyplace we could get food or water. We kept to ourselves but learned that the others who were stealing a ride were farm laborers or professional rail riders, all poverty-stricken.

The train was remade at Marysville. Our group of cars was left standing while the forward section moved off. We hopped another freight, which was remade somewhere in northern California. We ended up on a gondola carrying huge logs. The gondola had a flat wheel, and the logs were heavy with pitch that promptly transferred to the seats of our pants. The flat wheel hammered so bad that we often had to stand with our knees bent to absorb the shock. Later, as we gained altitude, we were unable to sit because of our burned backsides. Again we stood for hours, this time in increasing cold. Finally, when the train stopped at Shasta, we were almost unable to crawl from the log car.

By then we had learned that the forward section of a freight train was going the farthest. We ran ahead to some boxcars that had empty reefers containing dried-out paper that had been used to control transfer of heat from ice blocks to the cooled section of the car.

It was late March. The temperature at Shasta was probably in the low 40s. We wrapped up in the paper and, with glowing backsides, got some much-needed rest. The next day we arrived at the Portland makeup yard, where we identified a train being made up for Seattle and hopped a boxcar. After a long wait, Jack left to get cigarettes. A few minutes later, the train started. I didn't know whether to jump off or plan to meet Jack at the Seattle post office as we had agreed to do if separated. Soon the train was going too fast to jump. When it arrived in Seattle, Jack ran up from a rear car. He had his cigarettes.

For six weeks, we looked for work while trying to get passage to Alaska. An acquaintance of my father's couldn't help. Jack, who had worked briefly in a Detroit auto factory, applied at Boeing as a sheet metal worker. We lived in a dollar-a-night second-story hotel room on Seattle's skid row, looking out on a fascinating totem pole at the foot of Yesler Way at First Street, near a penny arcade where we occasionally squandered a nickel. Our room was also near a venereal disease museum, where wax representations and photographs of that group of diseases made temporary saints of sinners.

We were nearly broke, and we began to get desperate. If Boeing ever called Jack, the message never got past our Chinese hotel keeper. We had moved from our dollar-a-day room to one in the same building that went for 35 cents. Our meals, which had cost 15 or 18 cents three times a day, became a six- or seven-cent bowl of stew twice a day at a skid-row eatery. I occasionally shared a Bull Durham cigarette with Jack, a habitual smoker, but gave it up when both the money and the bag of tobacco ran low. We sent a steady supply of shirts and pants to a Chinese laundry so we would look presentable when we made the rounds of employment offices and potential employers. Only Boeing had offered any hope at all.

At first we had indulged in an occasional 10-cent double feature. Now we were considering the savings that would accrue by giving up our 35-cent hotel room for two 10-cent admissions to an all-night theater.

I messaged my parents that I was trying to enlist in the Marine Corps. They sent me $10 and the permission slip the Marine Corps required of anyone under 21. I would also have to lie about my age, since I was not yet 18. Jack had gone through the initial stages of enlisting while I awaited the permission slip. He failed his physical because of an incipient hernia. Then he tried the Navy, but ended up with the same doctor. We were down to about a dollar and a half when I was tentatively accepted into the Corps—providing I gained two pounds to make minimum weight. I ate bananas and drank water, weighed myself at the penny arcade, and went back and ate more bananas. When the needle pointed to 128, I returned to the recruiting office, was weighed, and was told to come back the next day to be sworn in, which I did.

It was May 28, 1938. I was handed a train ticket and a $10 bill. The recruiting sergeant told me two things. "If you learn to look somebody in the eye and tell them to go to hell, you'll make a good marine." And: "It's a federal offense not to be on the train when it pulls into San Diego."

Jack had found an ad in which a Seattle car owner wanted someone to help drive to Cincinnati. I gave him the $10, and he made the decision to go back to Detroit. That evening, I boarded the train to San Diego and a new kind of life. I was 17 years and one month old at the time—18 and one month to the Marine Corps.

I was met at the station in San Diego by a sergeant who persuaded me for a reason I never knew to store my suitcase in a locker. The suitcase contained my toilet articles, some unwashed underwear, an extra shirt, about 50 Indian head pennies, several hundred baseball cards, my school ring and my high-school sports letters. I never went back for it, maybe because I wanted to make a complete break with my life to that point. When my khakis were issued on the base, I also discarded the clothes I had worn. After a $5 salary advance and a visit to the canteen, I dropped my broken comb into a trash can. A brief encounter with a barber's chair left me essentially with nothing I had brought to San Diego.

2

Fools' Paradise in China

I wasn't a hit in boot camp, and it wasn't a hit with me. I had an intestinal disorder and my shoes rubbed my feet raw. The alternative was to go to sick bay and then start all over. Drill instructors Roland and Bradshaw put me at the tail end of every exercise until my grades on written exams and some successes in athletics changed their view somewhat. Instructor Smith, who was on final assignment before retirement, became a shadow adviser. Boot camp was designed to drive the faint-hearted and weak-willed to desertion, he said. My platoon lost 10 or 15 percent on the first liberty—which I was denied by Sergeant Roland, for some vague infraction.

Corporal Bradshaw had roughed me up on the rifle range. He stood on my back while I was firing at 600 yards from the prone position. I rolled over quickly and he fell on his face across me. That drew a lot of laughs, and Bradshaw threatened to run me over the hill. I told him I wouldn't always be a recruit and would see him then. I ran into him three years later when the 4th Marines were evacuating China. He was a private.

After boot camp, I was assigned to sea duty aboard the aircraft carrier Lexington, which appealed to me because of the travel it involved. We put to sea from Long Beach headed for Bremerton, Washington, in the 13th Naval District. We hit heavy seas off northern California and I was sick the entire trip. When we arrived at Bremerton, I was transferred to the naval hospital with a kidney infection and dehydration. The Lexington left on a cruise and I was reassigned to the naval district prison as a guard.

It was good duty, with all the liberty I could handle and a chance to earn extra money by running the bowling alley at the post exchange. Prisoners set pins and I got half of their five cents a line. I soon had enough saved to buy a 1933 Chevrolet. It was brought to me by Jack Maddock and another lifelong friend, John McGrath. The car had Michigan license plates, which I prized and which remained on the car as long as I had it. I used the Chevy to explore the Puget Sound area, the Olympic Peninsula and the apple-growing district east of the Cascades. With my newfound mobility, I roamed as far as Portland, Oregon.

Late in 1938, a call went out for volunteers for an Antarctic expedition. I promptly signed up. It was months before I was notified that I did not have the "necessary qualifications," which were survival training and radio expertise. About then I came to realize that I did not have qualifications of any kind. I had my name entered on the Asiatic duty list as soon as a call was made. I had been promoted to private first class in May 1939, with a $10 monthly increase in pay.

I also began providing transportation to Portland once or twice a month for marines and Navy personnel. This paid for visits to a girl I had become acquainted with in Canby, Oregon. It was easy to get three or four days' liberty by trading watches with other guards. I headed out several times a month, changed to civilian clothes, ate bologna and cheese sandwiches and slept in the car. Occasionally I took someone from the prison guard detachment with me, or I took fellow marines to visit their families around Puget Sound. Their sisters were never pretty and their girlfriends always were. I became disillusioned and usually went alone. The people of the Northwest were courteous but distant to service personnel, and the regulation haircut stood out.

In September I was given travel orders. I sold my car and departed for Mare Island Naval Ship Yard near San Francisco to await transfer to the Far East. After two months, I received orders to board the naval troop ship Henderson bound for the Orient.

It had been a good two months. The world's fair was in full swing on Treasure Island; the mood of the country, now beginning to emerge from the Depression, was on the upswing; the weather was superb; I had become acquainted with one of the great harbors and cities of the world. And I was ready to move on.

Honolulu was my first exposure to the tropics. I loved it. Incredible vegetation, outstanding climate, sea, shore, mountains and sky made it as close to paradise as I could imagine. We had four days, with liberty every day. Dole pineapple, Kamehameha's Palace and the nightspots near Pearl Harbor all had their turn, but I spent most of my time at Waikiki. I rented goggles and bought rubber slippers to protect against the coral and spent hours floating on the surface and watching the panorama of sea life. Diamond Head was to the east. The Royal Hawaiian Hotel, with its restricted beach and high-class clientele, lay to the west. East and west framed a picture postcard view of ships, boats and outrigger canoes. I made up my mind to return for a long stay as soon as I could, but I saw Waikiki again only from the window of a Navy seaplane.

We left Honolulu in early evening. A band played a series of Hawaiian songs ending with a haunting "Aloha-o-ee." It was a charged moment. The islands were part of the United States; now we were heading into the unknown. We carried a little of America with us, but most of it was being left behind. What was ahead would be what we made of it. I felt no more qualified than I had been rated for the Antarctic expedition.

We spent Thanksgiving 1939 on the high seas. The first week in December we were negotiating the San Bernardino Strait between Samar and Luzon and on into the islands from which the U.S. riverboats on the Yangtze took their names, among them the Panay, sunk by the Japanese to show the Chinese that America was a paper tiger. We arrived in Manila at the end of the week.

Our stations had been posted some time after we left Guam.

Shanghai and Cavite, in the Philippines, were scheduled to receive about 90 percent of the troops from the Henderson. North China was to receive the other 10 percent, equally split between Peiping and Tientsin. I was assigned to Tientsin. I determined to make the most of our short stays in the Philippines and Shanghai.

Manila was fascinating in all respects. It was as modern as San Francisco and as old as its Spanish fortifications. In a few blocks I went from Embassy Row to ageless and primitive barrios, from limousines to calesas and carramettas, from stores that sold the finest work in gold, silver, jade and silk to a 10-year-old boy who offered his sister for 25 centavos, from English and Spanish to Tagalog.

The Henderson had disembarked a small contingent at Guam without picking up the men who were being replaced. The same practice was followed at Cavite; the men being replaced would be boarded on the return trip. The thinning ship's complement was reflected in the sleeping quarters, the mess lines and the quality of the food. We came and went almost at will. The relaxation of regimen and authority was noticeable already. Asiatic duty was looking better with every mile from the States.

The trip to Shanghai was uneventful except that the climate changed from tropical to temperate, and we were soon reminded that this was not summer but mid-winter. The sea reflected the geologic processes of the Asian continent, changing from clear gray blue to a murky yellow as we neared the coast between Taiwan and the China mainland. The Strait of Taiwan was very busy, and junks were seen increasingly as we approached the mouth of the Yangtze.

We laid off for most of a day and moved into an open area where we dropped anchor in the Huangp'u early in the morning. The anchorage was populated with thousands of ships and boats. Sampans surrounded the Henderson and hands reached out for food and coins. Against orders, we threw food to those thin hands. Much of what fell into the water was salvaged with fine-mesh pole nets. Just up the river from the Henderson was a concrete battleship taken by the Japanese from Russia in their brief encounter early in the century. Now, with a skeleton crew, it made a Japanese statement to all who passed by.

I went ashore only once in Shanghai. The weather was foul, with sleet driving from the north and collecting on soot-covered mounds of snow scraped from the sidewalk. We had been given maps showing the British concession and the parts of the city open to us. Beggars lined the route from the launch that brought us to quay. I was studying the map when a withered man reached up and grabbed my sleeve as I went by. When I looked down, I saw a smear across my coat and a hand covered with mucous and traces of blood and looking not like any living thing. I took off my coat and gave it to him and returned to the launch. Back aboard the Henderson, I told the officer of the deck what had happened. He sent me to the medical officer, who told me it was probably leprosy. I was given a new coat by the quartermaster without question after he checked with the medical officer.

The incident shook me up considerably, and I stayed on board for that and the following day. The next day was Christmas, and I again failed to explore Shanghai. The day after Christmas I had duty on the launch, counting heads and balancing the load. There was no liberty the following day. We departed for North China that night.

The trip north was unforgettable. A great storm out of Siberia hit the coast of China with a blast of Arctic air. The sky and sea were the color of lead except for wind-formed whitecaps that covered the vessel with salt spray. As we proceeded north, the froth turned to sleet and then to snow. I stood on the bow until my face was frozen, experiencing the power of the storm.

When we arrived in the Chihli Bay portion of the Yellow Sea, ice had formed nearly seven miles out from Chin Wang Tao and we were forced to lay off for several days. Finally we were able to approach the Kaolin Mining Administration docks, built by Herbert Hoover, and off-load replacement personnel and supplies for the U.S. embassy guard in Peiping and legation guard at Tientsin.

We now had our first encounter with the Japanese, who ran the railroad. The passenger and freight cars we needed were waiting and we boarded soon after arriving on the dock. Eight hours later, we were still waiting for the engines to appear for the trip to Tientsin. The temperature was in the low teens. The Japanese officials said nothing about the delay or when the train would start. When they determined we had lost enough face and were shown who was in command in North China, the engines appeared and the passenger cars were soon comfortable. I had burned my mouth and tongue badly on a cup of hot cocoa provided by the Marines detachment at the Chin Wang Tao rifle range while we were waiting to depart. As a result, I ate and drank little for several days.

At Tientsin I was assigned to "C" Company and began what was possibly the best duty a marine could have. The barracks were excellent, having been built for German troops in a concession given to the Kaiser after the Boxer Rebellion and lost by them after World War I. The food was superior. Duty was light. Services were tops in quality and quantity and low in cost.

For most items, money off base was worth 10 to 20 times what it was in America. Excellent beer was one cent a quart. A meal in a fine restaurant was six or seven cents. Scotch and Canadian whiskey cost 70 cents to $1.20 a fifth. European cloth was available duty-free at prices designed to earn dollars at any cost. A haircut, shave or rickshaw ride of about a mile was 10 sen, or half a cent. Ivory, intricately carved camphor chests, jade, cloisonne—anything a person could want—was available at five or 10 cents on the dollar.

The family of a Chinese person killed by an American driver was paid 10 U.S. dollars. A young girl could be purchased from her family for the same amount. Compared with the Depression economy I had known only two years before, I would be living in absolute luxury.

Tientsin was a very cosmopolitan city as a result of post-Boxer concessions granted to England, France and Italy, as well as Germany. Many foreign companies were represented because of Tientsin's importance as a port on the Hai River and the Grand Canal. It boasted two universities and a highly developed and structured society. Germans, Italians, French, British, Russian refugees and Americans were liberally represented. American moving pictures were shown soon after they appeared in the States. Medical, cultural and spiritual facilities equaled those in many of the world's great cities. Many non-Oriental residents spoke excellent English and much of the Oriental population spoke enough English to transact business.

Eurasian girls modeled clothing and served as hostesses in better establishments. Marines had an excellent club of their own that was frequented by girls of many nationalities. They enjoyed American music and food and were often fine company. Occasionally, one of the marines would form a permanent relationship with a Chinese girl, get a room and "go Asiatic," but it wasn't common.

Free time was devoted to a wide range of athletic activities, to souvenir hunting in the bazaars, to searches for new restaurants and, in the evenings, to cabarets. There were several nightclubs where you could bring your own girl for dancing, food and drinks; or you could dance with hostesses provided by the management. Drinks served to the hostesses were non-alcoholic; we were not supposed to know, and we paid as though the drinks were real. And, since the girls got little of what we spent on them, it was common to slip them a few yen supposedly unknown to the management. Nonetheless, one could be assured of a good evening on the town for a dollar or a dollar and a half.

We traveled several times to Peiping, as Beijing was called when it was not the seat of the Chinese government, to participate in sports competitions. These trips afforded the Tientsin marines their only opportunity to see the national treasures of the Chinese. There was always enough time to visit the Forbidden City, the Temple of Heaven, the summer residence, the Great Wall and many of the lesser wonders of that ancient culture. Teihard de Jardin, the great anthropologist and philosopher, was at that period in either Peiping or the Gobi Desert. The last emperor of China was a pleasure addict in Tientsin.

English-speaking guides were available for about 10 cents a day. We provided the cost of their transportation and bought them food, but it was obvious they would rather have the money.

Europeans often said American marines made things hard by overpaying the Chinese, but we would normally take up a collection and give an all-day guide and interpreter two or three dollars at the end of a day. We would have been lost without them.

World conflicts and tensions and American relations with Japan, if measured by our reaction to them, were poorly understood at all levels of command. Although we were proficient in small arms, there was no instruction in tactics. We knew our weapons but nothing about the various arenas in which they might be used. It may have been that in the event of war with Japan, it was believed that American embassy and legation guards would be exchanged for Japanese in the same situation, as provided by the Geneva Convention—which the Japanese scorned as alien to their culture of Shinto, bushido and samurai.

Although officers' wives were required to leave China in 1940, we lived in a fool's paradise. We competed in water polo with the Italians, with whom the English were at war. We played baseball against the Japanese. The Italian commandant and Japanese General Homma were given honor guards at the Marines compound, a fact that was not lost on either the Chinese or the Durham Light Infantry and Seaforth Highlanders, who protected the concession along which our compound was situated. Before long, Homma would be leading the Japanese invasion of the Philippines.

We received information on the war in Europe only in most summary form. The geography and the significance of the battles described was lost on us. We knew that the United States was the most advanced and powerful country in the world. That meant that we had the most advanced weapons and most powerful Army and Navy in the world. We also knew that a Japan that could not subdue China was no threat to the United States. We dreamed on.

Foreigners and rich Chinese were buying American dollars with yuan at a rate that drove their value even higher, a situation we enjoyed but did not question beyond a vague uneasiness. With 56 of those dollars, I bought two camphorwood chests large enough for me to climb inside and pull the tray over my-

Jack Maddock (right) didn't become a marine at the end of our trip west. But he came to Washington state when I was out of boot camp and brought me this '33 Chevrolet.

Shipping out in '38. That's the carrier Lexington looming beyond the administration building at Long Beach.

Nick Spono (left) has a drink with me at the Tientsin Marines Club. Nick brought my surviving carved camphor wood chest back to the States.

China was a world away from a young NCO's rural Michigan upbringing. Yes, I shot the Great Wall on one of my excursions.

The surviving carved camphor wood chest. An American in North China could fill such a chest with treasures — on a corporal's pay.

self. The carving must have taken an artisan years, perhaps many years. I was able to fill those chests with ivory, jade, silver, wood carvings and cloisonne and send one back to the States on a corporal's pay without crippling my acquired level of self-indulgence.

The contrast with my life in America was so great that I considered extending both my tour of duty and my enlistment. I also considered being paid off in China if I could sign on with an American or European company there. To that end I began a formal course of education in the Chinese, French and Italian languages. At the insistence of the refugee Russian woman who was my instructor, I devoted a small portion of my Italian sessions to studying Japanese. After spending an hour on Italian, we would discuss the importance of learning Japanese over a can or two of American beer. The beer, at four or five cents, cost more than the session. Her poverty level was such that she was shocked when I wrote double-spaced and on only one side of my notebook pages. One day she asked me why a man would ask her why I was learning Italian, as was known at the compound, and Japanese, which wasn't known. I never found out who the man was.

Hard as I tried, I could not repeat the sound of French words to her satisfaction. She did not have the same problem with her British students. I also never was able to master the inflections of Chinese.

I wanted to learn Chinese sufficiently to conduct everyday affairs with merchants and servants. I wanted to learn French because it was the Caucasian language most likely to be known in the Far East. And I wanted to learn Italian because I occasionally went out with Yolanda, the daughter of an Italian legation official, and her friend. I wanted to be able to communicate with her friend and know what they were talking about. Yolanda spoke almost flawless English, except for our slang, but her friend, with whom I was often paired, spoke almost none. I also visualized myself as a potential man of the world, in which role I would need to know several languages.

In March 1941 we were notified that most of the embassy

guard from Peiping and legation guard from Tientsin would be leaving on the next two rotations and would not be replaced. My tour of duty was to end in December but had been moved up to September. No reasons were given. No one seemed to believe that a conflict with Japan was imminent. In fact, with the exchange of recent guards of honor between the Japanese Army and U.S. Marines and the meeting of our baseball teams, we were even less inclined than a year before to believe there would be trouble.

In July I gave up my apartment with its fine carved furniture, its beautiful handcrafted carpet and drapes and the amah (housekeeper) I never saw. The apartment had been mine for only four months. The return to a bunk in the corner of a room with the members of my squad was not easy. I had grown to love the quiet luxury and the opportunity for study and reading, as well as an occasional drinking and snack party until the early hours. We had been required to notify the command when we had a residence away from the compound. Few complied because the location would become known to other marines and to the shore patrol. I could have maintained the apartment, but two non-commissioned officers had been demoted recently for similar infractions and I did not want to jeopardize my year-old corporal's stripes.

A curfew was imposed and it became difficult to achieve any privacy. The command, recognizing the effects of the change, greatly increased intramural and club activities. There also was much more drinking, encouraged by a decision to reduce the club treasury and inventory by halving the price of drinks. I continued the language lessons, but with less sense of purpose.

Orders went out to bring all personnel up to grade on weapons, which was accomplished on the parade ground, in the squad room and in the basement firing range. Physical conditioning was attempted with pushups and a medicine ball, both of which did little except to emphasize how soft we had grown. I was about 10 pounds over the 165 I considered my ideal weight. Our commanding officer was the author of the Marine Corps Handbook, but it was a document for a peace-time Corps. We were unprepared for combat on water or in desert, field or jungle; we in North China were parade ground soldiers and we did not know it.

"C" and "D" companies were consolidated. I was given the low performers and the screwups. Now I had to bring a group of seven men I barely knew up to speed on the .30-caliber machine gun, the pistol, the hand grenade and the bayonet. Progress was mixed. Orders that came down were clear, but follow-up was rare or non-existent. There was a great air of uncertainty of purpose. The officers seemed as bewildered as the men. The blind were leading the blind.

In mid-summer, all but token weapons were ordered removed from North China. All weapons were old and removal simply meant we didn't want someone else to have them. Chinese carpenters were brought in to do the crating. We packed sensitive mechanisms in cosmoline against the salt air of the sea trip.

Late in September, most of the command boarded trains for Chin Wang Tao. We arrived well in advance of the USS Chaumont, a Navy troop ship. The freight cars were left on a siding with an intense security presence 24 hours a day. Eventually all but a fraction of the U.S. military capability was loaded on the Chaumont, and the trip—back to the United States, I thought— began. I had eight months to go on my enlistment and wondered where I would be stationed and if I would have a choice. I was grateful that it was too late in my enlistment for sea duty. Anything was going to be drab after China.

We loaded the Chaumont without delay and set out as soon as cargo and troops were aboard. In a few days, we were once again in Shanghai. There was no shore leave, but I had launch duty several times as we loaded the 4th Marine Regiment and all its equipment, leaving only a small contingent to protect U.S. interests and personnel on the Central China coast. We set out to sea, again in record time and fully loaded. A Japanese naval vessel accompanied us at a considerable distance until we left the Strait of Taiwan (or Formosa, as the Japanese insisted) and entered the South China Sea.

3

A Tragedy of Errors

Just three or four days out from Shanghai we anchored in Manila Bay. The 4th Marines were a complete fighting unit. Many of us were intimidated by their sense of organization, confidence and professionalism. They knew who they were and what they were. Before we dropped anchor at Olongapo where the 4th Marines Regiment disembarked, all North China marines on board were advised they would disembark at Cavite and would be held there indefinitely at the government's convenience. The plot was thickening. I still had three months of Asiatic duty to serve and normally could be kept for six months after my enlistment was up. I was philosophical about it.

I was concerned about the second camphor chest I had acquired and the souvenirs in it, particularly some bolts of Harris tweed and a walking cane that became a shotgun when a silver band was twisted to expose a trigger. Most other items were pretty much duplicated in the first chest, which I had sent home. The second chest, I was told, would be kept in storage at the Cavite Naval Yard. I never saw it again.

The next day, with a seabag and a backpack, and a new squad of men, I took up residence in a tent under the low frequency radio towers on Sangley Point, separated from the rest of the naval yard. I remained there about two weeks, then was reassigned to Mariveles at the southern tip of the Bataan Peninsula, at the mouth of Manila Bay.

The Navy was building tunnels into hills that came down to the water on the east side of Mariveles Bay, an inlet on the big bay that provided Manila its outstanding harbor. The harbor would be a major goal of any Pacific foe, and any plunder that an enemy might wish to take from the heart of the Philippine economy—to Tokyo, say—would have to pass through here. The tunnels at Mariveles were to be storage facilities for the submarine fleet. A few miles off Mariveles lay the main defense at the mouth of the harbor, the fortified island of Corregidor.

We were fewer than 100 men at Mariveles, led by a fine young lieutenant named Vroom, and again we had no real idea why we were there. We had nothing to do in camp and, except for several places to buy beer, there was no commercial life in the area. Several enterprising Filipinos set up thatch-roofed tiendas just outside camp, but they were poorly stocked. Their San Miguel beer, though good, was warm. We had a small commissary, but it, too, was short on supplies.

The jungle came down to the bay. On early excursions, we rustled up wild chickens. At first, with their screeching and flapping, they frightened us more than we frightened them. Even more scary was coming upon a wild boar or sow. They would crash off through the underbrush, leaving us with hearts in our throats and breathing stopped until we came to know what they were.

The most frightening creatures were ones we never saw. The hills were drying out, and pythons left five- to eight-inch paths across the fine dirt surfaces of the road near camp as they came down the mountains seeking water. Occasionally a band of monkeys would object to our passage through their jungle, scolding from branches of trees on all sides, but they were seldom seen unless you sat silent and motionless for a while. I went to mass several times in Mariveles and was an object of curiosity to the priest and his parishioners, and probably an object of suspicion. I soon lost track of Sundays.

We were under blackout from the first day we arrived, but tunnel work went on night and day seven days a week. Earth-moving equipment excavated for buildings that were never to be built. Bits drilled into rock that was never to hold munitions. It was now late October 1941. Communications about international tensions were even more woeful than they had been in China. I did not know the name of the top Marines officer in the Philippines nor the admiral in charge of naval forces in the Far East, but I did know that General Douglas MacArthur was in charge of the U.S. and Philippine army forces in the islands. I had no knowledge of our armed forces, except for the garrison a couple of miles across the water on Corregidor and the fact that Clark and Nichols fields were receiving B-17s.

It did not take a genius, however, to conclude that the blackouts, the tunnels and the B-17s were for the dubious benefit of the Japanese. The sudden exodus from China and the holdover of short-timers for the convenience of the government pointed in an ominous direction, but we were still not overly concerned. That troops at our level would fail to assess our military capability correctly was of no consequence. The way MacArthur and his staff assessed and deployed their forces was another story.

With the winds of war about us, I concluded that neither I nor my squad was in good physical condition. I decided that a hike with light gear up Mt. Mariveles would acquaint us with the jungle and bring us together as a unit. We had much greater respect for each other after just two or three of these expeditions; before long, men from other squads were asking to accompany us.

It was highly satisfying to lose ourselves on an arm of that great mountain with the ever-present cloud over its summit and then know that we would find our way back to camp together, or, if separated, we would find each other again or find our own way back. It was also satisfying to meet each other on the parade ground, in the mess hall, or over a beer and see a faint smile of satisfaction on each other's faces, knowing we had done something the others had not. Of such is confidence born. We were never to know what thorough jungle training would have done for us.

I was 20 years old. I was a corporal. I had proved to myself that I had college potential. I had great plans for myself, indefinite as they were.

Then, on December 8 west of the 180th meridian, we were awakened and told that the fleet at Pearl Harbor had just been destroyed, that we were at war, and that we were at present risk.

We were assembled and marched to the tunnels under construction just east of Mariveles. The construction people were there, but there were no tunnels ready for munitions or for us. The blackouts had told us there were spies in our midst. It was natural, perhaps, to assume that the eyes in the shadows were Filipino; time proved that too frequently they were Japanese in Filipino clothing, or Germans, or even Americans—but rarely were they Filipino.

We stayed near the tunnels the rest of the night. At dawn, feeling foolish and not a little cowardly, we went back to our barracks. With dawn came reason. That Japan would waste an early strike on a facility that was scarcely begun was ludicrous. We knew that they had destroyed a great target and would be looking for others of military significance. It was clear to all that the United States was not prepared and had failed to anticipate even the most probable events. The command would now have to plan for a war that already had begun.

Directions were not long in coming. Within a day, we boarded PT boats for Corregidor and almost immediately were ordered to the south dock to board a Navy inter-island vessel for a quick trip back to Cavite.

Amid this confused hopscotch appeared a vision of the old pre-war Marines, of a Far East duty that would never be the same. Before leaving for the Orient aboard the Henderson, a marine who was to be paid out of the Corps in a few weeks had come over to me and transferred possession of a backless folding chair with a canvas seat. The chair, he said, had been across the Pacific nearly 30 times, mostly on the Chaumont and the Henderson, each time in the possession of a marine who wrote on the underside of the canvas his name, the name of the transport, the destination and the departure and arrival dates. Many were barely readable. I was to put it in the hands of someone on the return trip who would in turn see that the old chair continued its journey. And now, I saw it again—on the deck of the vessel ferrying us to Cavite. It probably had traversed 200,000 miles of the Pacific Ocean. This little journey was undoubtedly the chair's last.

At Cavite we were reorganized. I was given 14 men, including only one of those I had at Mariveles. We were assigned immediately to the naval ammunition dump in the old wall erected by the Spanish conquerors. It was about 20 feet above the Manila Bay high tide that lapped at its base. Its parapets, common to Spanish fortifications of that vintage, looked down on the water on two sides. On one side was moored a submarine, minus its engines. I was given four cannon, three-inchers normally mounted on small boats or on shore installations to repel small craft. It was the first time any of us had ever seen one. An officer whose name I do not remember said we were to fire at incoming Japanese aircraft. He gave no further instructions. I had never seen him before; I never saw him again.

I gathered the men around one gun, opened the chamber, inserted a shell, removed it and gave everyone a turn at the controls. Apparently the cannon was designed to be fired at distances of about a mile. I designated the four oldest-appearing private first-class marines as crew chiefs, each with two men. Jim Barna and I would resupply the ammunition, two guns each. Our orders were to man the guns around the clock. We had no lavatory and no idea what we were going to do for food. Shortly after noon, I told Barna, whom I knew to be a street-wise kid from Hamtramck, to scout up food and water for us. He soon came back with coffee and directions to the mess hall. Eventually, we all got to eat. We also learned that the sick bay was only about 100 feet beyond the base of the wall, so we had a source of water at a reasonable distance.

It wasn't long before we knew that the old fortification under our feet was the Navy storehouse of mines, torpedo warheads and ammunition. It didn't take much imagination to know what a well-placed bomb would do. The knowledge left us weak-kneed and speechless.

On December 10 we watched the bombing of Nichols Field south of Manila. The bombing lasted perhaps an hour and a half.

Columns of smoke filled the air, and we knew we had been hurt. Rumors had been circling that Clark Field, 100 miles north-northwest of Manila, had been hit and that the damage to the B-17 fleet, never off the ground, had been extensive.

With Clark and Nichols fields destroyed and Army installations offering scattered and poorly concentrated targets, it was obvious that the U.S. naval capability in the Far East was a worthy and logical Japanese objective. Confirmation was not long in coming. Admiral Rockwell and the naval command under him cooperated fully with the Japanese in the same way that MacArthur and General Brereton had lined up the B-17s and P-40 interceptors on the ground at Clark and Nichols fields while Japanese air armadas were known to be bearing down on them.

U.S. Navy and Marine personnel were concentrated at the prime target, the Cavite Naval Yard, without a single adequate weapon of defense. The result was predictable and catastrophic. We had learned nothing from the bombing of Pearl Harbor and the two airfields on Luzon. Fifty-four Japanese aircraft bore down on the naval base without air or ground resistance. They came in two waves of 27 aircraft each at about 20,000 feet, well beyond the range of our three-inch guns. We watched as glints of silver emerged from the bellies of the aircraft. One of my young men said: "They're dropping leaflets." I replied that it didn't take a squadron of planes to drop that kind of message.

Soon we saw the bombs tumbling nose over fin. Slowly the tumbling turned into a nose-first wobble. Then they straightened and their conformation could be made out. I was terrified beyond anything I had ever known. Hell above and hell below. Hundreds of bombs could be seen heading straight for their targets, and the target was us. Below us was a quantity of explosives exceeding by far that which was being dropped by the incoming bombers. The descending noise made by the incoming bombs changed from a shudder to a howl to a scream. It was almost impossible that one of those bombs would not find its way to the warheads and mines stored beneath us. But the impossible happened. The naval ammunition depot was missed. I had been praying as never before. Several thousand other sailors, civilians and marines also were praying, and not all were missed.

A stick of bombs raced across the naval yard, and the first blast struck the dispensary where we had been given water by some friendly corpsmen. They and the building ceased to exist. As the bombs raced across the yard, I looked around to see what had happened to my men. Only Jimmy Barna was there. He shrugged and put it out of his mind; I couldn't stand. Of the men who disappeared after that initial bombing, I only saw one again—a quiet little fellow from Staten Island. We never talked about it.

By this time, fires were raging everywhere. Huge columns of white and black smoke converged over the area, obliterating both sky and horizon. Barna and I, after a few minutes, left the wall to see what damage had been done. Other than at the dispensary, there was surprisingly little loss of life in our area. We saw four bodies and no other casualties. Two of the dead appeared untouched and may have died of concussion. The others were no longer recognizable as human.

In about 20 minutes, the siren wailed again. Somehow I knew the Japanese would be coming out of the sun. We returned to the base of the wall. My legs were weak and I struggled to get to the top. Barna got up with much less of a problem. This time the bombs and the planes were invisible in the sun and the smoke, but we had learned from the first pass to recognize the distance of the bombs by their sound. It was almost impossible that we could be missed a second time, but we had something in our favor—any bombs that hit in the water on the north and east would almost certainly not damage the ammunition dump. If the wall were going to be hit, a bomb would have to be placed in a strip that covered 30 or 40 feet. They missed. The first bomb in a stick hit between the dispensary and the wall; all the rest fell harmlessly in the bay. The bombs aimed at our section must have come from the easternmost plane in the flight; all of the other bombs hit west of us in the main part of the yard.

I watched Barna shove a shell into a three-incher, point it

upward and pull the lanyard. Only two others that I knew well as soldiers made as great an impression on me as Jimmy Barna.

I was too weak to leave the wall. Barna said he would be back soon and left. I didn't expect him to come back up. But in about 20 minutes he was there with a half-dozen wristwatches and a Waterman pen and pencil set. The canteen had been hit but was not burning. He said an officer told everyone there to take what they wanted before it went up in smoke. I refused a watch but accepted the pen and pencil set. Soon a runner came by with instructions to assemble at the main gate. I was wobbly but could now walk.

When I got to the gate, I was given about 10 men I had never seen and told to report to a lieutenant at the lumberyard to fight fires. We fought them all night but saved only a small percentage of the stacks. They burned too fast for us to make a fire break. I found two instances where piles of sticks under the stacks had been set afire and had gone out. I reported it to the lieutenant and went back to the task of putting out fires without water. We didn't need light for the work; the flames reflecting from the smoke above us gave us all the illumination we needed.

Food was brought to us as we worked, and I found I had recovered some of my appetite. We finally got a break between the burning and non-burning stacks. That left us only burning embers, which were falling everywhere, to put out when they landed on the untouched stacks. In early morning, we were no longer needed and I took my men, now down to six or seven, and checked with an officer at the gate. Major fires were still burning, but it was surprising how much had not been severely damaged. As a functioning base, however, Cavite Navy Yard was a total loss.

In mid-afternoon all marines were assembled at the main gate of the yard. Cavite was being evacuated. We would march in a column of four to a staging area. We would not be organized into units for the march. Privates walked alongside gunnery sergeants. I had left my seabag on the wall. I had my backpack, bedroll, rifle and cartridge belt. Few had more, many had nothing. We marched about four hours, arriving at a small banana plantation as night fell about 7 p.m.

I was looking for a place to bed down near the officer in charge so I could learn whatever I could about what was going to happen. That was a mistake. An officer collared me and told me to get two men and patrol the road in the direction of Cavite. I picked one private first class. Barna, who had stayed with me on the march, volunteered to be the other. I asked for orders and was told just to "patrol the road." As we got a few yards beyond the edge of the encampment, I looked back and saw a large luminous cloud several hundred feet away and across from the encampment. We puzzled over it for a few minutes debating whether it was natural or supernatural. I sent Barna back to investigate. He returned in a few minutes to announce that it was a tree. It was, indeed, a tree—either an ilang-ilang or a guava and covered with fireflies. We went back to our patrol. About 10 o'clock we were relieved of our post, telling our replacements to alarm the troops if they encountered anything threatening. It was all the instructions we could infer from the assignment.

A field kitchen was set up during the night and was in full operation by dawn. The meal was hotcakes, served as long as anyone wanted them. In mid-morning everyone was required to identify himself by name, serial number, rank, expertise and origin—Shanghai, North China or Cavite. We were organized into companies, platoons and squads and marched as units back to Sangley Point. The tents were still in place inside the main gate in the shadow of the gigantic low frequency radio towers, which were used for submarine communications. Some of the tents were already occupied by marines who had not made the trip to the banana plantation. Among them was a private first class named Edward Duggan with whom I had frequently gone on liberty in Tientsin. He had been editor of the Tientsin Marine.

I again had seven men, most of whom I had never seen. Two were extremely young. We were designated part of a rifle company and assigned as guards at the main gate, as were two other squads in the tent area. Our assignment was to man the gate and patrol the fence and waterfront areas on both sides of the point. Fences ran down both sides of a road that traversed the length of the peninsula at its center. On the Manila side of the road was a water tower, the chapel, the hospital, a number of administration buildings, the officers' quarters and officers' club.

On the Corregidor side of the peninsula was a large well-groomed field where the radio towers were situated. The tents were organized near the center road beyond the tower farthest from the guardhouse at the main gate. A number of trenches had been dug in the loose black sandy earth and more were being dug. A covered bunker to the east of the main gate was reserved for Admiral Rockwell and several members of his staff. Another bunker was being constructed to the west of the guard-house and near the exterior fence. It was covered about three deep in sandbags. Beyond this bunker was one end of a row of aviation fuel drums stacked two and three high and extending in a semicircle around the towers, almost to the field kitchen that served the tent dwellers.

Shortly before noon toward the middle of December, I escorted Carlos P. Romulo, head of the Philippine scouts, over to Admiral Rockwell, who was standing near his bunker. A few minutes later, we heard the characteristic drone of Japanese bombers and I went over again to the admiral and asked if the alarm should be sounded. He said, "They won't bomb here," and I went back to the gate. A few minutes later, two Filipino girls came to the gate to inquire after their boyfriends. I took them inside to go over the list and see if I could identify the men from the unfamiliar pronunciation of Tagalog-speaking girls. Harry Dunlavy, a corporal from Shanghai, was also there. We had been together in Mariveles, where he and the company clerk, Corporal Tully, occasionally went on beer runs together.

Soon we heard the whine of bombs. We told the girls to flatten on the floor, and did so ourselves. They stood there. Harry grabbed one by the arm and dragged her down. I did the same to the other. It was the first time I had thought of anyone but myself in a moment of crisis since the war began. I remember a vague sense of satisfaction about it when the whine changed to an angry howl. Milliseconds later, the guardhouse seemed to rise off the ground. I was looking up, my cheek pressed hard against the floor, when a string of holes appeared in the side of the shack about four feet above the floor.

The first bomb in the stick nearest the guardshack landed just within the point of the peninsula on the north, and the last bomb landed about 30 yards from my post, on civilian property beyond the gate. Again I had been missed.

The Japanese were accurate, but they had failed to damage any of the radio towers seriously. Again they had come from the northwest. Many buildings on the peninsula were damaged and several tents appeared to be on fire. The aviation fuel drums looked intact.

The bomb that damaged the guardhouse had made a crater about 20 feet wide and eight feet deep. Its edge was less than 20 feet from the northwest corner of the shack. The bomb had hit the unfinished trench intended for the gate guards. The trench was empty at the time. The officer of the day had been racing to a trench when the bomb exploded. A fragment entered one side of his metal helmet and went out about six inches later, spinning it off his head. In a few minutes, after regaining his orientation, he was unscratched and amazed at his good fortune.

I became concerned about Ed Duggan and the graveyard-shift marines who were asleep in the tent area. With Dunlavy away, I left the gate in charge of a private first class and raced for the tents. About half a dozen of them were on fire. I looked in each as I ran down the line. One marine was dead on the floor of his tent, showing no sign of being hit. Another was stretched across his bunk in a burning tent, his feet on the floor. I dragged him into the area between tent rows.

I continued to the field kitchen, where I saw a marine struggling to get up. His right buttock had a moderate amount of blood on it. I grabbed him by the shoulder and turned him enough to see his face. It was Private Vieux, a Cajun from Louisiana, with whom I had gone through boot camp. I asked him how bad he was hit. He said he wasn't hit but he couldn't get up. I looked at his buttocks and saw that a fist-sized chunk was missing. He said it didn't hurt.

There was no sign of Duggan. Most tents were afire, small-caliber ammunition was beginning to detonate, and marines and sailors were materializing to fight the fires and render first aid. I was headed back toward the main gate when I heard the bombers again.

A long trench had been dug extending westward from the fence that divided the peninsula, past the base of the tower nearest the tent area. I waited until the bombs changed in sound to a fluttering howl and dove into the trench, my head toward the central fence. A second later I looked up to see a sailor in whites trying to climb the fence and get to the trench. Suddenly he flew apart. Bombs landed all around me. They seemed to lift me out of the trench and suspend me in mid-air.

After the explosions subsided, I tried to conclude whether I was alive or dead. In a moment I knew I was alive because my right arm and shoulder felt ablaze. I looked and saw that they were covered with huge red ants. I got out of the trench and ripped off my shirt and undershirt and wiped off the insects, grateful to them for showing me I was alive.

When I looked around, I saw the radio towers were intact but the water tower was spouting in a dozen places. Buildings from one end of the installation to the other were either burning or were a mass of rubble. The tent area was half destroyed and the aviation fuel was belching flames and black smoke in a dozen places. Again, we had concentrated men, materials and equipment into a convenient target for an enemy against whom we had no defense. We had incurred five major bombings and still we had not learned. Our respect for the Japanese was growing. Respect for our own command was being greatly degraded. From that moment, I never had full confidence in anyone in authority over me in the military—or, for that matter, in my post-war career.

I returned to the main gate. The officer of the day left me there to control it, giving me a private as a runner. He then took all others to fight the fires and take care of the wounded, the dying and the dead.

There was no rank until late that night. Officers, non-commissioned officers and privates did whatever had to be done. At about nine in the evening I was taken off the gate and directed to carry injured sailors and marines into the chapel, where lamps had taken the place of destroyed electrical service.

My friend Corporal Tully was assigned to patrol the beach on the east side of the peninsula. He went to his post, found a chair to sit on, put the muzzle of his rifle under his chin and pulled the trigger.

We put Tully in the chapel, too, and wondered about the course he had taken—what had he known that we did not? It was not the first time Tully had considered suicide. He had once told me that he would know when the price of living was too high. He professed to be an atheist; but every once in a while, especially after a few drinks, he would break out with strains of "In the Garden," echoes I suppose of his mother, who had died when he was young.

The barrio outside the main gate had been evacuated. Within a day or two, I was handed a .22-caliber rifle by my platoon leader, a second lieutenant, and was told to take several of my squad out into the barrio and kill every dog I saw. The dogs had no food and the medical officer was afraid of rabies.

The first shot I took during the war was at a furry little puppy, probably about 10 weeks old. He rolled over on his back in submission and I shot him through the neck. We had no shovels and left him for the rats. No one said anything. We shot four or five more dogs during the rest of the afternoon and returned to the base.

A day later, I was approached by my lieutenant, who was looking for 10 volunteers to go out on a mission that had some potential danger. He would not provide any details. In an hour, I managed to come back with six men besides myself, all armed with Springfield rifles. I took a Thompson submachine gun from the guard shack and left on a troop carrier, the lieutenant driving, me in front with him and the other men in the back.

We went less than half a mile toward Cavite but somewhat south of the road between Cavite and Sangley Point. We stopped the truck and hiked several blocks in a loose formation, the lieutenant and myself leading. He had a map. As we came within sight of a house that was built to the ground rather than elevated with bamboo and slat floors typical of Philippine dwellings, the lieutenant ordered us to stop and stay out of sight.

He stared at the house for almost an hour. There was little activity in the area and none near the house we were observing. Finally, he told me it was suspected that the dwelling housed a radio that provided a beam for incoming Japanese aircraft. I asked him what our orders were, and he said to observe suspicious activity. The quiet around the house was ominous, and we concluded we had to see inside before leaving. We decided to prepare to open fire and make a show of force. The lieutenant and I approached together, he at the left with pistol in hand and me with the Thompson held at ready. He tried the doorknob and pushed the door open. The house was empty.

It had one large room with a table, two chairs and a mattress. In one corner an escrow partition hid an opening in the floor. It smelled of excrement and looked like it had been occupied but not in the last several days. We returned to the rest of the men and went back to Sangley Point, where the lieutenant made his report.

It was now 10 days since Pearl Harbor. U.S. military capability in the Far East had been reduced to a small fraction of its pre-war strength. In the Philippines, rumors abounded. The islands' defense was in disarray. Morale plunged.

I knew nothing of the lieutenant I reported to and knew the names of no one up the chain of command. This was not true of the 4th Marine Regiment out of Shanghai, but was universal with the North China and Philippine marines below the commissioned officer level.

Scuttlebutt had Germans piloting Japanese lead aircraft, and

Japanese troops were said to have made at least four landings in the islands. Two landings were later confirmed: in Batangas, southwest of Manila, and at Legaspe, some 200 miles to the southeast. Common sense told us we were not capable of a long-range strike against Japanese airfields on Formosa, or it would have happened. MacArthur had his troops strung out across hundreds of miles of Luzon and Mindanao. An untrained and poorly armed contingent of the Philippine Army—the soldiers MacArthur had assured Washington could hold their own against the Japanese Army—threw down their weapons and fled into the jungle when the Japanese landed at Lingayen. Confidence in MacArthur and the naval command deteriorated drastically, with good reason.

We began to discuss the possibility and then the likelihood that the Philippines would fall to the enemy within weeks, maybe within days. We openly talked of fading into the hills and becoming guerrillas if the situation came to that. We knew almost nothing, however, of Philippine geography and topography. Tropical diseases, snakes, aborigines and having to forage for food dominated our image of the jungle. Nonetheless, I started to make a collection of two items: quinine and matches.

On December 22 or 23 we were ordered to Manila. Some went by bus, some by truck and some by launch. We had only small arms at Sangley Point, but other weapons were being salvaged at Cavite.

The trip to Manila took less than an hour. Several hundred of us went in a caravan of buses and trucks. We all had been attached to units at Sangley Point, but we did not leave as units nor did we assemble as units when we arrived near the old wall on the waterfront. There was a broad lawn east of the old wall, where several Filipino boys were performing close order drills with sticks instead of rifles. They appeared to be in their mid-teens.

We were ordered to stay in the area and were given our first issue of C-rations. I ate sitting under a palm tree and noticed a newspaper under another tree where a civilian had been sitting. It was in Spanish. I couldn't remember when I had last read a newspaper, so I went several blocks until I found a tobacco store that had an English-language edition. I remember only that the Japanese had landed in Lingayen, and that there was discussion of declaring Manila an open city. This told me all I needed to know about the status of our military position in the islands.

Before long, with the Pacific becoming a Japanese fiefdom and America needing a hero, MacArthur would be getting a Congressional Medal of Honor for his heroic defense of the Philippines. In late December 1941, my own view was quite to the contrary. It would grow even more contrary in the months and decades to follow.

During the chaotic events on Luzon in the early weeks of the war, nothing was heard from MacArthur. He had pushed for a plan named Rainbow Five, which called for defending the entire Philippines. He thus abandoned War Plan Orange (Orange for the Rising Sun), which precisely foresaw the enemy's tactics. War Plan Orange would have concentrated men and material for a defense of the Bataan Peninsula and the fortified islands just off its tip, mainly Corregidor. As long as Corregidor was in American hands, Manila Bay would be useless to the Japanese. And Manila harbor was the main objective of the emperor's troops who were now advancing across the map of Rainbow Five.

MacArthur had seen himself as a grand master of the coming war rather than the commander responsible for a limited and localized confrontation. His vainglory had overpowered his reason. Now, with Christmas upon us, and with marine corporals contemplating life as jungle guerrillas, he was coming to his senses—too late. Vast stores of munitions, gasoline, food and medicine would be abandoned or destroyed at the Rainbow Five outposts. War Plan Orange would go into effect with pathetic shortages of the two things an army needs to survive and fight—food and weapons.

After wondering seemingly a long time what would happen next, with only a few minutes' notice we were put on a caravan of trucks and buses and informed that we were headed for Bataan.

4

Retreat Toward the Enemy

The trip was expected to take half a day. We would be going north through the part of Bulacon Province that touched the bay, then northwest into Pompanga Province to San Fernando, its capital, 35 miles from Manila. Because of extensive marshlands between San Fernando and the bay, this was the shortest route available. From San Fernando, we would proceed southwest some 25 miles around the marshes to Bataan Province and another 25 miles down to Mariveles at the peninsula's tip.

There was, however, somewhat of a problem. The Japanese were coming down from their landing site at Lingayen Gulf toward San Fernando. Our progress was stopped repeatedly by a large number of trucks, buses and automobiles from military installations near Cabanatuan in Nueva Ecija Province. American and Philippine forces to the northwest were fighting a delaying action to allow as many troops and as much material as possible to escape to Bataan. We were retreating toward the enemy, intermingled with hundreds of military and civilian vehicles carrying U.S. and Filipino troops from Legaspe, Nueva Ecija and Batangas.

Progress was incredibly slow. An endless line of vehicles crossed the Calumpit bridge bumper to bumper. The shoulders of the road were bad, and one vehicle with mechanical problems would obstruct the convoy until a place could be found to dispose of the vehicle and transfer its men and cargo.

Late that night we were off-loaded in a clearing just south of Orion. We slept wherever we could find a place to lie down. The next morning we were ordered to walk to Mariveles, about 20 miles away. I had some C-rations, but my canteen was empty. Walking was difficult because of the vehicles on the road. We walked out of formation and wherever the footing was best. Late in the afternoon, suffering from thirst, I stretched out in the shade of a bush and saw the metallic glint of a can. It had no label but, when shaken, clearly contained a large amount of liquid. I opened it with a bayonet and took a drink. It was green olives in brine.

Somewhere between Lemay and Mariveles we came upon a field hospital and water. We stayed overnight, sleeping near the bay where the mosquitoes were less of a problem. We made the last few miles into Mariveles before noon. There appeared to be thousands of Filipinos between Orion and Mariveles, including a large number of women. The village of Mariveles had become a town almost overnight. We were directed to an area above the town in an incredible banyan grove. Kitchens already had been set up and we were fed as we came in. For several days we ate and slept beside buttress roots of banyan trees high enough to walk under.

Shortly after we arrived, a small contingent of marines was organized to oppose a small landing of Japanese marines between Bataan's southern extremity on the South China Sea and Olongapo, about 35 miles north. Apparently the Japanese forces were seeking information rather than combat. One squad of marines was headed by a Corporal Sutton I had known at Tientsin. The two forces soon made contact in the jungle.

As we heard it, the U.S. marines engaged the Japanese. The Americans heard someone from the other side announce, in excellent English, words to the effect of: "Don't shoot, we give up." Sutton stood to take his prisoners and was shot through the head. He was the first fatality I heard of among my friends from North China. The Japanese landing force was later destroyed, but I never heard the details.

We were bombed only once while bivouacked in the banyan

grove. The dive bombers probably were targeting a small landing strip where three or four P-40s were being refitted to carry bombs. There was damage to the field but none to our encampment, to the planes or to the now critical supply of aviation gasoline, which had been effectively camouflaged and separated into small caches. The lessons of Clark and Nichols fields, of Cavite and Sangley Point, were not lost on us by the time our aircraft had been reduced in numbers to four.

We remained bivouacked in the banyan grove for two or three days. We had almost no duties and no knowledge of or preparation for a role in defending Bataan. The Army units that had been so apparent when we first entered the peninsula and so dominated the Mariveles area when we first arrived were for the most part gone. Army vehicles were frequently seen on the road, but large movements of troops and equipment were confined to the front on both sides of the peninsula.

A lieutenant I did not know took command of us. We numbered about 150 men, but no attempt was made to organize us into units. I knew perhaps 15 of the marines in the bivouac, either from Tientsin or from brief encounters in the Philippines.

About December 26 we were treated to a turkey dinner. It was to be my last "Stateside" meal for almost four years. I probably weighed about 160 pounds. We were in fighting trim, caused more by irregular eating than by sustained work or marching. Food at the banyan grove had been available only twice a day. The quality was poor, heavy in starches and low in protein. One of the problems was water, which was available only from heavily chlorinated lister bags. Without water, it was difficult to swallow food. The hotcakes or corn fritters that had tasted so good the first day or two soon became mildly repulsive. Burnt-flour or corned-beef gravy on rice became equally unappetizing in the evening. However, because of the low level of our activity, food was not an overriding concern.

Anxiety undoubtedly affected our appetites, but in different ways with different people. If we had been kept busy, the apprehension level would have been considerably lower. As it was, nothing could compete with thoughts of the last three weeks' events, unless it was the specter of what the next few weeks might bring. Idleness and inaction breed fear, a fact that was amply proven to us in the next few months.

On December 28, the marines in the bivouac received orders to leave for the harbor to be transported to Corregidor. We marched in a loose column, again not in units, to docks along the south shore of Mariveles Bay. We broke ranks along the road that skirted the shore and behind which the hills and jungle rose in a low chain to the point of land nearest Corregidor. While we were there, a lone Japanese plane swooped over the hills and descended on two small U.S. Navy vessels that were tied up. The plane dropped one bomb 100 yards or so from where I had settled down on the edge of the jungle. A sailor who had jumped to man a .50-caliber machine gun on one of the vessels took a bomb fragment in his chest. It tore away a grapefruit-sized portion of his rib cage. His last words were: "Look what those bastards have done to my hand." No one else was injured.

Shortly after dark, we were loaded on a barge laden with food from a ship that had been scuttled on the west side of the bay. A tug towed us across the bay to the island fortress.

We arrived at the north dock about 10 p.m. and spent most of the night off-loading and transporting cartons and bags under the cover of darkness. One barge already had been dive-bombed. It sank in the dock area after burning for several hours. Heat had turned sweetened canned milk into a type of candy, which the enterprising dove for during the long waiting for the ax to fall.

We rested for what was left of the night wherever we could make ourselves comfortable. I lay down on a narrow-gauge rail car loaded with cartons of food until it was moved, probably to Malinta Tunnel, shortly before dawn.

Bombing was a constant fear, but I had not heard of a night bombing by the Japanese and felt reasonably secure. I was glad to march off to Middleside Barracks shortly after dawn. I chose a bunk on the second floor, slept, ate C-rations, slept again, looked over the barracks and slept once more. Middleside was constructed of concrete and had a four- or five-foot slab between the first and second floors. The lockers of the U.S. Army soldiers whose bunks we were using, and who had been moved to the gun emplacements, contained many of their personal items. I took some bar soap, razor blades and a pen knife from a locker and later put the pen knife back.

The air raid sirens sounded several times that first day on Corregidor, but no bombs were dropped. After being in the open for so many bombings, the extremely thick layer of concrete between the first and second floors gave a sense of security that I hadn't known for a while. I would sleep on the second floor and find shelter on the first floor when the sirens sounded. My sense of security lasted until mid-morning the next day, December 30. Japanese planes raided the island for nearly three hours. The main targets were the Topside and Middleside barracks. It should have been obvious to the Japanese that the Army troops were no longer there. The bombs ranged up to 500 pounds, and damage was extensive.

I was taking a shower when the sirens went off and Middleside Barracks was hit by a dive-bomber. The attacker was downed, the first loss of a Japanese aircraft that I was aware of. Two batteries claimed the hit. The bomb either came through the top two floors or through an opening in the roof before detonating in a service shaft. The blast was numbing, but damage to the building was negligible. A marine corporal was killed instantly; no one else was injured. Now we knew that the Japanese already had put an airfield in operation within several hundred miles of the fortified islands, or that a carrier was operating with impunity within dive-bomber range. We also learned that Middleside Barracks did not offer the protection we had thought only a day earlier.

The road from Middleside to the dock areas descended in a series of switchbacks, each with a culvert where the road crossed over an arroyo that drained the hillside. I discovered such a culvert shortly after the air raid. Only a hit at the upstream entrance to the culvert represented a danger to anyone seeking protection there. For a brief time at the bivouac, my thoughts had been directed at taking some kind of action against the enemy; but, lacking weapons, those thoughts soon faded. Now I thought almost exclusively about finding a place of safety during the bombing raids. It might have been different if I had some responsibilities, but we were still not formed into military units.

There were air raids every day from January 3 through January 7. I used the culvert every day, and so did 50 or 75 other marines, sailors and Army airmen. The sailors were from the Cavite Navy Yard, from the Yangtze riverboats that had made the perilous trip through the South China Sea just days before Pearl Harbor, or from boats or ships that had been or were to be sunk or scuttled near Manila or Mariveles. The Army Air Corps personnel were from units whose planes had been destroyed on the ground or who had arrived in advance of planes that never came from the States. They were the worst off of all of us because they had never handled field weapons and now had small arms issued to them.

After one of the raids, I was standing near the flagpole at the main entrance to Middleside Barracks when I saw a manhole cover lifted from below. Out of it came two American musicians, both civilians, whom I had known in Tientsin. They were playing their way around the world when the threat of war caused them to leave China on a freighter. Both were in Malinta Tunnel when the fortress of Corregidor fell to the Japanese. I never heard of them again.

Topside and Middleside Barracks and the coast defense batteries at the west end of the island were major targets of the raids from December 30 through January 7. Almost 400 Japanese aircraft participated. Damage inflicted on surface structures ranged from severe to complete. But the gun batteries were not seriously damaged until Bataan had fallen to the Japanese and artillery was trained on them. I never went to Topside. A bomb hit Battery Geary and killed about 30 men, but there was little other loss of life that I learned about.

The hospital was just below the culvert I used for shelter. It was hit, but not seriously, while I was at Middleside. However, the isthmus docks on either side of Corregidor were targeted frequently. Many buildings that were so important to supplying and servicing defense capability of the fortified islands and Bataan were either destroyed or seriously damaged.

The Japanese soon determined that our three-inch anti-aircraft guns had limited range. The problem was with the fuses, which detonated the shells before they reached their full range. Fuses with longer delays were brought in shortly before the surrender, and several formations of bombers were surprised by them. The new fuses forced the planes to come in at higher altitudes, bombing with less accuracy.

I remained at Middleside Barracks about 10 days. Every time a flight of bombers came and went without losing an aircraft, without breaking formation, or without being intercepted by American planes, the truth of our situation became clearer and morale sank lower. We hoped against hope for a relief convoy, but the information circulated about the extent of damage to the fleet at Pearl Harbor and our first-hand information of American preparedness and training in the Far East gave our heads a message that our hearts were having a hard time receiving.

Near the middle of January 1942 I was put under a young lieutenant from Shanghai, along with 16 other marines. Several were from Tientsin, but most were from the Philippines. Some were very young; all were very green. I was the only non-commissioned officer in that group.

Another young officer had 12 or 14 men. They, too, had one non-commissioned officer, another corporal. My group was assigned .30-caliber machine guns, with which I was thoroughly familiar having had machine gun, Browning automatic rifle, Thompson submachine gun and small-arms training often since leaving boot camp. The other lieutenant's group was responsible for the .50-caliber machine guns. Both groups were to deploy on a small island two miles southeast of Corregidor. It would be my last military assignment.

We mustered on Corregidor's south dock, which was still functional, late in the afternoon and were transported the short distance across to Caballo Island in the middle of the mouth of Manila Bay.

A fairly large contingent of Navy personnel was based on the island under an officer of commander rank. He and his men had crewed the Mindanao, the Oahu and the Luzon, Yangtze River gunboats that had been stripped and were to be scuttled near Caballo. The riverboat crews became highly skilled 12-inch mortar crewmen almost overnight on Caballo.

Battery Idaho, an anti-aircraft unit, was also located on the lower part of the island, well-hidden from both land and air observation in the dense 15- or 20-foot trees that covered the central part of the island's flat land. Camouflage disguised the breaks in tree growth where the three-inch guns and a range finder had been placed. They were manned by an Army unit that gave every indication of being completely professional.

We bivouacked in the dock area on the north side of Caballo that night, under blackout. As I looked at the stars I somehow knew that this was the end of my wandering about Manila Bay. There was no place left to go. With a thousand thoughts racing through my mind, it was sometimes difficult to sleep. Before the war, I had resented lying in bed awake. Now it was sleep that I resented, as if by sleeping I was stealing from myself some of the little life I had left.

5

Besieged in the Bay

Manila Bay is one of the great natural harbors of the world. It has a shoreline of some 120 miles and a diameter averaging 35 miles. It empties southwest into the South China Sea through an opening 12 miles wide. The Bataan Peninsula on the northwest is guarded by Mt. Mariveles, with its ever-present crown of cloud. To the southeast, the bay is flanked by Cavite's Pico de Loro Hills, with their innumerable defiles that so well hid the rifles and mortars of the Japanese. When isolated, the U.S. and Philippine forces on the fortified islands would fall under fire from both north and south.

Caballo, known as Fort Hughes to the American military, lies a little north of the halfway point between Bataan on the northwest and Cavite Province on the southeast. It represents a small portion of the south rim of an ancient volcano, most of which lies submerged in the mouth of Manila Bay. Three miles farther north, the major portion of this long-silent natural fireworks is Corregidor, rearing high out of the depths along 120 degrees of the crater's circle. The westward portion of Corregidor looks like the head of a giant pollywog; the main portion of its tail points toward a sliver of volcano rim, Caballo, the only other visible volcanic remains.

Caballo is perhaps half a mile long, shaped somewhat like an old flat iron. The western two-thirds of the island comprises sheer cliffs rising as high as several hundred feet on the north, west and south, with a 45- or 50-degree slope extending to the east. The eastern one-third's 20 or 25 acres lie just a few feet above high tide—flat, very rocky, moderately wooded with 15-to 20-foot trees. The northern cliffs rise out of the water and are impassable at their base; on the south side there is an extremely difficult passage to the western tip of the island, passable only by climbing over boulders met by waves and spray.

The dock was on the northeast side between a promontory and the steep slope to the west. A narrow gauge track led from the dock to the center of the island, which at that point was 150 yards wide. One branch carried a searchlight from a small tunnel out to the eastern end of the island, another led west into a steep tunnel and was pulled several hundred feet by cable to the top of the island. Halfway up were the dispensary, a 12-inch mortar emplacement, supporting facilities and an auditorium where moving pictures could be shown. All were underground, carved out of rock.

The track serviced two 14-inch disappearing rifles, Batteries Woodruff and Gillespie, that could hurl three-quarter-ton projectiles far out to sea but not toward Batangas to the south nor Bataan to the northwest. The magazine for the rifles, the mortars and the anti-aircraft weapons was buried deep in the rock. The top of the island was well wooded, like the slope to the east. The only substantial soil on the island, however, was a porous volcanic material on the slope, which could be dug into without immediately encountering rock. What little soil existed elsewhere filled the spaces between rocks.

The track also led to a 12-inch mortar emplacement on a low shoulder of the southeast slope where it falls away to the flat part of the island on the east and the sea on the south. A spur off the main track led to the southeasternmost part of the island and into a concrete-lined cave that housed the searchlight. This track was on a berm that had been built out of rock from the area immediately to the north, leaving a depressed area that showed evidence of holding water during monsoon season. A stooped figure could traverse one end of the flat land to the other behind the berm without being seen by an observer in Cavite Province.

It took about four hours to off-load our equipment, which included five .30-caliber water-cooled machine guns, two .50-caliber machine guns and a 75-millimeter rifle known as the French 75. We also off-loaded our small arms, our personal effects and many boxes of food and gear. Every item was painfully winched from boat to dock, loaded on rail cars and off-loaded 100 feet inland under a large camouflage netting. Everything was later removed to an area farther from the dock.

At 11 o'clock we were given coffee and sandwiches and told to sleep in the dock area. I had a shoulder pack, the Springfield rifle I had been issued in boot camp, a cartridge belt full of ammunition, a canteen and mess kit, a scabbard and bayonet, a few changes of underwear, a second set of khakis, a Corps field scarf, a towel, some toilet articles and stationery on which I faithfully maintained a journal I had begun December 8. I also had a Waltham wristwatch I had won in a bowling competition in Bremerton $3^{1}/2$ years before, the Waterman pen and pencil set Barna had retrieved, a rosary, a King James version of the New Testament, about $30 in cash and the .45-caliber pistol Barna had lifted from the dispensary after it had been destroyed at the Cavite Navy Yard.

We did not have to exchange words. Everyone knew this was the end of the line. It was here we would meet the enemy. The whole of the Western Pacific Rim had fallen to the Japanese. We were the only meaningful resistance between Mukden and Port Moresby. This had been accomplished in seven weeks. Except for what was now transpiring on Bataan, we had been proven inept at all levels of command and in every type of military action. The smoke from the ruins of Pearl Harbor mingled with that of Clark and Nichols fields, of Indochina and Malay, of Guam and Wake, Java and Sumatra, Borneo and the Celebes. New Guinea, one of the world's largest islands, with a small military contingent on its southeastern tip, was all that stood between Tokyo and Australia other than those with their eyes to the sea, the land and the sky on Bataan and Corregidor. Only China had put up more than token resistance.

We were asked to give our country time. The Japanese Navy had bested our Navy, their air force had bested our air force, their land forces had bested all they had met. Now they were mounting their forces for a drive down the eastern and western slopes of the Bataan mountains. Our air capability was now down to three P-40s. We had abandoned vast stores of war material in Manila, in Legaspe, in Cabanatuan, at Clark and Nichols and in Batangas and Nueva Ecija provinces. We had been outflanked at sea and were now surrounded on a strip of land and bit of bay 40 miles long and 20 miles wide. Our Navy was licking its wounds 2,000 miles away to the south. Our bomber force, except for a handful that escaped to Mindanao, was being salvaged by metals-poor Japan's smelters. Our rifles, machine guns, hand grenades, torpedoes, artillery and support capability were of World War I and Spanish-American War vintage. We were physically unprepared, tactically unprepared and strategically unprepared— and we knew it. MacArthur advised us that help was on the way, thousands of men and hundreds of ships. Not even the most ingenuous believed it for a moment. We went to sleep that night convinced that here we would make our stand, and the world's most powerful nation was powerless to help.

For me, it was not a hasty conclusion. It started with being held over in the Philippines when my enlistment was nearing its end. It was reinforced on being sent to Bataan and finding construction at a furious pace. The destruction of our airfields and most of our Army Air Corps convinced me that we could no longer keep the enemy at a distance and that something was seriously wrong with our high command, both at Pearl Harbor and in the Philippines. When no attempt was made to conserve either men or war material at the Cavite Navy Yard and Sangley Point, it became obvious that our major problem was not so much equipment and troops as a deficiency of command. MacArthur, Brereton and Rockwell had squandered our resources, and they were not renewable. Our leaders were in good company with the British, French and Dutch commands in Southeast Asia.

We assembled the next morning and were told that we would report to the Navy commander assigned to the island. The two marine lieutenants would report to him separately. Lieutenant Leone of the 4th Marines would be responsible for the .30-caliber weapons and Lieutenant Hagan would be in charge of the .50-calibers. I was given components that were to be assembled into five .30-caliber guns and the responsibility for defending the entire perimeter of the flat eastern third of Caballo. Oddly, the two .50-calibers assigned to Lieutenant Hagan were to be interspersed between the .30-caliber weapons on the eastern shore. This meant that to coordinate beach defense, it would be necessary for information to flow separately from the different caliber weapons to the common command post, there to be analyzed and separate orders then issued to the two commands.

I toured the beach scouting positions for the .30-calibers.

One would be about 25 feet above high tide near the 12-inch mortar on the southwesternmost part of the flat area. It would protect the island from a landing among the rocks under the south cliffs and would traverse eastward through a fairly dense stand of trees to protect from a landing below the 12-inch mortar. It would also cover a short stretch of rocky beach to the east, including where the French 75 was to be set up 25 yards east of the 12-inch mortar and just off the searchlight track.

The second emplacement would be about halfway between the 12-inch mortar and the southeasternmost point of the island. This position overlapped the coverage of position one and protected the French 75 and the 12-inch mortar to the west, as well as position three at the end of the track. It also protected the .50-caliber machine gun to be established in trees to the north of track's end.

Position three provided coverage for position two and swept north to the sandy beach area once rocks at the end of the tracks were removed to lower the terrain below the muzzle of the gun.

The fourth emplacement was in a shallow cave near the dock. It covered the area from the sandy beach westward to the dock and was built up with sandbags to just below the level of the gun's water jacket and was nearly invisible under camouflage netting.

The fifth machine gun was a Marlin air-cooled weapon I had neither seen before nor heard of. It had no literature and no spare parts. I worked with it for hours but was never able to get it to fire more than a single shot at a time. We were forced to settle on four positions.

The second .50-caliber machine gun was set up in the edge of the trees at the northeasternmost point of the island overlooking the beach. It was unable to fire south along the beach toward the other .50-caliber and was too far inland to sweep the beach to the west effectively. As it turned out, it was the only one of our machine guns to fire at the enemy.

Position one required only a moderate amount of earth and rock removal and, because of the trees, did not require careful disposition of the diggings. In preparing positions two and three we had to loosen rocks with bayonets or iron pry bars to a depth of about two feet. The rock was piled on three sides, making a pit about four feet deep and seven feet in diameter above two feet and perhaps $4^{1}/_{2}$ in diameter below two feet. This gave us a ledge for equipment. Over the rocks, and cantilevered two feet to the front of the pit, we placed timbers from a gymnasium that had been dismantled before we arrived. Corrugated sheet metal from the gym was placed over the timbers and covered with several layers of rock. Camouflage netting was draped over the front and sharp edges of the emplacements, making them scarcely visible from any direction or from the air. The front legs of the machine guns were embedded in the rock and covered with sandbags, and the rear legs were covered with a sandbag that alternated as a seat. The guns traversed nearly 180 degrees and could be elevated about 20 degrees under the cantilevered roof. The gunner would have to lean over the cartridge belt man as he swept from east to west and fight for footing among the ammunition boxes and cooling tanks, but it could be done.

At each emplacement, ammo boxes were cached in the rocks

where only a direct hit could destroy them, and additional ammunition was stored in the 12-inch mortar emplacement. Ammo could be placed on rail carts and taken down the track to supply positions two and three or could be carried under cover of the berm.

I made a command post between positions two and three and achieved a telephone link to the lieutenant's command post before the gun emplacements were completed, which was about a week after we arrived. The first order over the line was to eliminate all activity on the beach except just before sunrise and just after sunset. If we had received that order on the first day, we never would have been ready.

I assigned three men to each Browning machine gun, one as a gunner, one as his assistant and one as an ammo carrier. Most had never fired a .30-caliber machine gun and only one was qualified with it. I needed to school them in handling the gun, in recognizing and resolving problems and in maintenance. The latter was critical because of salt spray. Three things go wrong in operating a machine gun: failure to feed, failure to fire and insufficient gas to eject a spent cartridge and pick up a new one. Under battle conditions, each must be diagnosed immediately and corrected without delay. We spent hours together cleaning, oiling, learning nomenclature, introducing problems and monitoring the reaction of each crew member to each situation. At the end of the third week on Caballo, I felt they were ready and that it was time to test-fire our weapons.

I gave the men a two-hour-on, four-hour-off schedule. The special orders for those on the "off" portion of the schedule were to stay away from their guns during daylight hours and within voice of their guns at night. The next man on was to relieve the man on duty during mess call. All men on duty were to stay inside the emplacement during their watch, keeping constant lookout for any sign of activity in the water or in the area of the Cavite hills or shoreline. Occasionally, a flash of light from the shore or hills, or something floating in the water, would be observed in daylight. Early in March, the night watch frequently reported flashes of light, always about 11 o'clock. We were told by Army communications not to worry about it, and realized we had people helping us over there.

Sleep was sporadic for most of the men. It was not uncommon to see two or three engaged in conversation, sharing a cigarette, or just sitting and thinking as I made my rounds two or three times each night. I used Jim Barna as a supernumerary, having him fill in on one of the guns or make the rounds for me or with me. He was from Hamtramck, a largely Polish enclave in Detroit, home of the Dodge Main auto plant. I trusted him to act with a cool head after I saw him in action when Cavite was bombed. He probably wouldn't have been good in charge of other men and didn't want to be in charge. He was the only one on the island I called by his first name.

I was now 20 years old, had not finished the 11th grade, had never read a book deeper than Jules Verne and probably had never had what could be called an informed, reasoned and non-superficial conversation. I did not know religion, philosophy, literature or science—and I was sometimes convinced that I never would. I had never truly loved or been loved by a woman and was convinced that would not likely be my lot, either. This may have been our greatest fear—that we would never participate as a link in the chain of humanity, that this was indeed for each of us the end of the line. Whenever my thoughts turned to this, I experienced a vast emptiness, a loneliness that was beyond words and almost beyond thought. Barna was an Eastern Rite Catholic. He believed and did not question. I was of the Roman Rite; I thought much but not well. What should have been accepted on faith, I submitted to reason, and for that I was ill-equipped. My spiritual and intellectual life was born on Horse Island, as Caballo translates; but after its birth, it was to remain quiescent for many years.

Miller, a private first class, was crew chief of the .50-caliber machine gun at the end of the searchlight track about 20 yards from our position three. He was a complete soldier. He knew his weapon and he knew what to do with it. He was fearless without being foolish. Barna believed himself somehow exempt from mortality; Miller recognized his and minimized the risks without letting caution cripple him as it did so many. They were both men of integrity. Their codes of conduct were uncomplicated and innate; mine was studied. I would be there when the chips were down, but it was a matter of pride. They would be there with no strings attached. I learned much from both of them.

Barna would be executed for stealing on a work party; Miller would be beaten to death at Nichols Field by the White Angel for opposing the treatment of prisoners there. His head and face were so swollen from beatings as he stood in front of the Japanese officer in his last moments that he was unrecognizable. Ordered to salute the White Angel, so known for the gloves he wore, Miller spit in his face. He is my measure of a man. Among the military men I knew, only P.D. Armstrong, a squirrel shooter from Tennessee, could stand beside Miller. There were others, many others, or the lines would not have held; but Barna and Miller and Armstrong were men I had stood beside in the mess line. P.D. went back to Corregidor's Malinta Tunnel time after time for ammunition and help as the Japanese gained a foothold at North Point, captured Kindley Field and pressed forward to Malinta Hill. It was said Armstrong took a terrible toll among the enemy before one of his kind in a different uniform saw him before he himself was seen.

Making the rounds one night shortly after the emplacements were completed, I stopped at my lieutenant's command post and told him that all of the emplacements were ready, the men were trained, supplies were secured, the resupply system tested and that we were ready to test-fire the weapons and calibrate their sights. He was playing cards with Shaggy Marsh, crew chief of the second .50-caliber machine gun who spent most of his time at the command post, and with Lieutenant Hagan and their man in charge of communications.

Lieutenant Leone half stood up and said: "Hell no, we'll show the Japs where we are!" I asked him what we were supposed to do when the Japs came and the weapons wouldn't fire. He looked alarmed but wouldn't change his mind. He wanted to know why they were not in firing condition and who among our men knew machine guns. I told him I was the only person on the island certified as a .30-caliber machine gunner, that all guns were different, and that the salt spray in the sea air caused receiver action to change daily. When I told him to come down to the emplacements and see for himself, he told me to go make my rounds. To the day the islands fell, he never inspected the beach defenses we had set up.

Neither did I see Lieutenant Hagan far from the command post in the 3½ months we were on the island. They stayed put and fed each other's fears. Shaggy Marsh suggested, Leone and Hagan ordered, and all the crews knew that when the Japs came, there was nothing that either lieutenant could or would do. By the end of the first six weeks, all directions originated on the beach and were carried out there.

Hagan became so preoccupied that most of those who came in contact with him thought he had lost his mind. His train of thought disappeared halfway into a sentence, he frequently covered his face with his hands, and he turned away while talking to someone. Often he would fail to respond to conversation. He was well-educated and clean of speech and was a handsome man. I pictured him as a teacher in a small college. I pictured Leone as a used-car salesman and Shaggy as a gambler, and I was not far wrong.

Two incidents solved the problem of the test-firing ban. Position two proved to be about a foot and a half too far inland to protect the beach in front of position one. Either the whole position had to be moved that distance or the gun itself had to be moved. We chose the latter. The plan was to dig the rocks out of the beach side of the emplacement, push them out the front, move the gun forward and then extend the roof to cover it. Smith was crew chief, and I told him to let me know when he was ready to move the gun. It had to be dead level when in horizontal lock, or it would fire into the ground in one direction and into the air in the other.

A day or so later, Smith told me he was ready. He was in the pit. I told him to remove the sandbags from the legs, the cartridge belt from the receiver, clear the chamber and tell me when he was ready. I laced my fingers under the water jacket, straddled the muzzle and said: "Say when." He gave the signal and I lifted. At that moment, a shot went off between my legs and an instant later I found myself in the entrance to the emplacement, pistol in hand and pointed to his face. I cooled off about the time Barna came from the field phone with a message from Leone wanting to know "what in hell was going on down there." I told Barna to say it was an accidental discharge and that I would report later.

I figured out that from three to five shots should have fired before Smith's hand could be released from the trigger. The spent cartridge had been ejected, but the receiver had failed to pick up the next round. Either the receiver was binding or the recoil spring needed adjustment. The receiver was clean and free, so I concluded that the recoil spring was the problem. There was no way to determine the right adjustment except by firing the weapon, which I had orders not to do. I told Smith with little confidence that, in battle, he should loosen the recoil spring one-half turn at a time until the weapon fired as it should. Critical time would be lost as a Japanese landing party surged ashore.

A few days later, I was picking my way among the rocks under the cliffs to the west of position one. The surf was up and noisy, and when I was about halfway to the west end of the island I heard a shot. Looking up, I saw a soldier with a rifle in hand motioning me back. I did not argue.

I went to Topside and hunted down the Army lieutenant who had ordered the shot and asked him what was going on. He wanted to know why I had not responded when his man called to me. I told him the surf was too loud and that I was responsible for beach defense and had to know if it was feasible for the enemy to land undetected and threaten the island by overtaking the position one machine-gun nest at night. He agreed that I should patrol there, but when the area was in heavy shade.

When I arrived back at the little shelter I had built under some trees and where Barna was sitting in for me on the field phone, I was surprised to learn that no one had heard the shot.

The next day, with the wind blowing out to sea in a rare shift of weather and the southwestern face of the cliffs in deep shade, Barna and I took the machine gun from position one off its tripod, carried it around the bend several hundred feet from the 12-inch mortar, buried the muzzle and chamber in cotton mattresses, and squeezed the trigger. It, too, fired only one round. After several adjustments, I got off a five-round burst and took it back to its position. Within a few days, by switching machine guns between positions, the four weapons had been test fired and proven operable. If the test firings were heard, they must have been thought to have come from Topside.

I had a second run-in with Leone about three weeks later when, about 1 a.m., I approached position one, gave the signal, and nothing happened. I gave it again, two quick taps of a stick on a stick followed by a delayed tap. Still nothing happened. I climbed the 12 or 15 steps cut out of the soil and rocks slowly and quietly and listened at the edge of the pit. It had no roof over the front half but had a good stone cover over the back half to give protection from shells bursting against the cliffs above. The opening would allow quick removal of the machine gun if necessary.

I struck a match and found E.C. Cummings asleep. He had arrived in the Philippines straight out of boot camp, just a month before. I took my .45-caliber pistol from its holster and edged around the slope to the left of the carved stairs. Intending to teach Cummings a lesson he would never forget, I slid the receiver back on the pistol. At the same time, I began to slide slowly down the steep western slope. When I tried to stop my slide, I released the receiver with my left hand while my finger was on the trigger. A bullet slammed into the inside roof of the emplacement. I had nearly killed Cummings. He never completely lost the wild-eyed stare that he had when he first woke up. I swore at him and told him I'd kill him if it happened again. He never said a word. Position one was extremely important because it was the only position that had no backup in one direction. If the enemy had landed to the west and overcome the position, they could have infiltrated behind our beach defense and taken the whole flat part of the island, including Lieutenant Leone, with 30 or 40 men. They could be displaced only by shelling ourselves from Corregidor and Fort Drum—one of two other small fortified islands in the bay. Fort Drum (Fraile Island) lay 2½ miles to the south, and Fort Frank (Carabao Island) lay a mile and a half farther to the southwest.

Leone did not call until the next morning. Again I told him "accidental discharge" and "my fault." I never again let Cummings stand watch alone. Shortly afterward, he was standing in the mess line when a lone incoming shell hit near the field kitchen, killing a Filipino mess boy and wounding Cummings in the hand. He was the first marine on Caballo to qualify for the Purple Heart.

The father of the Filipino mess boy killed by what turned out to be a 150-millimeter rifle shell also worked in the field kitchen. I spoke to him about it. He told me his other son, a radical left-wing Hukbalahup, had been killed a month earlier. The father was dry-eyed and philosophical about it. "We will be following them soon," he said. I left thinking more about myself than his sons.

Corregidor was being bombed daily. One day, without warning, 27 planes flew over Caballo in tight formation and the island's anti-aircraft weapons opened fire. The projectiles were well-placed but detonated several thousand feet below the flight. I later spoke with one of the anti-aircraft crew with whom I had talked before. On that occasion, several weeks after we arrived on the island, the air raid siren sounded while I was visiting a gun site near the sandy beach. I immediately ran through the trees toward the rail tunnel. The battery consisted of three guns and a range finder. I tripped over the cable to the range finder and fell hard. Having been bombed at Cavite and Sangley Point and at Middleside on Corregidor, I was more than a little bombshy—terrified might be more accurate. The sergeant picked me up unhurriedly, looked me in the eye and said: "You're scared, aren't you?" I denied it but was soon babbling about the previous few weeks. Suddenly I was ashamed. When I left, I walked. That was the last time, I believe, that I ever reacted to enemy action without being in full control of myself. Later I asked the sergeant why the anti-aircraft guns were fired if they could not reach the planes. He replied that they were expecting longer fuses and were trying to draw the planes down where they could be hit. I never saw one hit.

A day or so later, a Japanese fighter casually flew along the north coast of the island, probably no more than 500 feet above the water. As the pilot rounded the sandy beach on the northeasternmost part of the island, he thumbed his nose at the men swimming in the water and those staring at him from the beach. He swung to the left slightly and headed toward Nichols Field south of Manila. Long after he had shrunk to the size of a toy in the sky, someone opened fire at him with the .50-caliber machine gun just inside the tree line. This was the second and last time a marine unit I was associated with had fired at the enemy. The first was equally futile. Our role, it appeared, was to be shot at.

When the alarm sounded a few days later, the anti-aircraft guns sent up their short-fused projectiles and the bombs fell. No one was killed, no one was injured, and no equipment was hit. I was at machine-gun position two and took shelter there while the bombs fell. The ground rumbled as the concussions tossed us about somewhat. When the dust settled, I looked up and down the south beach and saw that nothing there had been damaged. I went over the track, rang up the command post and reported that the south beach defenses were intact. I then hung up and started for position four on the north beach, wanting to get there before the planes doubled back for their second pass.

When the planes returned, I took shelter in a small cave a few feet from position four. Again, they caused no significant damage. Shrapnel scarred the command post and some storage buildings and the field kitchen again, but no real harm was done. About a third of the bombs missed the island and landed in the bay. Neither the dock nor the Navy vessels anchored several hundred yards out were touched. One of the bombs had landed 30 or 40 feet from shore, sending up a tower of water. When the planes left unscathed from their second pass and we came out of our shelters, we saw about 40 fish, some up to 18 inches long, floating on the surface. I ended up with four red snappers, which I knew were safe to eat. I took them back to the south shore and broiled them over coals of wood retrieved from the torn-down barracks. Split 14 ways, we all had a treat, just enough to remind us how drab our food had become. We joked that we hoped we would be bombed again soon. Attempts to obtain a further harvest with hand grenades met with varying success. Many unexploded grenades still lie on the bottom near the north dock, unless they have rusted away.

On February 11, the unmistakable rumble of PT boat motors caught the attention of everyone on Fort Hughes. Because of the mine fields across the mouth of Manila Bay, we were certain the boats were ours. The sound faded to the west, and we proceeded to speculate what was going on. None of the speculations included MacArthur. Suicide PT boat attacks on Japanese shipping off the coast of Bataan had been carried out early in the war and this seemed most likely a repeat of that heroic adventure. It was a day or two before we learned that MacArthur had turned his command over to Jonathan Wainwright and left on one of several PT boats on a desperate and perilous trip through waters over which the Japanese held absolute and unchallenged control. We knew now that our situation was hopeless.

Despite all the hype and stage managing, MacArthur had few admirers among the troops. His failures were too obvious and his posturing too transparent. His refusal to visit his troops on Bataan was followed by his criticism of Wainwright for the premature fall of Bataan, which was the fruit of MacArthur's own folly. Wainwright earned the loyalty and affection of his troops by his presence with them on the field of battle; MacArthur sought it through the press. He never changed.

It was probably early March that I was passing time with the crew of the 12-inch mortar battery at the base of the steep slope leading to Topside when I was asked to furnish some men to back up the skeleton Navy crew assigned to the mortar. I got Barna, one man from the French 75 and one man each from the three positions on the south side of the island. I wasn't aware at first that it was to be a live drill or that we had been given targets in the Pico de Loro Hills of Cavite Province. We were shown by an Army sergeant named Pharr how to roll a rail car into the magazine, load a 700-pound projectile in its canister, push it to the emplacement and open the breech of the mortar, the muzzle of which had been lowered to the horizontal position. The canister was then opened, the projectile inserted in the breech, powder bags packed behind the projectile, the breech mechanism closed and screwed shut, the muzzle elevated and the circles set.

The blast was followed by a screech like all the demons out of hell. The howl was caused by the compression ring that had detached from the projectile and followed it for hundreds of yards before it fell into the bay. We fired five or six rounds when someone reported seeing a splash in the water a few hundred feet out. Someone shouted: "Ranging shot! Clear the area!" We all ran to the heavily concreted magazine. Moments later what was probably a 105-millimeter mortar shell exploded in the emplacement on the steps down to the base of the mortar pedestal. After one shot for range and deflection, safe in a mountain defile, the Japanese had managed to put a shell directly on target. We were in awe of their marksmanship. There was no follow-up projectile from the Japs or ourselves.

Shell fragments had damaged the threads on our mortar's breech mechanism, which had been left open, and entered the magazine. One fragment ricocheted around a corner and took a chunk out of Pharr's left arm. He calmly let someone apply a tourniquet and left for the dispensary. No other damage was done that affected operations, but the scarring of the concrete was a daily reminder. The mortar was not fired again until preparations were being made by the Japanese for their landing on Corregidor from Bataan.

Toward noon a few days later I found myself in the hospital ward halfway up the tunnel to Topside. I was there to get the weekly supply of quinine pills for the men on the beach and to obtain a package of "poison" for the lister bag. I stopped to watch a game of penny ante poker being played by some recuperating patients and staff. Also watching, from his bed in a corner away from the mortar pit and looking out on it, was a patient in a hospital gown. He wore a sailor's hat, which accentuated the malaria or jaundice pallor of his face and the yellowed whites of his eyes. I was leaning against a stanchion, my back to the mortar pit, looking toward the game at the center of the room. The sailor moved closer to the game by lying stomach-down on his bed, his heels where his head had been. Without warning, a Japanese mortar shell exploded in the mortar pit, its shrapnel ricocheting around for a few seconds. The elevating gear of the mortar was moderately damaged; the only other damage done was the removal of part of the sick sailor's heel by the shell fragment. He, too, was awarded the Purple Heart. We received three or four additional incoming rounds, none of which did any damage to personnel or equipment.

A library of books was available for those who were interested. I checked out a volume of Shakespeare's plays but was unable to concentrate on it. I then tried to get into a novel by Henry James but couldn't get interested in it, either. I tried my hand at writing verse, but it invariably embarrassed me the next day, so I gave that up as well. A moving picture, one of three saved by being on loan when Corregidor's film storage building was destroyed in an early bombing, was shown in the small auditorium once a week. It was a good film with top actors and actresses, as I remember, but it no longer seemed important.

One night shortly after the movie began, one viewer was stung on the arm by a scorpion, which made the seats suspect and cost what little patronage the screenings previously had. The victim's arm swelled so that his elbow and wrist were no longer discernible, but he was in little pain and in about two weeks he looked normal again.

A "beast" of another kind made an appearance at position one on my rounds one night. As I climbed the improvised ladder to the pit, I heard a scuffling in the underbrush followed by a shout of alarm in the emplacement. As the commotion continued, I stuck three or four matches together and saw a 2$^1/2$- or three-foot iguana climb over the rocks and out from under the overhang.

Miller, who was a genuine outdoorsman, heard about it and sought it for days in the tac-a-mona plants. The plant name literally means wait-a-minute because its reverse spines let you in but not out. That iguana saved its highly prized tail by climbing where Miller could never go. Its ancestors had been on the island for a million years.

That lizard may now be the sole guardian of a small treasure. A soldier from New Jersey had fashioned a Las Vegas-style dice board. He took a percentage as the troops played against each other, and soon "the house" had most of the money on the island. He scrounged a shell canister from the French 75 and came back from the slope broke and looking like a grave-digger. That ended all but penny ante gambling on the flat part of Fort Hughes. It is almost exactly even money that he never lived to come back for his cache.

Around the middle of March we were bombed with picric acid. It turned a large area of the slope a sickly yellow and accomplished its mission by ruining our water supply. From that time, water became a major concern. Some may have come from the distillation system of one of the Navy boats anchored off the island, but most came from sumps or rain, I suppose, because all we got had to be heavily chlorinated. It left you more thirsty than before you drank, yet at some point everyone had to drink it. Between the water and the food, which was now about 37 percent of normal, our weight steadily declined, mine to about 140 pounds.

It was a long 12 hours between our two meals each day. Corn fritters and sugar syrup was a common breakfast, with hotcakes a close second. Fresh meat was infrequent at first and then absent altogether, replaced by corned beef mixed into red rice. Vegetables and fruit were unavailable. When the corned beef was gone, it was replaced by a burnt-flour gravy, which was eaten because of its oil content.

The food problem was worst on the inactive. But they had a much worse problem. Inaction is the enemy of courage. The fearful kept with the fearful. Their worlds closed in on them. They lost interest in whatever was outside of self. Their rehearsals were all concerned with the day of the great test. Men who were drinkers, sports enthusiasts, woman chasers, pleasure-seekers or even shy observers of civilian and religious codes, shorn of those interests, rehearsed one life-terminating scene after another. Miller was eager for the day; Barna would see what happened and go from there. I built a boat.

There were several scenarios. One was that Fort Hughes would be taken, at least the flat eastern portion, and Topside would be allowed to wither without food or water. Another possibility was that Corregidor would fall without Fort Hughes being taken. A third was one in which Fort Hughes would run out of food and water and its men would weaken, starve and die of thirst. A fourth scenario, one I never considered, was being taken prisoner without a final showdown.

Fort Drum and Fort Frank, the other two small fortified islands, were now under daily siege. Fort Drum may have taken more hits for its size than any target in history. It's a credit to its designers in the second decade of the century that it withstood every assault the Japanese could mount against it. The siege began with four 105-millimeter guns, followed shortly by ten 240-millimeter howitzers. From early February to the end of March there must have been little sleep on Fraile Island. We stood on the south shore of Caballo and watched and listened.

The Japanese also pounded incessantly at Carabao Island's Fort Frank, which guarded the entrance of Manila Bay from the southeast. The Japanese finally penetrated one of its magazines, the blast vibrating Fort Hughes and filling the southwestern sky with black smoke.

Bombing and shelling of Fort Hughes was mild in comparison. The reason was a matter of constant concern and speculation. Whether we were not important enough, whether they were saving us for later, whether they felt we had not been able to recover from their direct hits on our mortar emplacements, we were never to know.

The shelling and bombing of Corregidor has been too little understood in the United States. It happened too early in the

war, and was too negative when upbeat news was required, to
have been widely known and fully understood at the time. Immediately after the war, too much momentous news had inter-
vened for Corregidor to be generally appreciated. Perhaps if it
had been better publicized, greater care would have been taken
to see that the effect on those who lived through it, and through
the 41 months that followed, would be minimized. It was truly
an experience too deep for words. When telling was tried, the
very emotion of the words, oddly, cost them their impact. Besides, to recount it meant to relive it.

General Wainwright had his men make an estimate of the
number of pounds of Japanese shells Corregidor absorbed from
the hundreds of enemy guns and howitzers on Bataan and
Cavite. The estimate was 1,800,000. Corregidor has a target area
of about two square miles, which may be easier to imagine as
1,280 acres. That translates into 7,680 residential lots. If on Corregidor, your average home lot would have absorbed 234 pounds
of incoming shells up to 240 millimeters in diameter. Your lot
would also have been raked by flight after flight of heavy bombers, light bombers and dive bombers. Most of the shelling and
much of the bombing would have occurred between April 10 and
May 5, 1942. If your lot were located in James Ravine, as were
Battery E of the 60th Coast Artillery and a platoon of the 4th
Marines, or along the north shore on the eastern half of the
island, where the bulk of 4th Marines were dug in, your piece
of turf would have absorbed 10 or 20 times as much as the average lot. Yet the Japanese landing forces incurred staggering loss
of life. Skeletons came out of holes all over the island and, with
World War I weapons, laid considerable hurt upon a modern army.

It took the Japanese five months to open Manila Bay to their
ships. It was by far the longest period Japan had been denied a
local objective since the beginning of the Sino-Japanese War in
1938, and possibly in their entire 2,000-year history.

Many men on Corregidor were not assigned and had no unit
to call their own. They were Army personnel from Bataan, Navy
personnel from sunk or scuttled ships, or Army Air Corps per-

sonnel who had lost all the equipment they had been trained to use. Most of these men would have made good backup personnel for any of the batteries or emplacements. These units, however, were short of weapons and supplies and did not want them. There was no equipment to form separate units, so the unwanted became the "rats" of Malinta Tunnel. They chose to stay alive in the tunnel instead of being useless targets on hills or beaches. In the tunnel, fear fed upon fear until the men passed the point of no return. The fault lay, again, with high and middle command. When extra shovels and picks were needed, the tunnel rats should have and could have had those picks and shovels in their hands. They were wasted. Some wasted themselves, but most were wasted by others.

Much has been said about how MacArthur stood fearlessly without cover while hoards of planes dropped tons of bombs on the rock, which is true. It should be noted that when this took place, it was Topside that was being bombed while the general had Malinta Hill, Bottomside and Middleside between him and the target. Before the bombing became more indiscriminate, he moved his quarters into the tunnel, as he should have. MacArthur, by that time recovered from the catatonia he appears to have exhibited in the first two weeks of the war—those critical two weeks in which his air capability, his naval support and his supplies were lost—was trying to reverse his self-image and the image others had of him.

For Fort Hughes, the shooting war started in earnest near mid-March, with Battery Craighill dumping about ten 700-pound shells onto the defile emplacements of the Japanese in the Pico de Loro Hills. The guns there had been pounding Fort Frank and Fort Drum mercilessly. Their bombardment stopped. On the next day, or soon after, Craighill again fired on Cavite and this time received moderate counter-fire.

Something else happened at that time that gave us temporary hope. An Army ordnance expert modified a 12-inch mortar shell to explode at the level of the bomber flights. The round was duly fired at airplanes as they came out of the sun. The shell failed to detonate, falling into the bay several miles south of the mortar that fired it. It was felt that there was some danger of a muzzle blast, and a second attempt was never made.

Firing from Battery Craighill ceased with the receipt of heavy return fire on March 16 or 17. Apparently the island command wanted the enemy to believe that the batteries had been damaged. It became more and more apparent that the island's offensive capability was being reserved for the anticipated invasion.

The final punishment of Corregidor began several days after Bataan fell on April 9, 1942. The Japanese consolidated their position between Cabcaben on the east and Mariveles on the west with the emplacement of hundreds of heavy-bore rifles and howitzers. Tens of thousands of shells pounded U.S. defensive positions with deadly accuracy. The bombers that had been diverted to the reduction of Bataan now had free rein over Corregidor, whose three-inch anti-aircraft capability soon ceased to exist. While bombing had leveled all but the most rugged nonmilitary installations on Corregidor before Bataan fell, the damage to true military capabilities had been negligible. Each battery was highly independent, with its own magazines and crew facilities. Now, in support of artillery firing from Bataan and Cavite, the bombers prevented transport of food and water and movement of the wounded and sick.

That man or beast, any men or any beasts, could survive the bombardments of those few weeks seemed out of the question. I sat by our machine-gun emplacement at the north side of the island by the hour watching and listening as the explosions savaged the south side of Corregidor. At night the flashes were brilliant and the roar was constant. Ten years later, I stood in a canyon in the Santa Susana Mountains in southern California watching and listening to, but especially physically possessed by, a test firing of what was then one of the nation's great military rocket engines. It imparted just a glimmering of what it must have been for the men who were the target of the apocalypse on Corregidor.

A lone night shell received by Caballo before the final days landed about 30 yards from me while I slept on a small platform under a mosquito net just beyond the searchlight track from position two. The searchlight crew had moved the 48-inch mirror from its concrete bunker under cover of darkness. It was positioned at the end of the track about 150 feet east of my makeshift floor, its generator motor running. After waiting several hours for it to be turned on, I left to get some sleep. About 2 a.m., I learned later, it was turned on and its trial beam swept the bay south of the island from Battery Craighill eastward past Fort Drum, then northwest toward Cabcaben on the Bataan Peninsula. The light was greeted within minutes by a single volley from the Pico de Loro hills in Cavite. It landed over the track in a drained and dry rocky tidal basin. I was sleeping on my back, my left leg bent at the knee. The first thing I was aware of was that I as sitting half upright and that an explosion had taken place. The netting had billowed in toward me. I rolled off the platform to the rocks eight or 10 inches below and waited for another shell. It never came. After a few minutes, I heard the searchlight crew pushing the light back to its bunker. At about that time, I rubbed my hand down the outside of my left leg. It came up sticky. I picked an occasional small piece of stone out of my leg for many years.

On April 12 or 13, heavy fire from Battery Craighill's four 12-inch mortars brought counter-fire from Bataan and Cavite, but not with their heavy equipment. The next day we again directed a heavy barrage on Cabcaben, this time with no counter-fire. Night and day, Corregidor was taking an incredible beating from Bataan and, to a lesser extent, from Cavite. The mortars on Fort Hughes were silent until April 30 or May 1, when Craighill again hammered Bataan. The Japanese response was little delayed and overwhelming. To the shelling were added nearly 100 Japanese aircraft sorties, mostly against Corregidor. There was little sleep and no activity in the field kitchen. We ate C-rations or neglected to eat. There could be no doubt that the moment of truth was imminent.

The shelling of Corregidor became still more intense May 4, and we readied for an invasion. We had been given an opportunity to write a last letter home around April 26. I'm afraid that what I wrote exhibited a little more than a touch of self-pity and schoolboy philosophy. The letter left on a submarine that had negotiated the harbor mines. Several days earlier, two PBY amphibious planes had landed between Fort Hughes and Corregidor and departed with an unknown cargo. We saw the handwriting on the wall; the message was the one we had been telling ourselves but did not want to believe.

On the night of May 4, the crescendo reached an unbelievable pitch. Soon the 14-inch rifles on Fort Drum began a barrage directly over us. Each projectile sounded like a freight train and must have been in a very low trajectory. They were firing on landing craft in Cabcaben and Mariveles. The Japanese had failed after months of shelling to silence these lethal weapons. A little later, our mortars on Fort Hughes opened in a continuous barrage. We were lofting nearly half-ton projectiles of a high-blast, low-penetration type barely over Corregidor to the bay beyond North Point. At the same time, the Japanese on Cavite were shelling us from the south and southeast. The Corregidor invasion was a reality. I had long since positioned my men and readied for an invasion of Fort Hughes that I now was not sure would come; Fort Drum so protected Fort Hughes that it was not likely to be used as a stepping stone to Corregidor.

Around midnight, the shelling from both Bataan and Corregidor came to an ominous stop. Shortly afterward, the sound of 37-millimeter artillery took the place of the Japanese 240-millimeter howitzers, interspersed with an occasional louder report, probably three-inch cannon. When the wind was favorable, rifle fire could be heard. It was impossible to imagine how a defense could be mounted against a landing party after the pounding of the last month and especially the last four or five days. Yet the firing continued until around 11 a.m. May 6.

At noon, the flag of the United States was hauled down and a white flag hoisted. I was a member of the largest group of Americans ever to surrender in battle. Some 17,000 Americans and more than 120,000 Philippine Army soldiers throughout the islands were to lay down their arms.

We milled around silently on Bottomside while codes and

equipment were destroyed by officers and high non-commissioned officers. I threw the receivers and spares kits of the .30-caliber machine guns into the bay. The recently bombed food storage warehouse was opened and C-rations were made available, as well as some cases of fruit. There was little talk.

I was filled with conflicting emotions. It would be false and cowardly to say that I did not feel great relief that I would not now likely become a casualty of battle. That I had never once squeezed a trigger with an enemy in my sights would, I knew, be a lasting self-reproach. That I took so long to learn to control my fears was a shame I shared with many. I was not now going to be able to slide away in the boat I had constructed of corrugated iron sealed with roofing tar and equipped with shell canisters for outriggers. It was beached at position four, and the plan was to paddle to safety under the cover of night to the hills of Batangas Province a few miles south of Manila Bay. "All must surrender," we were told, "then you should try to escape." With no quinine, no food, no maps and no knowledge of Tagalog beyond those words used in public transportation and shopping, I resigned myself to becoming a prisoner of war. Given a second chance, I would not choose that course.

Suddenly, early in the afternoon, the shelling of Fort Hughes from Cavite began again, one shell hitting near Battery Craighill. We all hurried to the tunnel or the mortar emplacement. The shell bursts were moderate and I guessed they were 105s.

Lieutenant Leone, in a jovial mood after successfully abandoning his command post, was talking to anyone who would listen in the mortar magazine. I caught his eye and turned away. Moments later, he came over to me and told me to take my men back to their positions. I stared at him in disbelief and finally told him I would go but I wouldn't order any of the men to go with me and that I would report the incident after the war. The shells were now hitting well away from our positions. Barna came with me.

When we got to the French 75 between incoming shells, Barna looked in and called me back. Squeaky Myrick and the tall, quiet college boy whom everybody liked were sprawled inside. Both were dead. The position had taken a hit just outside its front opening, doing little damage to the emplacement. Neither of the dead showed any significant physical damage; apparently the blast had ruptured the capillaries in their lungs. It would have been quick if not instantaneous. They had lived to the surrender and a few minutes more. I stayed.

Barna went back to the mortar and called the medics. Then we ran down the tracks and into position three, where we discussed stupid and cowardly lieutenants. Just after dark, the shelling stopped. We went back to Craighill, and the bodies and the lieutenant were gone. I did not see him again until he asked me on Corregidor to verify to some acquaintances that he had met the Japanese upon their coming ashore to arrange the time and place for the official surrender of the island. I conceded that he had.

It was about 11 p.m. and we were in the 12-inch mortar emplacement when we were called out by a tall Japanese who repeated "comma outu" several times. I was the fourth or fifth of perhaps 30 marines, sailors and Army men to exit the magazine. I came out with my hands up. After a few more followed with their hands up, the Japanese said, "Handsu downu, don'tu be afraid."

The myth was ended. That the little people with the round eyeglasses and gold front teeth who kowtowed to everyone but the honey barge operator, the people from the little island that had so recently opened their country to Western ideas, could conquer half of China and run the Americans, the British, the Dutch and the Anzacs out of the Western Pacific was inconceivable. Yet here we were throwing down our arms before those same people.

My mind was filled with a wild confusion. It was impossible to absorb the reality. Shame, ignominy, wild speculation, anger, frustration, resentment and defiance fought to dominate my mind and emotions. I would never know if this would have been the frame of mind in which I would have greeted a Japanese assault force. I had much left to prove.

Part II
KORAH!!!

"Korah" is an expletive used
by the Japanese to warn or get
the attention of an inferior.

6

The Degradation Begins

The 400 soldiers, sailors and marines stationed on Caballo at the time of the surrender roamed around for almost two days after the white flag went up on Corregidor. Our captors showed their contempt by ignoring us. We had little contact with Japanese except when they had a stealthy look at our wrists for watches or made an awkward search for something of value in our pockets. Otherwise, we milled about the island near the slope to Topside.

On the second day, the food storage warehouse was opened by a Japanese officer who designated what would be loaded on a barge and taken to Corregidor. Fewer than 100 cartons of packaged and canned food were in the warehouse: sugar, fish, prunes, corned beef, peaches, coffee and a few tins of jams and jellies. It would have carried us another month or six weeks. A Japanese soldier opened a flat can, stared at its contents, smelled it, took out a whitish disc and tried to take a bite. Disgusted, he spit it out and threw the can aside. During a break, I retrieved the can and the four or five flat discs that remained. It was abalone. The disc proved just as inedible as the Japanese found it. When my jaws began to ache, I gave up on it too.

We loaded the cases for the Japanese, ate C-rations when we found them and drank chlorinated water, which made us more thirsty than before.

Toward the end of the second day, we were herded together

in the service area near the dock on the north side of the island. The camouflage was damaged but still afforded some shade. Two or three guards patrolled the outside of the area while we were separated by branch of service under the canopy. The Army, about 300 troops, was positioned nearest the dock. There were 50 or 60 sailors, about 30 marines and a handful of Filipino civilians. About 30 boxes were stacked near the center camouflage pole.

No provision was made for food or water. The bay was our latrine. If there were non-ambulatory cases, I never saw them. The soldiers and sailors had fairly large duffel bags or seabags of clothing and personal items; the marines, who had lost everything except what they were carrying in the Cavite Navy Yard bombing and who had accumulated little since then, had a variety of containers for their personal effects. I had an officer's musette bag; some had backpacks; others pulled the four corners of a towel or piece of canvas or cotton sheeting together around a few belongings.

My cache included a toothbrush, half a can of Colgate tooth powder, a Gillette double-edged razor, a 10-pack of blades, the Marine Corps field scarf, an almost empty bottle of Vaseline hair oil, a canteen and cup, a mess kit with a cover and a fork and a spoon, a rosary and my King James New Testament. I later acquired a U.S. Navy hospital bath towel that was to become very important.

I had made a major mistake when I gave up my cartridge belt along with my pistol and the rifle and bayonet I had been carrying since boot camp. Several marines had Marine Corps issue blankets, which they rolled up and formed into a horse shoe; I lost mine in Cavite at the same time that the warehouse was destroyed along with my second camphor chest of China souvenirs.

Toward noon the second day under the camouflage, a Japanese soldier entered the area, walked directly to the 30 boxes— which contained dried prunes—saw that several had been opened and emptied, and quickly walked out. We all watched him with interest and anxiety.

Soon a Japanese officer and an interpreter appeared. We were lined up and the officer, through the interpreter, demanded to know who had broken into the boxes. No one volunteered. We were stood at attention until late in the afternoon, with the interpreter asking periodically who had taken the prunes. Shortly before dark, Barna stepped forward. After 15 or 20 minutes, five more stepped out. They were lined up about 10 paces from the area in which we were concentrated, stood at attention and told that the penalty for stealing what belonged to the emperor was death. The rest of us were dismissed, while Barna and the other five stood at attention all night. In the morning, they were mildly dismissed.

Later that day, all of the Army personnel and most of the sailors and marines were loaded on an intercoastal steamer and taken to Corregidor. About 30 sailors and marines, myself included, were told we would stay on Caballo to salvage metal and clean up the dock area and storage facilities, which turned out to be a two-day job. While still on Caballo I asked a Japanese officer by sign for food and water. He shook his head and went away, but he sent a bucket of rice, a half bucket of vegetables heavy with soy sauce and a bucket of the best water I had tasted since our water supply was bombed with picric acid. The portions were small, but it was the first cooked food we had eaten for more than two weeks. The water was the best.

We boarded a small launch and made the 20-minute trip to Corregidor's south dock, where we milled about for several hours while the Japanese paid little attention to us. The sun was intense and our breathing began to come quick and shallow. In mid-afternoon we were assembled and marched to an area southeast of Malinta Hill known as the 92nd Garage. It had been the motor pool and originally was built as a beaching ramp and service area for amphibian aircraft that landed in the somewhat sheltered area between Corregidor and Caballo. The Garage comprised five or six acres of volcanic soil and broken rock sloping gently into the bay, where a large concrete ramp disappeared into the water. The 12,000 to 14,000 survivors of the battle for the fortified islands—from the Army, Navy, Marines, Army

Air Corps, Philippine Army and civilian life—were jammed into this small area.

There were no pathways, making it necessary to step over each other to get to a lone spigot that issued several gallons a minute of good water. We formed groups of five or six that would be represented in the water line 24 hours a day, taking turns— often in pairs—that ranged from one to several hours. Our container was a five-gallon lard can, the side of which had been torn open, probably by a bomb or shell fragment. Tilted on its side it would hold a gallon and a half, but one gallon was supposed to be the limit. We would get the water, then struggle over innumerable bodies of the sleeping or stretched-out prisoners of war until we arrived back at our spot near the main gate. There was little talk in line, but it was the best place to be for information. You were more likely there to see someone you had known in the States or in China and find out what had happened to mutual friends or acquaintances. It was best at night, without flies or sun.

Despite having more and better water than on Caballo, the sun sapped us of much of our moisture and strength. Our tongues began to swell until we could not get them between our teeth without biting them. It became common to talk with the upper and lower teeth a half-inch apart and the lower jaw held rigid to avoid a painful bite on the side of the tongue. Before I arrived at Corregidor, the water line had been the scene of a great deal of anarchy, but only one incident occurred while I was there. A red-haired marine I had known in Cavite, with his face flushed a more livid red than usual and a wild look in his eyes, brushed aside the person getting water and lay face up under the spigot. No one interfered until it was obvious he could hold no more water. Then he was dragged a few feet aside, where he lay for several minutes before staggering away.

Diarrhea, the prelude to dysentery, already was making its rounds at the 92nd Garage. There were no latrines and no tools to dig them. As a result, our excrement formed a thin line at water's edge or was spread over the slope at the edge of the area. As one of the last group to arrive, I was positioned within a few paces of the Garage entrance at the outer perimeter of the prisoner concentration—within feet of the slope used as a latrine. Flies were everywhere. They landed in the drivel on our chins caused by the enlarged and bitten tongues. They landed on food as it was spooned out of a mess kit. They gathered ferociously on the mouth, nostrils and eyes while we slept. We were given broken red rice but had no fire, no cooking water and no containers in which to cook. So we hammered the rice in the bottom of our mess kits or pulverized it by rolling the ball of our spoons over it. We then added a little water to make a paste and ate it, competing with flies all the way. At first I threw away small portions where flies had landed; later I shoved them off and ate it all. The price was high; in a few days most of us had roundworm and diarrhea.

With incipient dysentery spread in a semicircle around the area, and being tracked back into the center where we were concentrated, it was a ghastly scene of stench and filth. There was no paper to clean ourselves; all we could do was sit in the water a few feet from shore, our bottoms bare. But the water itself was a carrier of our waste. Degradation, something with which I would become intimately familiar, was at hand.

Being near the gate, I was twice chosen to leave the camp. The first time was as part of a work party to clean up the area between Malinta Hill and the south dock. I was given a reed basket and told by demonstration to pick up pieces of metal that once had been bombs or shells. I had picked up eight or 10 pounds when I saw something glisten at my feet, partially covered by the red earth. I picked it up and couldn't let go. It was a small human hand, dried to the point that it looked almost transparent. I finally scratched out a trench and buried it five or six inches deep.

The experience unnerved me more than I thought possible. I could not get out of my mind that I had shaken hands with death. For days I looked at the hand that had picked it up, wondering if it was clean, then it faded from my mind. I never understood why that hand was more chilling than the dead I saw and handled at the navy yard and at Sangley Point.

On the way back from that work party, one of our group threw himself over a cliff that rises between the bay and the southeastern face of Malinta Hill. We stood for 10 or 15 minutes watching him move spasmodically on the narrow beach below. He had bounced off protruding rocks as he plummeted the 40 or 50 feet to sea level. We went on. I never heard anything more about him.

The second time I was chosen to leave the area was when a Japanese civilian selected five of us to climb Water Tank Hill, where he took pictures of us in the foreground and 12 or 14 thousand of our comrades 150 or 200 feet down the hill. The stench on Water Tank Hill differed from that of the 92nd Garage. It originated from the rotting bodies of friend and foe alike, buried too close to the surface and too lightly covered with the porous soil.

I was blond, as were all but one of the others chosen to pose for Japanese newspapers or magazines. If pictures of nearly six-foot, blond, disreputable, filthy, unshaven American Caucasians was what was wanted, the photographer had chosen well. After about a half hour of positioning us for the photos, he walked over to us, handed me a package of American cigarettes and said, "Here," and left. The armed escort took us back down the hill into the camp.

Near the end of the second week I was at the 92nd Garage, we were marched to the south dock. Being near the gate, I was one of the first to leave. That was early morning, probably May 24 or 25. It took until mid-afternoon before the area was largely emptied of prisoners. We stood at ease but in formation the entire time. Occasionally we would sit on our haunches. Sometimes we would be prodded to our feet, but for the most part we were left alone. We had neither food nor water. The sun was merciless. From time to time a prisoner would dart to the edge of the area and lower his pants. The guards did not interfere.

When the last group arrived from the Garage, we were brought to attention and counted over and over again before boarding a freighter. As we went up the ramp, we were issued an eight-ounce can of sardines. Mine had no opener. I immediately found a place on deck and pierced the can with a piece of angle iron that formed part of a winch. I drained the fluids into my mouth, shaking the can to get every drop. Then I succeeded in opening the can enough to pick fish out of the hole. I shook the remaining contents to where they, too, could be picked out with a fork. It was pure nutrition.

The freighter crossed the bay that night and anchored about a half mile off southern Manila. As the sun rose, we were transferred in groups of 300 or 400 to a landing craft. It stopped about 50 yards off shore, the front end opened and we were forced down the ramp into the water. Holding my musette bag above my head, I waded chest-deep to shore. We stood and watched thousands of prisoners repeat our performance.

Late in the morning we were herded to Dewey Boulevard, lined up in a column of four and marched through Manila. The march, with its prolonged stops, took about five hours. Only a few pockets of expressionless Filipinos watched along most of the way; but in the main part of the city, the sidewalks were lined as many as three or four deep.

Japanese women had set up tables with tea and small cakes along Dewey Boulevard, and we were brought to brief halts in front of them. The prisoners refused to accept the food and tea, so—after some talk among guards and Japanese photographers— groups of prisoners were forced over to the tables to have photos taken accepting the largesse.

It had been demoralizing to see the quality of design and workmanship that went into the landing craft, but what was more demoralizing was the ratio of Japanese guards to the prisoners they were escorting. Frequently it was difficult to see a guard at all. Nothing could have told the story of our humiliation quite so well as the disparity in numbers between the guards and the guarded.

Among the onlookers, the Caucasians and many of the Filipinos were in tears. Many were business families from uncommitted countries, some were citizens of Italy or Germany. Many placed their index and middle fingers over their noses pointing toward tear-filled eyes—a forlorn sign of distant victory. Occasionally a girl's or woman's mouth would open in horror mixed with relief as she recognized a skeleton in the column of prisoners. There was no doubt where the sympathies of most of the spectators of that grim scene lay.

The march probably was only four or five miles but it felt many times that. Our shoes were wet and we were unable to get all the sand out of them. Diarrhea was a problem with many, and I used the last of a roll of toilet tissue I had kept to the last possible moment. Embarrassment over having elimination problems in front of the only women and girls we had seen in six months was humiliating beyond anything I had ever experienced. After a mile or so, I was a filthy mess, as were many others, and chafed raw.

Finally we left the broad avenues and entered an area of old buildings and narrow streets without sidewalks. As we approached a turn, an old woman held out a banana-leaf package to one of the prisoners. A guard hit her on the hip with the butt of his rifle and she collapsed without a sound except that of a steel plate against bone. Other guards had allowed food in banana leaves to be passed, but not this one. There were to be many like him, arrogant and brutal with an unaccustomed power.

In another several blocks we arrived at Bilibid Prison. Before the war, it was used to hold the Philippines' most hardened criminals. It was enclosed by a brick wall some 10 feet high, with rows of cells and a fairly large service area containing the galley and offices. We were given a bowl of cooked rice and a cup of sweet potato vine soup, then assigned so many to an open cell that not all could lie down at the same time. We adjusted to each other as best we could and passed into a fitful sleep. The next morning, we all had fleas, lice and bedbugs. Constant trips to the latrine made adjustment of bodies in the dark almost impossible. We shared each other's filth.

I got up early the next morning and made a trip to the latrine, musette bag in hand. I hurriedly washed off with my Navy hospital towel, then washed the towel and made a G-string of it and a piece of rope. I washed my khaki pants and shirt, wrung them out and went back toward my cell.

July, 1940

Fifteen Cents

THE TIENTSIN MARINE

Vol. II

No. 7

經中華郵政登記認為第一類新聞紙類

LOCAL AMERICAN & JAPANESE BASEBALL TEAMS

A threat to the Yankees we were not: the company baseball team in Tientsin. (That's me back row, center.)

Edward Duggan in Tientsin. He was the first I sought when I wanted a tennis game in China. When Sangley Point was bombed, I thought I'd never see him again.

Yolanda, daughter of the Italian legate at Tientsin, is one of the reasons I became a student of foreign languages. I never learned what happened to her during the war.

How naive were we in North China? We prepared honor guards in Tientsin for both the Italian legate and Japanese General Homma — who was to capture us in the Philippines.

This calesa in pre-war Manila's Spanish quarter illustrates the city's fascinating combination of the old and the new.

On the way I passed the galley, where morning rice was being prepared. I looked curiously at one of the cooks, who had a heavy limp, and he looked at me. It was Private Vieux, the marine I had pulled from a burning tent on Sangley Point, his right buttock partially removed by a bomb fragment. We talked for half an hour while he worked. He told me about mutual friends who had passed through. He had been taken prisoner from a hospital near Sangley Point before mid-January and had been well-treated. He gave me a spoonful of guava jelly on a piece of banana leaf, which I savored for an hour. I never saw him again.

Two days later we were awakened while it was still dark and given a rice ball as big as a good-sized orange. Then we were mustered outside the wall and marched to a Manila rail freight yard. We were lined up along a row of boxcars and told by a Japanese officer, through a disdainful interpreter, that our highest officer was lower than the lowest Japanese soldier, that we were permitted to live only through the benevolence of the emperor, that we would be executed for disobedience or disrespect. He then related a string of Japanese military victories on islands of which we had never heard. We had no reason to disbelieve him. They were, he said, "creating a Greater East Asia Co-Prosperity Sphere."

After being regaled with Japanese successes and their vast superiority over all their enemies, and after being made to bow several times to the Japanese officer, we were herded aboard the narrow-gauge freight cars, all of which were small and without openings other than a sliding door. I got in among the first and took a position halfway between the sliding door and the rear wall.

Some of the freight cars were of metal. I was fortunate to get in one made of wood. Well over 100 of us were packed in each car, so tight we could hardly turn around. After about an hour, the door was partially closed and a Japanese soldier was stationed just inside it. If he were touched, he raised his rifle menacingly.

Even before the train jolted to a start, the stench of uncontrolled dysentery was thick in the air. Soon a half dozen or more of the prisoners slumped to the floor unconscious. Those nearest straddled them with their legs and said nothing. It was not even possible to fan them or give them water to drink if they regained consciousness.

We were probably five hours in the freight car through the hottest part of the tropical summer day. There was some relief when the train was in motion, but the oxygen was greatly reduced when the cars were standing still; we inhaled our neighbor's exhaled breath. My knees buckled several times, but I never went down. Few maintained complete control of their bowels for the entire trip. Most, at least, had a canteen of water.

When we arrived at Cabanatuan, about 60 miles north of Manila in Nueva Ecija Province, we learned that four had died along the way. Many more were unconscious or out of their heads in the heat. I had been lucky. I was on the sun side of the car when we boarded, but as we turned north and the sun traversed west, I had both the shade side and the portion of the car that got most of the fresh air.

The train reached Cabanatuan well before dark. We were hustled a short distance to a schoolyard, where cauldrons of hot rice awaited. But more inviting were multiple water faucets and drinking fountains with water of superb quality. After about half an hour, my head and neck still throbbing but my breathing back to normal, I obtained a good ration of rice in my mess kit and ate slowly until dark.

On the far side of a street that ran along a field bordering the school grounds stood a row of two-story, almost American-style houses. From many of the windows we were observed by the local population. The field between us was our latrine. Shame gave way to necessity.

Shortly after sunset but while there was still light, I found a free faucet, took off my khakis, soaked my pantslegs in water and used them to wash myself. I then washed the trousers thoroughly without soap, wrung them out, laid them near my musette bag and, wearing my Navy hospital towel G-string, squatted down to talk with some fellow prisoners for several hours. The future was a main topic. Finally I went to sleep with my head on my musette bag and my trousers spread out to dry.

We were roused soon after daybreak and cauldrons of rice appeared. Then we were lined up and the very weakest were loaded on trucks. The rest of us were informed that we would be on a march for most of the day, and that those who fell out of line would be shot. We were given a last chance to use the field and were lined up. We formed a column of six with our backs to the row of houses, where faces clouded with concern watched the proceedings.

Sailors and marines headed the column, followed by Army personnel. There were no Filipinos or civilians in our group. We marched out of town and into largely uninhabited, gently undulating countryside.

The sun rose, and the temperature rose with it. The pace was slow, and there were frequent stops. The road was made from dirt of the realm and alternated between rutted and passably smooth. About 10 o'clock we came to a few Nipa huts with a number of makeshift tiendas between them and the road. They were staffed by children, with an occasional old woman in the background. On their shelves and counters were displayed a small variety of the candies, cakes, cookies and drinks of the Philippines.

The guards had no objection to our breaking ranks and buying from the young shopkeepers. Some of the prisoners had money; I had long since lost mine in a Caballo poker game. The youngsters sold all they could. As we were called again to marching order they came out from behind their counters and gave what they had left to prisoners. A girl of 10 or 11 with a great questioning in her eyes gave me a small home-made coconut candy wrapped in waxed paper. The kindness was almost more than I could stand. I turned away with tears in my eyes. For that alone, I would always love the Filipino people. There was much more reason to love them.

Toward noon a tall, blond, freckled marine asked me for a swallow of water. He had an empty canteen at his side. I told him one swallow but he wouldn't stop drinking, so I banged the canteen harder than necessary against his teeth and pulled it away. He had gotten away with about a fourth of my carefully hoarded supply. Caballo Island and the 92nd Garage had taught me an unforgettable lesson about water.

My feet were now raw in my sockless shoes, which—as I lost weight—had steadily grown too large and were fastened only partway with broken laces. The mucous was beginning to flow and dry between my buttocks and down my legs, making walking a small torture with each step. The weaker were beginning to fall back in line and the guards watched them closely. As we approached a small stream and some fairly large trees that followed its banks, we were called to a halt. Suddenly a tall, blond marine broke ranks in front of a startled guard. He staggered toward a tree that stood somewhat away from the stream and the other trees. As he approached the shade, he went down on his hands and knees, his whole body convulsing and a sound seeming to come out of his stomach like the yelping of a dog. The guard took a number of marines down to the stream, where they filled their mess kits with water, brought it back and dumped it on the unconscious figure. We somehow knew that he would not be shot.

Early in the afternoon we came over a rise and saw a large camp—we had made it! This was Camp 1. It spread out about 1,000 feet in two directions on flat, rice-paddy land. It was surrounded by a fence and contained dozens of buildings laid out like a military compound.

Our hopes were shattered as the head of the column passed the road that led to the main gate of Camp 1 and continued to skirt it on the west. Long after I passed the access to the compound, I looked back and saw the Army personnel stopped while we continued our painful march. We didn't know for several months how lucky we were.

Late in the afternoon, as we emerged from a grove of trees and around a bend, we saw another camp. We stopped on the road between a fenced compound on the northwest and what proved to be Japanese administration and guard quarters on the southeast. We were quickly counted by the camp commander's people and released by the escort troops. They had been very decent. An interpreter counted us off in groups of about 100, told us which building we were assigned to, and released us to find the buildings ourselves. Those who had arrived before us stood and looked for familiar faces as we found our way to the northeastern perimeter of the camp, one building removed from the road. The floor consisted of flat, round rocks up to three or four inches in diameter. It was a shell, having only walls and a roof.

I stretched out immediately and went to sleep in Camp 3. A 10- or 11-mile walk that would have been no challenge six months earlier had tested the limit of my endurance.

7

A War of Nutrition

Late the next morning when the barracks was awakened to answer a call to muster, I found I could not move. A deep breath caused excruciating pain in the lower ribs of my back. When the Navy chief in charge of the barracks saw that I could not respond to the muster, he brought the Japanese guard in to count me and later brought in a Navy corpsman who determined that I had pleurisy.

The marines were assigned almost immediately to a different barracks. It had the typical two-tiered shelving of split bamboo on each side of a four-foot aisle. After a day or two I could drag myself out into the sun and was soon walking about with little pain.

In about a week I joined a party to bathe and wash clothes in the Pompanga River a short distance from the camp. The Pompanga's headwaters rose about 50 miles to the north and east in a mountain range that formed a barrier to the eastern coast of Luzon from its northern tip to south of Manila. I picked up small pieces of soap that had been discarded by the other prisoners and washed myself, my towel and my khakis until all were thoroughly clean. Wearing a wet G-string, I carried my clothes back to the camp to dry.

The prisoners were surveyed, identifying us by name, rank, serial number and service. I was relocated to a barracks exactly opposite the one I first occupied, one building from the road on the Cabanatuan side of the camp.

It was now early June. I weighed 51 kilos on the galley scale: 126 pounds. The pleurisy had caused me to miss many meals, which consisted of a small bowl of red rice and a cup of eggplant or comote (sweet potato) vine soup three times each day. The rice was broken but largely unpolished, retaining some of its germ and vitamins. But soon we were told there would be only two meals a day. We were to get the same quantity of rice; but in practice, the portion was reduced to the same amount we had been receiving each meal—a decrease of 33 percent. The effect was catastrophic.

About the same time, we were gathered together to receive some "good news." The interpreter told us that the Japanese camp commander had graciously decided that he would allow the enlisted men to be placed under officers of their own services—which made no difference, as there was little to command. The interpreter also gloated that America had suffered a terrible defeat at Midway, losing most of the ships that had survived Pearl Harbor. We were appropriately dispirited, based on our record to date. However, when we were told in August that the fleet destroyed at Pearl Harbor and Midway was again destroyed at Guadalcanal, we knew we were back in the fight. The Japanese, seeing our reaction to the news, seemed also to have second thoughts; we received no more news of their successes while still in the Philippines.

The Pompanga River on first sight looked like a tailor-made avenue of escape. Many others thought the same. My own plan was to slip past a guard at night, get to the river and follow it to its source. Then I would drop over the low mountain chain to the sparsely populated east coast, living off the land. Such fantasies were quickly dashed.

Early in my time at Camp 3, four prisoners traded some personal effects to a Japanese guard for a bottle of gin. Drunk, they slipped out of camp and were gone three or four days. With nothing to eat and not enough strength to go on, they turned themselves in. The camp was denied rations for one day. The four escapees were placed on a platform in the center of the camp near the road where they could be seen from the Japanese headquarters and by anyone passing by. Their heads were tied to their knees and their heels tied with a rope over their shoulders again to their knees. They were placed in a kneeling position under constant guard for nearly two days. Then they were cut loose, given a cigarette, and later water and food.

The next day the entire camp population was assembled on one side of an arroyo that led down to the river. The four were forced to dig their own graves. They were ordered to stand at the ends of the graves, which were about three feet deep, and were shot. Each crumpled back into his grave but the one on the right end, who attempted to crawl out. The officer who had issued the command put a pistol to the prisoner's head and pulled the trigger. Four spectators were chosen to cover the graves. The four Japanese in the firing squad threaded their way through the prisoners, tears in their eyes and heads lowered. There was a limit to how far a human being could sink, and they, too, had been forced to that limit.

The next morning there were four crosses on the new graves. That practice would not long be observed. I remember only one epitaph, etched into a makeshift wooden grave marker, at Camp 3. It said:

> Tell America, oh passerby,
> That here obedient to our word we lie.

A day or so later we were formed into groups of 10. If one of the 10 were to escape, the remaining nine were to be shot. It was no idle threat. On a ship to Japan I was to learn that a marine I had known in North China had watched while his brother was shot after one of his 10 was taken by Philippine guerrillas while on a work detail in Laguna Province.

Our health continued to deteriorate. What food we got was poorly digested because of diarrhea and dysentery. It was commonly referred to as "rice stomach." Few had any doubt that it was basically a nutrition problem. The health of some was better than mine, the health of many was worse.

After several weeks of relief, my dysentery came back with a vengeance. The presence of mucous caused dozens of brief trips to the slit trenches each day, with accompanying wretching of the abdominal muscles. My journal—first the blank pages, then everything I had written—disappeared sheet by sheet.

Marked graves and then unmarked graves began to populate the slope below the latrines. The steps in the process were known to all. First you became too weak to make the frequent trips across the shallow ravine to the slit trenches. Next you moved down to the slope across from the trenches and smoothed out a "bench" to lie on, waiting for the call. Then came the first show of blood. Few recovered from the blood stage.

The Japanese gave us tools to dig the slit trenches but refused to leave them so we could cover the diseased human waste. Flies became so dense it was impossible to keep them off food as it was carried in buckets or placed in mess kits. The Japanese reacted by offering a bread roll for each 100 dead flies delivered to the dispensary. The big change came when the guards started leaving the shovels at the slit trench site. With the reduction of flies, new infections were reduced dramatically.

Before that happened, however, I moved to the side of the arroyo, being present only for roll call and frequently for chow call. If I was not present when rice was distributed, Pat Ryan brought it down to me. Pat asked for nothing. His health was better than most. I was not the only one he helped. More often than not, he went to the galley to get the buckets of rice for our barracks. I never went once. I gave my daily ration of one-half cigarette to Pat. He would put it in a bamboo holder and smoke slowly and thoughtfully, but you never knew what he was thinking. Ryan went out on a work party late in 1942 and stayed with it until he was loaded on a ship with a marine named Ruzicka whom I knew in North China. Both went down with the ship when it was bombed, I heard, off the coast of Luzon in 1944.

About a week after I moved to the latrine area I realized my health was improving. I walked around the camp a bit and visited the rumor mill, as the galley and storeroom were known. It was there that the only contact with the outside world was made, when trucks delivered wild rice and vegetables about three times a week. Occasionally even a guard would become a news-bearer. One might hit his index fingers together like swords clashing and say "senso Raboul" or "senso Rashia" or "senso Eikoku"—fighting in Raboul, Russia, England. Sometimes a newspaper in Japanese ideograph but with maps that were recognizable would tell us where the action was.

Before long I began having vicious headaches. I would feel fine in the morning; but from early in the afternoon until 3:30 or four o'clock my temperature would rise and I would be virtually blinded by pain. It was Ryan who put wet cloths on my head to ease the pain until it lessened in late afternoon. One day, he brought me a doctor recently arrived from Camp O'Donnell, terminus of the Bataan Death March, along with some medicine. The doctor, named Weinberg, pressed under my rib cage and immediately diagnosed malaria. He gave me fractions of a dose of quinine for about 10 days, after which the headaches and blindness left and never came back. However, probably as a result of the malaria, I developed yellow jaundice. It had no symptoms other than discoloration, but it was a matter of interest to Weinberg, who thought it might be hepatitis. There were a number of cases of both in the camp.

The next three months proved to me that the body has remarkable powers of self-recovery. I already had overcome a serious case of diarrhea or dysentery in a remarkably short time and, with a fraction of the quinine ordinarily required, had been cured of cerebral malaria. There had been pleurisy; and a jaundice condition, perhaps a result of hepatitis, had come and gone. Much more was in store.

Many prisoners' feet had begun to be hot and very sensitive to the touch and particularly sensitive to sunlight, even through shoes. If anyone came near, they would shout a warning. I soon knew the feeling. Sunlight on any part of my body caused a scalding sensation on the skin atop my feet. I could squeeze a foot without flinching, but could not draw a finger lightly over the skin. It was agony to put on or take off shoes. Apparently a vitamin deficiency was affecting the nerve endings. The foot condition lasted for years, but with reduced intensity, and was especially sensitive to changes of weather. Occasionally a sensitive area appeared—still appears—on another part of the body, but normally for only a day or two. We called it dry beriberi.

I developed another type of beriberi about the same time. At first there was a puffiness on the tops of my feet. Pressed with a finger, the depressed spot would slowly even out. I knew from what already had happened to many others what the course of the affliction could be. The feet of a marine named Levitt in my bahai had swollen to such an extent that his ankles and knees were no longer distinguishable. It wasn't painful and the victim merely walked stiff-legged, throwing his feet ahead like a man with artificial legs. One night his friends put his seabag under his feet. In the morning, his feet had pretty much drained, but he was dead. Apparently the fluid had drained to the area of his heart and lungs; either he had suffocated or his heart could not function surrounded by it.

I watched my legs take the same course. First my feet were swollen late in the day; then they swelled early in the day. Within a few days, my legs were swollen well above the knees and they became extremely awkward. There was no pain associated with the disease and only one complication: The skin broke on the lower leg and seeped a clear fluid. The problem was keeping flies off to prevent infection. Within about two weeks, the symptoms slowly began to disappear for me and for many of the others. There had been no positive change in the quality or quantity of food, so the body must have risen to the occasion once again.

Another problem was not long in coming. I woke up one morning and could not get my eyelids open. I felt around for my canteen and managed to get some water on them. When I got my eyes all the way open, I discovered in a piece of mirror that both the upper and the lower lids were heavily coated with matter. I had a similar problem shortly before in which the corners of my mouth and nostrils were coated. Other symptoms followed. My navel became highly inflamed and sensitive, and my mouth and eyes both were stuck shut in the morning. Finally it spread to my scrotum, which became enlarged, glassy, and assumed the look of alligator hide. It cracked, bled and scabbed over, making it very painful to walk.

This disease had still other symptoms: Liver-colored splotches appeared on the lower legs; the skin of the affected area became transparent and lifeless and peeled off; then the splotch itself dried out and flaked off and the surface gradually returned to normal. There was a bloating of the abdomen and considerable discomfort. Probably more than 60 percent of the camp experienced this disease in some of its manifestations.

At one point in Camp 3, blisters appeared on my legs, almost an inch across and several inches long. Many prisoners had them. The outermost layer of skin seemed to separate from the inner layer, and the space created by the separation filled with fluid. Soon the skin holding the fluid would die and break, and the fluid would run down the leg, soaking whatever it touched. Often there was a mechanical incident that ruptured it but, in either case, there was no pain. The condition lasted several weeks; again the body somehow cured itself.

One last problem associated with diet was visited upon us. This happened late in our stay at Camp 3 and afflicted perhaps one in 10 or 15 prisoners. Our testicles enlarged to an incredible degree, becoming the size of small grapefruits. I had heard of the phenomenon in China among the beggars in Shanghai and Tientsin. Now it was happening to me. A great deal of anxiety arose from a facetious statement by a camp doctor who said we wouldn't have to worry about a shotgun wedding. I confused sterility with impotence for a long time, but was concerned about both.

The condition was very awkward. Again, my Navy hospital towel came into use. I fashioned it as a sling and managed to get about as needed while the condition existed, which was two or three weeks. I was not alone.

I never knew the cause of this latest affliction, but I may know its cure. About the time it first occurred, the food suddenly improved in both quality and quantity. Work parties were formed and went into the countryside killing two or three carabao a week for three or four weeks. The Philippine bovines, used as wallowing draft animals, were boiled until tender if almost tasteless. The grease on the top of a cup of soup was something we had not seen for a long time. We were also now frequently finding squash, onion and eggplant in the soup with the occasional chunk of carabao.

I was also making tea from guava leaves, which were plentiful in the compound. I was warned about it by Ryan, who had asked a doctor, but I felt I had little to lose. The fear was that the leaves may have been toxic, but 40 years later I learned that they were a native remedy.

As summer ended, the only symptoms I retained were the painful beriberi feet, occasional swelling of the ankles and periodic diarrhea. I began to entertain a cautious optimism.

Several prisoners had portable chess sets with pieces about a half-inch tall. Ryan said he knew how to play chess, so I thought it over for a while and decided to try to make the pieces. I made white pieces out of a balsa-type wood from trees in the compound and the dark pieces from the small branches of lignum vitae. In about two weeks I had a passable set and Ryan taught me how to play. We spent hours playing chess. The kibbitzers occasionally borrowed the board. Others made backgammon boards, again of local wood with pieces scratched out with broken glass after having been sized by a saw from the toolshed.

I also kept myself occupied, and attracted much attention, by starting a garden between the bahai and the perimeter fence. I got the seeds with the help of the galley crew, which got them through the interpreter. I churned up the soil with a stick and soon had several corn, bean, squash, eggplant and pepper plants growing. Prisoners came from all over the compound to see it.

It had been a difficult four months at Camp 3. Barracks after barracks had been closed down as prisoners died and units were consolidated. The empty spaces in my own bahai remained empty. There were seven of them, a loss of about 10 percent in four months, which projected to 30 percent over a year. But the situation was not as bad as that; most deaths occurred in the first half of our stay. If the food situation were to remain as it now was, I could foresee few more deaths unless from heart attack or epidemic. There was general optimism. Better food, some attempts at sing-alongs, the board games and an occasional rumor had turned us to looking cautiously outward. There were several types of religious exercises, ritualistic for the Catholics and ministry of the word for the Protestants.

A few attempts at a camp-wide variety show were eerie and bittersweet. A prisoner we knew as Rimshot Rabinowich made the only overt attempt at humor I heard during my entire confinement. I do not recall any laughter. Some solo renderings of semiclassical songs reminded us of our cultural heritage and resulted in great longing and nostalgia. The shows were canceled anyway when some of the songs drew applause, which was heard across the road at the Japanese commander's quarters.

Nonetheless, the camp had gone from a fly-infested hell to a reasonably fly-free environment. The odor of several hundred bodies buried too close to the surface was a frequent reminder of both our own mortality and good fortune. Most of us would have been satisfied to wait out the war as we were.

Before long, however, it became clear why the food had improved; we were advised late in October that we would be moving to Camp 1. We would be gone before my garden could yield its increase. When the order came to move, we prepared with both expectation and anxiety.

8

Hell Below Deck

The march to Camp 1 was not as difficult as the march in the opposite direction had been four months before, but neither was it easy. It was the most sustained drain of energy any of us had experienced since arriving at Camp 3, and a further weight loss had reduced our energy reserve to near zero. My own weight was about 115, actually up a few pounds from the days on latrine hill.

Whatever cautious optimism had gathered in the latter days at Camp 3 evaporated as we approached Camp 1. The prisoners we saw through the fence were skeletons. Worst of all was their eyes, which stared at us almost without comprehension. Two objects on poles at either side of the gate we were to enter captured our attention when they became recognizable as human heads. Two Filipinos had paid that price for throwing food to the American prisoners.

We stood in formation for an interminable count while the escort guards transferred their authority to the Camp 1 guards. We were given the news that we would soon be leaving on work parties, were assigned to bahais, and were dismissed.

The death rate in Camp 1, populated by Army personnel from both Bataan and Corregidor, had been staggering. The prisoners had been accorded the treatment given to stubborn defenders in the Western world when the Turks, Mongols, Goths, Visigoths and Huns were ravaging Europe a thousand years before. This was a final destination of many of those who had made the Bataan Death March during the shelling of the fortified islands. And this was the destination of those Army troops I had seen turn off behind me while we marched on to Camp 3.

Probably 25 or 30 percent of the camp had died in the previous four months. Those we saw as we approached were candidates to die next. The others had been shipped out on work details— the healthiest, then the next, then the next. The hopelessness of those left became a searing memory: abject misery without prospect and without mental function allowing them to comprehend, lower than animals because of what they had been. The guards joked and teased with each other at the gate and stepped off vigorously at the changing of the guard, indifferent to what was happening within the compound. It was inevitable that we would ask ourselves: "Who is the more animal, who is the less human?"

The burial detail was given extra rations for its gruesome task. There was no lack of volunteers. They gathered soon after the morning ration, and before the sun became too hot they dragged four or five skeletons each day to the peace of the red earth. A chaplain accompanied them and helped remove and bring back the clothes of the dead. The bodies were rolled into mass graves and covered with a few inches of soil, which often washed away with the first rain, leaving shriveled skin to turn into glossy leather, bones to bleach and organs to putrefy and be carried back to the camp by flies.

I made only one burial detail. Dragging the litter caused the bones in my wrists, elbows and shoulders to strain out of their sockets. I dared to wonder why the God and Father to us all did not intervene to stop that obscenity. The price being paid seemed to be so far beyond that justified by the malice or frailty of the victim.

The second week at Camp 1, I was selected to leave the camp on a permanent work detail. However, I had to be taken off the list because of the drain of the march, the burial detail and the return to the same rations that had caused so much misery at Camp 3. At first I did not recognize what was happening. I picked up my mess kit early one morning in the dim light of the bahai and started outside. The moment I came into the bright light, my eyes flooded with tears. The pain was excruciating. I felt my way back into the bahai. Even with my eyes closed, the light through my eyelids caused tears to flood down my face. In the bahai, however, I was fairly comfortable in the early morning light. What had happened was that my eyes had dilated to their maximum and had failed to close down the pupils in response to increased light levels. A doctor examined them and my name was removed from the work party. My place was taken by Ruzicka, the marine who went to the bottom of the sea with Pat Ryan.

After four or five days my eyes returned to normal, except for a temporary night blindness that affected a large number of us. I was never bothered with the problem again. Several more work parties were named, and about November 10 I found myself on a list to leave the camp. The previous work lists were of 20 to 30 men. This one included nearly all the prisoners who had been in Camp 3. Most of those remaining, probably more than 1,000 prisoners, were on the hospital side.

Around November 15 we were trucked in shifts back to the Cabanatuan train station, where we waited hours for the last of the prisoners to arrive. We boarded passenger cars and made a quick and relatively comfortable trip to Manila station. There we were quickly assembled, counted and marched to the dock area. We milled around for several days while the rest of the prisoners from Camp 1 and other prisoners from work parties followed us to the dock.

After three or four days, about 1,500 prisoners had been assembled on and near the dock. We roamed the area at will, resting or sleeping on hundreds of tobacco bales being shipped to Japan. Also on the dock were a number of bales of compressed dried fish, which we tried to eat and later came to believe were intended as fertilizer. There was no food at all the first two days, but on the morning of the third day we had all we could eat because the last group from Cabanatuan was late in coming. I put a large sheath of tobacco leaves in my musette bag; then, remembering the prunes incident on Fort Hughes, I put the tobacco back. I did not want trouble with the emperor!

On the fourth day, some were allowed aboard a waiting ship and we wandered the deck until late afternoon. A pig was caged on the stern, and a dozen chickens were in another cage. The crew was courteous without exception, asking questions in their few words of "Eikokugin." Late in the evening, however, we were herded off the ship while the tobacco and some recently arrived cargo was loaded deftly into a hold amidship. About 11 that night, we were directed into the fore and aft holds. I went into the forward hold thinking the air flow would be better.

By now it was clear that we were bound for Japan. It did not seem grounds for terror. For one thing, we were too weak and too focused on survival to expend energy imagining what lay ahead. Besides, nothing could be much worse than Camp 1 and Camp 3 had been.

The forward hold was entered by a steep open ladder against the aft bulkhead. The ladder led to an open area about 20 feet long by 15 feet across. On three sides, triple tiers of shelves had been constructed, the bottom tier on the floor with about $3^{1}/_{2}$ feet separating each of the two above. There was considerably more headroom for the top tier. The ladder had a drop of 11 or 12 feet and extended about seven feet out into the middle of the hold, which came to be very significant. It had no handrail but was of sturdy construction. It was less than 30 inches wide. In the middle of the hold was a slop bucket. It was half of a large barrel of heavy wood, had split bamboo straps, and probably had been made to transport pickled Japanese turnip-radishes called daikons. A similar half barrel, set well away from it, contained water.

I had stayed near the gangplank and was still near it when we were called to order and counted. As a result, I was within the first 20 or 30 prisoners to enter the hold. It was a long and tedious process and required stepping over the elevated lip of the hold and onto a tread that was barely illuminated by the lights in the rigging or the single dim light suspended in the middle of the hold. The descent was further aggravated by the beriberi that plagued most of our feet.

I took possession of a bay in the bottom tier directly across from the base of the ladder. I reasoned that the air would be best at the bottom of the hold, and that even when the hatch was closed the portion above the ladder had the best chance of staying open.

It was more than an hour before the last prisoner entered the hold. We had no idea how many were to be in each bay, so we stretched out to stake our claim, which left so many in the center of the hold that those coming down could not get off the ladder. Those in the bays would not allow recent arrivals to squeeze in. Seeing the stoppage, a Japanese guard forced his way down the ladder shouting, "Korah!" and waving his rifle. We got the message quickly, and—by sitting up and interlacing bodies and arms and legs in the bays—everyone was removed from the center of the floor and into the bays.

The guard exclaimed, "Yosh!"—the vernacular for "Yuroshi" (good)—and left the hold. Gradually, starting with the bottom bay, prisoners started migrating to the open area at the center of the hold; then, tiring of standing, they sat down on the edges of the bays, the feet of those in the upper bays dangling in the faces of those below.

The slop pot near the base of the ladder soon came into use, and the problems it would be generating became obvious to everyone. Almost at once it was occupied by three at a time, with a queue of the impatient waiting in front of each. Some in the queues didn't quite make it. This left both the base of the pot and its rim a mess. To use the slop jar meant to step in someone else's excrement, to get it on the cuffs of your khakis, and to sit in it on the rim. This led to a further problem, that of not contaminating your bay. To keep from tracking it into a bay, it was only necessary to leave your shoes outside the bays and climb up. But this was agony at best and impossible at worst for those with beriberi. As a consequence, the rungs of the ladders leading to the upper bays were soon a filthy mess. To get down from an upper bay, it was necessary to grasp the rungs of the ladders. So prisoners cleaned their hands with the drinking water, pouring it over their hands and into the slop bucket. As a result, the drinking water was soon exhausted, and the slop bucket was soon filled. But diarrhea and dysentery wait for no man.

Those using the slop bucket, even though they removed their shoes before entering a bay, brought back human waste on their cuffs and on their buttocks. Before long, the hold was a cesspool. Dante looked forward to November 1942, not backward, when he recorded his vision of hell. For much of the rest of my life, this nightmare Pacific passage would color my impression of the Japanese culture.

The worst was not yet.

We got under way about eight the next morning, joining a convoy, we learned, in Manila Bay near Corregidor. The heat of the tropical sun became intense and the air in the hold lifeless. I gasped for breath. A young lieutenant took turns fanning me and another prisoner. He seemed never to stop. We were a tangled mess of human bodies, faces under knees, heads on legs or laps or chests, on knees in a corner, standing with back bent against the tier above, knees aching, tail bones and hip bones cutting into our flesh. In an extremity each element of a group knows what is good for the whole, so we knew when one could stay in a position no longer—and we shifted. We had perhaps $3^{1}/_{2}$ square feet per person. We all complained, but rarely was a complaint directed at an individual.

Around 3 p.m. a Japanese soldier appeared at the top of the ladder with two wooden buckets and made it clear we were to empty the slop bucket. It was necessary for him to menace with his rifle before two of the prisoners brought down the buckets and dipped them into the overflowing slop bucket. Typical of Americans, they overfilled them. The carriers then had to mount the ladder holding a bucket with one hand and skipping from rung to rung with the other. The ladder became as filthy as the floor. The slop bucket was finally emptied, and the guard held up his hands to indicate he wanted 10 men to get rice and water. Now it was necessary for the rice and water to come down the same filthy ladder, the carrier using one hand, that the excrement had gone up.

I don't remember eating or drinking the entire 17-day trip. I must have blocked it out completely. No faint image of getting out my mess kit, having rice put in it, eating or drinking water remains with me; but I am sure that much of the revulsion I have had for 50 years at any hint of contaminated food originates in the hold of a Japanese freighter late in 1942.

On the second day out the hatch was suddenly closed, and it was obvious the convoy had been threatened. Rice buckets were being returned to the galley, and the prisoners bringing them up the ladder were almost brutally forced back down into the hold. One of them had a dental bridge knocked from his mouth. The hatch remained covered about four hours. The other prisoner the young lieutenant was fanning died in the intense tropical heat and lack of oxygen. I faded in and out of consciousness, hearing my benefactor ask if I had ever tasted that fabulous St. Louis draft beer, the name of which he had forgotten, or what I was going to do when I got back to the States. He must have been a rare specimen.

The dead were hauled up to the deck with ropes and buried at sea. We lost 16 or 17 from our hold, most before we reached Taiwan. A canvas shunt on the deck, which directed air into the hold, did more than anything else to keep the death rate down while we were in the tropics and subtropics. About a day out of Taiwan we had a second submarine alert. The hatch again was closed, this time for several hours beginning in late morning.

We lay over in Taipei for two days, left, came back the same day, and left again the next day. It was now past mid-November and we were entering the Strait of Taiwan, where the weather was more influenced by the Asian landmass than by the warm Japanese current. Being below the water line and against the hull of the ship, the hold first cooled off, then, as we approached Shanghai, became cold. The convoy hugged the coast as it passed the outflow of the Yangtze and into the Yellow Sea, where the weather was dominated by the air flow from Siberia. Forward and well away from the boilers, our cesspool went from suffocating heat to freezing cold. We began to take advantage of the warm bodies on all sides of us. Prisoners who had placed their backs to the outer shell of the vessel now turned around so that as little body surface as possible touched a surface that could suck the heat from it. After the first five or six days, I had no more trouble breathing; it was now a matter of maintaining heat in a body that had lost all its fat reserves. We laid off what may have been Pusan for two days. The next day we disembarked at Shimonoseki on the Japanese island of Honshu.

We were called to order on a large surfaced area near the dock and told what came next. First, we would be sanitized, including our clothes; then we would be given our shots and boarded on a train for Osaka. The rail cars would be closed; we were not to look out.

We were stripped bare in formation, our clothes thrown out in front of us. The front line faced right and filed off to a spray bath where we were thoroughly soaked—hair, beard, armpits, crotch—with a disinfectant. We then were lined up for a shower that included soap and fairly warm water. We all stayed in the shower as long as we could before being hurried along by a Japanese guard. As we left the shower, we were directed, still dripping, back to our original places. On the way we received an inoculation and were weighed. I had shrunk to 49^1/$_2$ kilos— 109 pounds. Our clothes were gone and in their place was a pile of Philippine Army denims. The pair I ended up with were clean, in good condition, but far too short. I had lost my web belt. Our shoes were also gone, replaced by a pile of Japanese Army split-toed rubber and canvas shoes. I found a pair that fit. The weather was fair but there was a breeze off the channel, and we began to suffer from the cold as soon as we ceased to be active.

When the first section of prisoners had been sanitized and clothed, we were ushered to an outdoor customs. There I dumped my musette bag on a table where the customs official, wearing a white mask, said: "Yuroshi." I replaced my belongings and went on to the next table. There, for the first time since my group of 10 in Camp 1, I again became a name and not merely one of a group. A Japanese civilian advised us that our section of 500 men was to be known as "Wakayama." We were then directed to passenger rail cars waiting on a siding. The cars were sun-warmed, very clean and very comfortable. I chose a window seat on the north side of the car. The restroom was locked, but no one interfered with us using the facilities on the dock.

Late in the afternoon, some Japanese women came in with packages wrapped in large dried, but flexible, leaves. Each of us got one. They contained a large portion of rice, some vegetables, some kelp and a small piece of pickled fish. It was good to be in Japan.

9

A Slave in Japan

The sun went down, the wind came up, and the temperature in the motionless passenger car dropped, I estimated, to the low 50s. The Japanese guards in their padded pants and jackets and warm leggings seemed not to notice, but the prisoners suffered. It was a long and miserable night. My window seat proved to be a bad choice. The chilled air from the windows flowed down the inside walls of the car and over the seats to the floor. There was nothing to do but shiver; none of us had enough strength or endurance to keep warm by staying active.

Shortly after dawn, the cars jolted and we began to inch forward. Within minutes, warm air began to circulate through the car. In an hour, I was thoroughly warm.

The train sped along the north shore of the inland sea. A guard came through occasionally and would shout "Korah!" at someone peering through an edge of a drawn curtain. It wasn't taken as overly menacing. Someone soon yelled, "Hey Rube!," the circus warning, if they saw the doors open between cars.

The train made occasional stops. Before mid-day, possibly in Hiroshima, we received another bento, or leaf-wrapped meal. Few, myself included, were able to eat more than half. I was given a number of portions of kelp, but the iodine taste prevented me from eating much more than my own ration. We arrived in Osaka late in the afternoon and were placed on a siding. We spent the night only slightly less chilled than the night in Shimonoseki.

In the morning, we were lined up, 500 strong, loaded on buses and trucks and taken south around the eastern end of the inland sea and into the Wakayama Peninsula. In mid-afternoon we arrived at some brand-new barracks where the mountains came down to the sea. A tall wooden fence surrounded five large barracks buildings, a galley, a storage building, a dispensary and quarters for the Japanese guards. This was the Wakayama Camp of the Tanagawa group.

The interpreter's name was Hayishi. He spoke textbook English with an occasional idiom. Hayishi advised us of a prevailing south wind off the Pacific Ocean and informed us we would be excavating a hillside that would become a dry dock in about two years. The work would be heavy, he said, but our treatment would be good. We were again given shots, all with the same needles, separated into five groups of 96 and assigned to barracks. The other 20 men were assigned to the galley or dispensary, with quarters there. For the most part, we were segregated by service and put under the highest non-commissioned officer among us, in my case a Navy chief petty officer.

The barracks had four tiers, two on each side of a generous aisle that featured two charcoal braziers. Twenty-four sets of blankets were aligned with military precision at the foot of each tier, 96 in all. On top of each set of blankets was a new rice-hull pillow. The tatami mats were new—everything was new. It was a heartwarming sight.

I was assigned to an upper tier. When I couldn't climb up without help, a marine I didn't know exchanged places. Each of us was given a rice bowl and a soup bowl, of good quality china. There were to be two meals each day, the first at 6:30 a.m., the second at 6 p.m. We would receive a bread roll for lunch. We could make down our beds at eight each workday and at noon on non-workdays. At six the first night, we were given a large ration of rice and a bowl of soup thick with vegetables but lacking oil. At 6:30, we were allowed to clean our bowls at a fine multi-faucet wash station, behind which were about a dozen shower heads. We were also allowed to take about one-fifth of the coals left over from cooking the evening meal. It was good to be in Japan!

We were idle for three or four days. In the evenings the barracks, which were warm from the sun, cooled off suddenly and greatly. We were too weak to mill around extensively. It was a numbing, bone-chilling cold in which the body temperature itself seemed to fall many degrees.

The blankets proved to be ersatz. They were uneven in density, and we were able to pull what seemed to be pieces of wood out of them. A gentle but steady breeze came up through the flooring of the tiers. Those of us on the bottom tier would wrap the blankets around us, lie face down with chest on the pillow and knees drawn up underneath. Because of the beriberi pain, many of us did not take off our shoes when we bedded down. Often two or three prisoners would huddle together to cut heat loss.

On the second workday, reveille sounded as usual at six o'clock. A guard came through at 6:10 and found one prisoner still in his tier. The guard hit him on the foot, his shoe still on, with a billyclub. The prisoner did not move. The guard pulled off his blankets. He was dead.

It was now the heart of winter. We had only Philippine Army denims to keep us warm. We had no underwear, no socks, no headwear. The weather was blustery, with temperatures probably in the 30s each night and occasionally leaving a skin of ice on puddles well into morning. I wrapped my Navy hospital towel around my middle, and it proved to be a great help. Putting my hands into cold water was agony; they would turn blue almost immediately. The only relief was to put them between my legs until circulation returned. The pain in my feet was even worse, and the only relief was to get them cold enough to deaden the pain. At night, I kept them out of my blankets.

We worked six days a week. At first, the camp authorities allowed a five percent sick list, then 10 percent. The deaths rose to three or four per week. The sick list was soon raised to 25 percent and rations cut in half for each prisoner on the sick list.

It was share and share alike for the workers and non-workers, so everyone began to suffer from the curtailed rations. Our poor health became the pacing factor in progress on the dry dock. Construction officials came to the camp, followed by civilian Japanese doctors. The result was to form a sick barracks, into which the long-term sick were placed and those they replaced reassigned to the four working barracks. Camp officials insisted that the sick barracks go on half rations and that the others receive full rations, but the health of the whole camp continued to decline.

If the sun shone, there was little breeze in the pit where we worked. The first explosive blast would already have been made by the time we arrived at the pit, about 7:30 after a half-hour walk. The prisoners' task was to load the resulting rocks into mining carts and join the carts together on tracks laid by the Japanese. Once the prisoners pushed the carts together and linked them, they were pulled to the top by winch and cable. When most of the rock had been picked up, holes prepared by hand with a star drill were filled with explosives, the pit evacuated, and the charges set off. That gave the prisoners an additional welcomed break while the mining carts were pulled out of the pit and empty carts were brought down.

Late in December, it became a major task for me even to walk to the work site. My throat was swollen and painful and my mouth was raw. I seemed to have no energy that my will could call upon.

I was in the pit one day barely able to lift a three- or four-pound rock when the blast signal sounded. Everyone headed out of the pit. I knew I could never make it to the top, so I took shelter in an overturned cart on the side away from the impending blast. The charge went off and rocks rained down all around me, but I was in no danger. The crew returned to the pit and the Japanese honsho came over to me and said, "Nani?" (What's the matter?) I shook my head.

When the carts were again loaded, the honsho had me get on the tongue of the last cart and ride to the top. The carts were stopped and the honsho walked me over to the guardshack where he sat me down and offered tea. I felt my pulse pounding in my throat and put my hand there to take a count. The honsho lifted my head and looked at my upper chest.

In the middle of the afternoon, the kando, a male nurse, came from the camp, talked with the honsho and indicated that I was to follow him back. After a five- to 10-minute walk I had to rest, my head whirling. He looked at my chest and said, "Kokura kahki" (enlarged heart). He let me set my own pace. In about an hour we arrived at the compound. He took me directly to the dispensary and told the American medics, doctors Marsico and Campbell, about my heart. Dr. Marsico had me do a mild exercise and looked at my chest, about 60 percent of which was rising and falling with each heartbeat. He said: "Get your things and report to the sick barracks." The thought of half rations sent a chill through me. A few minutes later I was among a group that had little reason for hope. In a week or 10 days my throat was so swollen that I could hardly swallow. I was put on a ration of rice soup instead of rice cooked nearly dry, and watched daily as those around me were taken out to be cremated. I went to the latrine five or six times a day. Otherwise I did not get up.

Two things happened that saved my life. To replace those who had died, a group of marines taken prisoner in North China had been brought from Moji on Kyushu, the southwesternmost of the major Japanese islands. They were the healthiest prisoners I had yet seen. They toured all the barracks looking for marines they had known in China. As one of them walked slowly by looking carefully at each patient's face, he stopped in front of me. It was Russell Ormseth from Canby, Minnesota. I motioned to him. He stared and called my name like a question. I nodded my head. He spent about 10 minutes talking to me and bringing me up to date on those I had known. He then asked me what he could do. I told him I had scurvy and needed vitamin C.

Two or three days later Russ came in shortly before lights-out and stuck something between my blankets and my chest: one large, two small and two very small tangerines. On the way to the excavation he had swiped them from a household shrine that a local inhabitant had set out in honor of his gods on a festival day we did not understand.

It was agony for my throat but, over a two-day period, I ate the tangerines, skin, seeds and all. In another several days I was largely free of scurvy and never had it again as a serious threat to my life.

The second salvation was the arrival of a Japanese medical doctor. He passed through several days after I had received the tangerines, accompanied by the American doctors and the Japanese kando. He spent enough time at the foot of each patient to hear their medical report and sometimes to examine them. I suspected from the way he listened to the American doctors talk to the interpreter that he understood English, but he never spoke it. When he came to me, he heard what the doctors had to say, then asked, through the interpreter, for me to get up and open my jacket. My heart obliged, its beating visible over most of my chest. He spoke a few words. Later that day I was moved from the sick barracks to the dispensary, from which no one to that date had ever come back.

In fact, no one had been transferred back to a work barracks from the sick barracks while I was there, either. There had been three types of patients in the sick barracks: those who gave up and became terminally ill, those who became terminally ill and gave up, and those who refused to give up and died anyway or lingered between life and death. Nine of the latter already had been assigned to the dispensary when I arrived.

I was placed at the southeast corner of the dispensary sick room. I had the advantage of the morning and afternoon sun on the windowless south wall but also the wall that took the brunt of the prevailing south wind. At my feet with his head to the door of the lavatory was Lieutenant Pitkin. He never spoke, and was fed a little rice gruel—which he spit out after a while like a baby rejecting pabulum. He was suffering from scurvy and died three or four days after I arrived. They found two eight-ounce cans of sardines in his bag. One can went to the patients who could eat and one went to the doctors and kando. Pitkin had needed only five small tangerines.

In the southwestern corner of the dispensary was an emaciated young Army private. Soon after I got there, he got up, declared he was going back to work, waved to the doctors and the kando and went outside. The kando made a move to stop him, but Dr. Marsico told him the private would be dead in two days. The private visited around for half an hour making strange talk with guards and the galley staff, after which Dr. Marsico went out and led him back, announcing he had seen that look before in old people. The young man died the next morning.

Next to the young private was a 50-year-old Army sergeant named Carlsen. He had been heavy but now weighed barely 100 pounds. He was very fastidious and talked incessantly about roast rack of mutton. He rose quickly one day, heading for the latrine. He didn't make it. He washed his pants, put them on wet and said: "If that happens again, it will kill me." It did. They moved a tall, gaunt Texan by the name of Henderson into his place before the day was out and filled Pitkin's and the Army private's spots at the same time.

It was an odd sort of reunion for Henderson and me, two men at death's door. He had been a member of one of my gun crews on Caballo, a quiet one always seeming to have something on his mind. He was the last marine I had contact with who was one of my men on Fort Hughes. Henderson also would survive the war, only to die a year later in a San Antonio hospital.

A young marine by the name of Ditt was also brought in. He was very courteous, almost pious, and very grateful. He never complained. Next to him was another tall Texan by the name of Nesbitt. The tall men were hit especially hard in the prison camps because of their larger food requirements and poor circulation in their lower extremities. Nesbitt's toes were blue and cold; his small toes were almost black. He walked on his heels like a Chinese woman with bound feet.

Between Nesbitt and myself was a six-foot-six Army Air

Corps pilot. I never heard his name that I remember. He never made a sound except when his bed sores were being treated. I saw the ones on his right hip and his tail bone once. That was enough. The wounds were deep and wide and the white bone glared through. The doctors treated him every day, but he did not respond when they tried to feed him. One day soon after I arrived at the dispensary, I saw his lice leaving him and coming across the tatami mat toward me. I killed as many as I could by pressing them with my thumbnail. He died soon, and they replaced him with a Staten Island marine named Rossi.

The conditions in the dispensary were a great improvement over the barracks. The wind under the building was somewhat subdued; we had sun heating on two sides and were well-shielded on a third; we had the doctors and the kando with us; the guards occasionally gave us extra food, and they always brought in the coals from their braziers before they retired for the night.

I was normally comfortable until two or three in the morning, when the room cooled off and my body heat began to leave me. I would squeeze my blankets under me on both sides and fold my arms over my chest and try to get some sleep. In the morning I would be unable to move my arms off my chest except by rolling from side to side until they fell down by my sides and circulation was restored.

Deep head and chest colds swept the prisoner population shortly after we arrived on the Wakayama Peninsula. It is likely that in many it turned to pneumonia and caused many deaths. Heat in the barracks, padded trousers and jackets, and two or three weeks of highly nutritious food might have saved 100 lives. The bone-chilling cold of a Japanese mid-winter was to be the greatest source of suffering for myself and many others in our entire captivity.

About two weeks after I was moved to the dispensary, half its patients and several from the sick barracks were loaded on a truck for Osaka. I was the last to be put on what in the States would be a one-ton stake truck without a tailgate. I was unable to pull myself up onto the back of the truck bed, which was about four feet off the ground. Several of the prisoners standing around stepped forward and pushed me aboard. I was placed across the back, just inside the stake holes.

The truck springs were exceedingly stiff and the roads rough. It became three hours of torture. We bounced off the floor of the truck with the slightest bump in the road. Sometimes it seemed I was in the air half the time, and that every vertebra was being separated from every other. Those seated against the sides had their tail bone and hip bones pounded into the floor of the truck. Sometimes one would try to sit on his haunches, but the muscles in his thighs would not support him and the truck floor would bounce out from under him. Every ligament in our bodies was being tested and found wanting. The pain emanating from my entire backbone and radiating through my rib cage and hips made breathing a torture. If I exhaled, I feared I would vibrate apart, so I kept as much air in my lungs as I could and breathed in shallow jerks.

We went through Osaka and headed west around the inland sea. Another hour found us halfway between Osaka and Kobe at Kanaoka Military Hospital. We entered the compound and stopped in an open area. In a few minutes 30 or 40 Japanese gathered around and we were ordered off the truck.

I managed to get first my feet and then my legs off the truck, but when I slid my hips off I crumpled to the ground and could not get up. A Japanese woman of about 50 bent over me and asked in English: "Japan did not do this to you?" I looked at her and said: "Yes." She motioned to the observers and two stocky Caucasians came over, picked me up one on each side and took me into the nearest building. One was a medium-sized blond about 30 years old. The other was a large, barrel-chested man of about 25. They told me with unmistakable British accents that they were glad we came, then left to get the others.

The British pair and the newcomers bombarded each other with questions. When things calmed down, we all told a little about ourselves. We found that the pair were taken prisoner in the Malay Peninsula and had volunteered to become medical guinea pigs. Vincent Ennifer, he of the barrel chest, was a Yorkshireman and we had trouble understanding him at first. The other, Haydn D. Jenkins, was from Cardiff, Wales, and more educated than his countryman.

The beds were European style with heavy straw mattresses. We had all the covers we wanted. The first meal was typical of what we would be having for the next three months—rice mixed with barley. There was a rich hot soup with shreds of meat and strings of egg. Oil floated on the top. We were to have three meals a day. The breakfast and noon meals would not be as elaborate.

We slept warm that night and were free to stay in bed, roam around the ward or the hall, and open the windows onto the field behind and listen to the birds. After a day or two, we were invited to take a Japanese bath. I had to be helped out of the hot water, but I felt human for the first time in many months. The next day we were examined by resident doctors, who confirmed my heart problem and said nothing more. I never saw them again.

Small buckets of rice and soup came to us from the galley. We suspected it was at the suggestion of the nurse who had met us when we arrived. One small thing that helped a great deal was the furnishing of worm medicine. The effect was swift and dramatic. And my heels and the backs of my legs up from the heel five or six inches, which had split and cracked, improved dramatically. I rubbed off the dead cells and the cracks became increasingly shallow and then disappeared.

The hair on our arms and legs, which had broken off on the forearms and from the knees downward, began to push through again, first in stiff little whiskers and then as real hair. We were able to measure our improvement almost daily. My bed sores had healed, especially the one on my left heel that had hurt so much when I lay on my back.

Soon the skylarks were hovering over the field outside. A Japanese soldier who had screamed in agony for two days after coming out of the anesthesia he had been given for abdominal surgery started a garden outside our window.

Ditt and I and a tall Army private from Wyoming named Bond had beds against the window. At first Ditt had been able, with help, to go the 15 feet to the latrine. Then he had to be carried. He ate only a part of his rations. He said almost nothing. One day we were visited by a Japanese boy named Tani who had been born in California and was going to school in Japan when the war began. Tani had been inducted into the army, had gone to the tropics and contracted cerebral malaria, which he couldn't shake. He brought several of his friends one evening and we tried to sing American and British songs. Ditt broke a silence with a weak but incredibly pure "Bells of St. Marys," which faded out before it was finished. He never talked again. We hung a bottle to his plumbing, and it was quickly filled with calcium from his bones. Ditt died, the only death at the hospital among those I arrived with.

Nesbitt's feet did not improve and he was taken to surgery to have part of them removed, but he came back pretty much intact. They removed only one joint from each small toe and found no gangrene. His circulation was good enough to warrant optimism.

Henderson was the only one besides Ditt who did not respond well to the military hospital. He never got enough food and what he did eat failed to help him like it did the rest of us. He went on with me to Osaka Camp 1.

Throughout captivity I meticulously recorded my weight, in code, in my King James New Testament. The code was necessary because the Japanese were wary of any sort of recordkeeping— particularly anything related to prisoners' treatment. My own records became a gruesome barometer of how sorely the captor was testing the captive's mortality.

I weighed 44 kilos (96.8 pounds) when I arrived at Kanaoka; nearly three months later I had gained nine kilos, nearly 20 pounds. My heart no longer kicked up a fuss when I exerted myself. I felt well and at times vigorous. The nights started to be long as I slept too much during the day. For the first time since Caballo, I tried to do some directed thinking, but I was unable to maintain a train of thought when I tried to read my New Testament. Tani wouldn't talk about the war except to say that America was very strong.

A year earlier, I had passed my 21st birthday on the day the Japanese began shelling Corregidor from Bataan. Now I was to pass my 22nd birthday in one of their hospitals, 2,000 miles to the north.

A week or so later, on a few hours' notice, we were transferred to Osaka Camp 1, known as the Chikko Camp. It was the head camp for the Osaka group of POW compounds, so it also was known as Honsho Camp. We again went on the back of a one-ton stake truck with stiff springs. This time, I stood near the front and took the trip with little discomfort.

Camp 1 was devoted largely to longshoreman and stevedore type of work. We were given the choice of staying at Chikko or going to Ichioka, a stadium where prisoners who could not work were held. Our health had improved, but we were not strong and had no endurance. If it had been winter I might have chosen Ichioka; but with the weather mild and our hopes up, five of us chose Camp 1—Jenkins, Ennifer, Henderson, Rossi and myself. Nesbitt survived Ichioka; I never heard about the others. Ichioka had a British doctor named Jackson who won wide prisoner admiration for his medical ingenuity and his success in performing operations with razor blades and without anesthesia.

10

Signs in the Sky

At Chikko, the field of battle again was to change dramatically.

My military battle had lasted only six months. In it, I departed a make-believe world for one of grim reality. Before, I had looked outward and had survived, even prospered; during military action I was forced to turn inward for the resources needed to survive. It was a sudden and violent change, and the effects were to be permanent. I would never again—in military life, in society, in academia, or in religion—completely trust those in authority. I would want any such authority to prove itself first, when the chips were down. This attitude had life-shaping consequences.

My battle against disease had lasted almost exactly one year, and was now for the most part over. From it I learned something of the human organism's capacity for survival. I also learned it is better not to see too far into the future, or the price to be paid may not seem worth the article bought. Most of all I learned that tribulation can be made to be worth far more than its cost—but this was a complicated lesson, fraught with dangers, that I was not to understand until years later.

At Chikko, my battle would now become one against the awesome foes of fatigue and boredom. It is difficult to explain, particularly considering the horror of my earlier battles, why the next two years and some months—most of the time at Chikko—were so horrible. It was, in some ways, a subtle horror. Deep and sustained conversation was almost non-existent. Few friendships were formed. Nothing seemed important enough to expend energy upon. What conversation did occur often concerned food. The marginal nutrition we received was not mere punishment of some sort, and not just a husbanding of food resources by the emperor's troops. Focusing hollow-eyed upon survival, we were a docile lot—fewer calories meant fewer guards were needed. The brief fattening-up that often occurred when prisoners were to be moved, beginning in the Philippines, was livestock management, not human relations. The conditions under which many American larcenists and murderers live out their sentences—with television and libraries and three squares a day— leads me, quite seriously, to the conclusion that some commit their crimes for the privilege of incarceration. At Chikko, boredom had a more trenchant meaning.

I was fortunate, at that. Chikko was clearly one of the best camps in the entire Japanese prison system. Of the 700 in the camp, only 36 died while I was there. While Chikko lost two percent of prisoners a year, other camps in Japan were losing 20 percent. Starvation, cold, toil and disease took their toll.

The Japanese would, after the war, hide behind the code of bushido to explain their indifference to human misery. The Japanese warrior, bushido insisted, would kill himself before submitting to an enemy. And any enemy who surrendered was beneath contempt, undeserving of humane treatment. But among the Japanese warriors who guarded prisoners in the homeland, the code often disappeared when there were earthquakes below or B-29s above. The truth is, most of them simply despised anything not Japanese. We were not Japanese.

Nine of those who died at Chikko while I was there were East Indians taken from ships sunk or captured by the Japanese. Several of the dead were Filipinos. One, Pio, was sent out to work in the last stages of tuberculosis by Saunders, the American camp commander, who kept a fellow Mason off a work detail. But there wasn't much of that brand of justice at the Honsho Camp. The other deaths were random and caused by work accidents, infections such as typhus, and organic diseases.

At first I went out almost eagerly on work parties. I felt a new optimism but failed to understand my physical limitations. I lasted only a few minutes the first day out. I queued up for my turn at carrying a sack of grain 20 or 30 feet from a boxcar. I regained consciousness moments later flattened to the ground by the load. It probably weighed 50 kilos—110 pounds. Ten or 15 kilos was probably my limit, and that only every 15 or 20 minutes.

The Japanese honsho said, "Ginki nai" (not strong), and put me to work cleaning up spilled grain with a broom made of brush or twigs. In a month or so, I was able to carry a 110-pound sack and learned how to conserve enough energy to get back to the barracks in the evening. The first week or so, I needed help to mount the three steps into the camp, but I could measure my increase in strength and stamina daily.

The weather was ideal. What little news there was convinced us we were back in the fight in a big way. What we saw on work parties convinced us that Japanese production could never compete with that of the United States. I never met an American or any of our allies who did not think Japan would be completely and permanently defeated. We were half-right.

Unlike at many of the camps, the work at Chikko was greatly varied. Companies would contract with the Japanese camp commander on either a short-term or long-term basis. The camp commander merely furnished warm bodies. On long-term contracts a prisoner was appointed lead man and was a steady on the job. Others could shift between work details but usually stayed with the easier or more desirable jobs. Those who had no friends among the prisoner honshos or who had come late to the camp filled the less desirable parties. A stevedore or longshoreman job handling bales or boxes with slings and ramps one week might turn into a job shoveling salt or bauxite the next. Membership on one party one day gave a prisoner a priority for the next.

Sometimes the Japanese honsho knew and would divulge the work scheduled. This gave a clear advantage to those who learned enough of the Japanese language. There was a great deal of gamesmanship among prisoners. I initially selected only the lightest work; later, however, I tried to get on those parties in which there was the greatest opportunity to steal.

After six weeks or so, those of us who came from the military hospital no longer were given special consideration. One of my first jobs involved shifting timbers and rough boards at a lumberyard. It was easy work, with lots of down time; the Japanese and the Koreans who worked there were not much more interested in labor than we were. The Japanese officer in charge of the yard rarely put in an appearance, and the ride in a military truck to the yard was long and interesting, making the workday shorter.

One day, however, the yard commander showed up. He held a long, curved and polished piece of wood that looked like a Japanese officer's sword and scabbard. He called us to attention and walked down the ranks, hitting everyone two or three times on the buttocks or shoulders. If someone flinched excessively, he yelled "Keotski" (attention) and gave them double. It happened once a week or so for several months. One Japanese worker explained the officer's actions by saying, "Tomadachi shinda"— the officer's close friend had been killed.

Some of the work was at a cement factory. We loaded chunks of gray rock into mine cars and dumped them into huge horizontal cylinders. When set in motion, they ground the rock into a very superior cement. We had no masks and at the end of the day were unrecognizable under our coats of dust. The cement got into the pores of the skin and the eyes. If not thoroughly washed out, it would dry and fester or leave our eyes red for several days.

Only slightly less disagreeable was a bitumen storage area. When the temperature was high enough, the bitumen could be made to bend; but at normal temperature if struck sharply, it would shatter. Our job was to break large chunks out of a sheet many square yards in area and three or four feet thick. The smaller particles got into our shoes and clothes and were impossible to wash out. Worse, the fumes caused an allergic reaction in me and several others. It made our eyes and facial skin so puffy that I almost could not see, especially in the morning.

At Osaka Seiko, a steel mill, we stacked furnace bricks and chiseled impurities out of steel that had been hammered into bars 10 or 12 inches in diameter and seven to eight feet long. We quickly learned to make the metal flow into a widening inclusion with a dull chisel and then smooth it off with a sharp chisel, making it look as if the impurities had been removed. A Polish-American boy and an airman by the name of Lehman and I became very adept at the subterfuge.

The Japanese honsho was a gambler by profession who spoke passable English. If he had any interest, it was in quantity and not quality, and many of the ingots we processed came back from the furnace and hammermill and were seen over and over again.

Occasionally we worked at a military installation on the waterfront. It received and sent out shipments by sea and rail. We were involved in stacking and transporting bales of crude rubber, cloth, cork and soybean cake. We also handled barrels of various liquids and slurries. We loaded small rail cars, pushed them to another location, stacked them and often moved them again. The contractor could not always get a work party, so he often kept us even if he had no real work to be done.

Several acres of metal barrels were stacked three high at the waterfront site. Once we handled a shipment of about 60 drums of alcohol. One of them "got lost" in a stack of empty drums and the Japanese never found it. We siphoned the alcohol into our canteens for weeks and carried it into the camp, where it had great barter value for sugar or oil that had been stolen on other work parties. We even traded it to Korean civilians for an occasional egg.

The alcohol drum met an unfortunate end. A great typhoon backed the ocean up into the inland sea, flooding all the warehouses to a depth of 12 or 15 inches. It wet bales of cloth and boxes of military equipment and damaged extensive amounts of office records. But the only thing it did that bothered us was to set afloat those empty metal barrels, our half-full barrel of alcohol among them. We never found it.

My weight went up to 127 pounds in the summer of 1943. The beriberi pain in my feet never went away but lessened somewhat. Occasionally my feet and ankles would swell slightly, become sunburned and turn an ugly and painful bright red. I also developed a colitis condition that was a problem for many years. But all in all, it was a good summer and I was reasonably ready for the winter. I received an issue of Japanese Army padded pants that would have made a great difference a year earlier.

I began to learn some Spanish from a merchant marine named Angelo Manzano, whose freighter had been the victim of the disguised German raider Dogger Bank. Manzano's ship was American by registry and had been sunk in the South Pacific. The Germans apologized when they turned him and the rest of the freighter's crew over to the Japanese at Jakarta. I learned enough Spanish from him to skip the first two semesters of the language at the University of Oklahoma. Manzano's escape from Franco, his ingenuity in avoiding being sent back to Spain by France, his serving in a half dozen nations' merchant marines during the war, and his reunion with his bride of a month after 12 years was an odyssey worthy of Homer.

Lice, fleas and bedbugs were a constant annoyance, as were the rats that infested the waterfront. The bugs were much less active in the winter and colder weather was welcomed at least for that. The rice ration was cut early in the winter of 1944, and we began to lose some of the weight we had regained. The vegetables were not reduced for about another six months, so we lost more calories than nutrition. Occasionally we got a piece of fish or some squid. I longed for an onion, an apple or an orange—and a youthful addiction: cinnamon rolls. Day in and day out the food was monotonous to an extreme.

Ennifer was stabbed in the back that winter by a crazed Japanese civilian. The knife went in high and came out high on his left chest. The Japanese were highly embarrassed. They put the assailant in prison and Ennifer in a civilian hospital, from which he returned in two weeks completely healed.

After the stabbing incident, the escort guards, military and civilian, cleared the way in front and walked us in the middle of the street when possible. Beatings became more frequent and minor infractions in the camp were met with increasingly heavy punishment. I was made to kneel for gambling when merely playing acey-deucy with dice. My head was pulled back by my hair, my feet stepped on and water poured down my nose.

However, we learned how to handle the Japanese civilian honshos by telling them we would tell the kempeitai (secret police) they had been trading with the prisoners and selling and buying from them. Codes of conduct became understood that kept punishment by civilians within bounds and made the prisoners more circumspect as well.

I was caught stealing cooking oil once and soap on another occasion. For the oil theft, the honsho began to beat me on the head with the buckle end of a belt, breaking the cartilage in my left ear with the first blow. I grabbed the belt, jerked it out of his hand, threw it on top of a building and said, "Atama nai" (not on the head). He was furious and threatened to report me. That was the first time the kempeitai threat was raised. I later got a pole and retrieved his belt, which somewhat saved face for him. I held my breath when we arrived at camp, but I heard no more about it.

Chikko had received Red Cross parcels once, but the Japanese would not distribute them because "there were not enough to go around." Their sentries, however, opened the storeroom and stole from the parcels on occasion. As a result, two prisoners climbed one night to the roof, hung over the eve and broke into the storeroom through an air vent. They were caught coming out, reported, tried in a civilian court and spent six months in a civilian jail making baskets and brooms.

There was little else to steal and it was essentially no problem during camp life. Everything I owned at that time would fit in a cardboard box of 10 inches cubed. I hid only my Gillette razor blades. The 10 of them lasted all the time I was a prisoner. I would make a paste of rust resembling jeweler's rouge, smear it inside a glass and sharpen the blades by moving them back and forth with my middle finger. It worked fairly well.

The food got increasingly bad. We often received broken rice and sometimes had insufficient fuel to cook it thoroughly. The body does not process uncooked rice. And it constantly reinfected us with roundworm, which deprived us of both energy and sleep.

In the fall of 1944, Chikko received several baskets of beautiful apples. Prisoners from one barracks were assembled outside and made to pose, smiling, with an apple in each hand and the baskets in the foreground. Not only did the Japanese not distribute the apples, but tried to recover those that had been held for the pictures. The guards did not accept those that had a bite out of them, and Henderson ate his completely as he walked back toward the basket to which it was supposed to be returned.

One day we were offloading a 40- or 45-foot vessel at a small-boat dock when a Japanese worker fell into the water. None of the Japanese tried to save him. They appeared transfixed by the man struggling in the water. Finally an Italian-American dove in and pulled the Japanese toward the dock. Other prisoners fished them both out. The prisoners, openly disdainful of the Japanese who stood by and did nothing, made obvious remarks and gestures to them. Several days later, the camp commander sent a letter to be read to all prisoners cautioning them not to consider themselves better than the Japanese.

Late in 1944 I received my first communication from my family. The letter was six or eight months old. It was from my father, who said my mother had broken her arm and could not write. For several months I was convinced that she was dead. Then I received a letter in her handwriting. With the fall of Corregidor, my family had received a telegram from the War Department that I was missing and presumed dead. But in November 1943, a Japanese amateur shortwave operator had broadcast the names of American POWs in Japan. I was identified as one of them.

Overflights by American aircraft probably began in late 1944 and had become common in January 1945. We did not at first recognize them as American but saw their contrails at very high altitudes. The Japanese workers began to refer to a "Be ni ju koo" (B-29) increasingly and in increasingly concerned tones. Early in February 1945, more than 100 B-29s hit Kobe 15 miles across Osaka Bay. The attack occurred at night and the fires burned all the next day.

The raid told us that we now had air bases within bombing range, either in the islands to the south or in China. We had seen maps in Japanese newspapers of the landing at Leyte but did not believe we had aircraft that could make the round trip from Clark Field. The Japanese had said they were B-29s and we knew by their daytime reconnaissance flights that they were not carrier aircraft. They looked like the B-17s we had lost in the Philippines.

Shipping activity had tapered off greatly, and it appeared that Japan was being denied access to much of its former holdings. It was rare at this time for a prisoner to work a ship. This was reflected in further reduced rations and Japanese civilians' complaints about shortages. More and more, we were doing makework.

There was a feeling in the air that a crisis was near. This put both ourselves and the Japanese in a very difficult position. Their code called for them to die for their emperor if asked to do so. It might have been something they would do if asked, but on their list of things they wanted to do, it was not first. This also put the prisoners in a position of considering where they stood. It was not likely that all the Japanese would die for their emperor and leave the prisoners free to roam their land. There was no one of us who was not examining his options.

11

"You Will be Killed"

On the night of March 13, 1945, Osaka was bombed. Our camp was barely one city block inland. The first firebombs hit about two blocks inland and continued away from us for four or five miles. The raid lasted much of the night. (Military records reveal that 301 B-29s hit Osaka.)

In the morning, a vast area—later determined to be 25 square miles—was a smoldering desert. The firebombs would not have been effective against many of the "hardened" buildings at the waterfront, but they devastated the inland cottage industry. The bombs also reduced to rubble the homes of the population that supported Osaka's war effort. On the night of March 17, Kobe was hit. (This time the raid was carried out by 306 B-29s.) Kobe was now a mirror image of Osaka.

Our food situation became critical. The soup was always thin and frequently there was none. The rice ration was reduced to about two-thirds of a bowl morning and evening. I was beginning to feel weak and it became hard to concentrate. On occasion, my chest felt overfull. Visible heartbeats again appeared, sporadically, over much of my chest.

We were made part of a frantic effort to salvage material from damaged warehouses, where we were always on the lookout for food but rarely successful. Roof damage had allowed water to attack the contents of many structures. Mostly, we salvaged commercially valuable items such as bales and bolts of cloth. Some warehouses were heavy with the odor of mildew or mold.

What we assumed to be Japanese industrial officials were appearing at the work site more and more often. Surprisingly few Japanese were in the area. Groups of younger-appearing women came into the area several times to work, but their efforts seemed poorly coordinated.

During the Osaka bombing in March, we all expected the camp to be hit momentarily. There was no panic. It was something we knew had to happen. When it did not happen, it was for a while believed that our people knew where we were and had avoided hitting us. By this line of thinking, we attributed an accuracy to our Air Corps's night bombing that its daylight bombing never achieved.

(Kobe was to be hit again the night of May 7, with high-explosive ordnance rather than firebombs. Osaka was to be firebombed again with 458 aircraft on June 2; Kobe with 473 aircraft on June 6; and Osaka again with 409 planes on June 8. After a June 16 firebombing by 444 planes, Osaka became a non-functional city. Although much of its industrial and commercial area had not been seriously damaged, its work force had been dispersed.)

Until late April, work was restricted to salvaging from partially burned warehouses. The waterfront was only moderately hit and the major warehouses and wharfs not at all. We had different jobs every day—cleanup and removal of boxes and bales to undamaged buildings. Shortly after the major raid in which mile after mile of cottage industry had been destroyed starting a block from our camp, we were clearing out a warehouse of smoldering bales of cloth when the air raid siren went off.

As it had affected me so long ago in the bombings of Cavite and Sangley Point, the sirens now terrified the Japanese guards. They had been bewildered ever since the major bombing; now they didn't know which way to turn. Our young guard looked at us in terror. He had been kept out of military service because of "kokora dami"—a bad heart—and he looked near a coronary. He said "Be ni ju ku" and something we didn't understand and ran toward a concrete building where we had stolen so many cans of tangerines one lucky day.

The citrus heist occurred this way: Prisoners working inside the warehouse had moved crates against a loose piece of corrugated metal wall. Pulled back from the outside, the metal sheet allowed us to break open a supposedly secure crate. The contents would be emptied and those prisoners inside signaled others to throw the empty crate into the scrap heap and replace it with a full one. For men who hadn't had any vitamin C for three years, it was pure nutrition. We were caught on the second or third day when the honsho saw empty cans glittering six or eight feet beneath the inland sea in the late afternoon sun. He told us later that the bombing had saved him from the kempeitai. He knew that little would happen to us but much to him if he said anything, but I don't think he would have reported us in any case. We liked him before and we liked him more afterward.

When the guards scattered under the bombing run, leaving us unattended, we waited for the incoming planes, trying to anticipate where they would hit. Another honsho returned, herded us into the warehouse with the smoke-damaged bales of cloth, closed the door and, we thought, locked it. Bombs fell, but not in great numbers and at a considerable distance.

We piled bales to give us a stair to the metal roof about 15 or 18 feet above the floor. Gene Grimsley and Angelo, the Spaniard who had fought with the Loyalists against Franco, enlarged an opening in the already damaged roof, slipped out and dropped 10 or 12 feet to the ground. The lock had not been turned. The door had been open all along. We flooded outside and waited out the attack in meaningless freedom.

For the next few days six of us emptied military warehouses of what proved to be a relatively large amount of metal ingots and metal barrels containing an extremely heavy powder. The work party was headed by a Japanese colonel accompanied by two non-commissioned officers, one a driver. We loaded small convoys of trucks and took them to Takurasuka, a beautiful place where wooded mountains met fertile agricultural land northwest of Kobe.

The colonel's hoard was deposited daily in a school. It was always gone the next day. The same prisoners were picked up by the colonel each day. No Japanese honsho accompanied us. Another group, somewhat larger, was loading materials onto trucks and off-loading them to barges.

The colonel fed us well but spoke, as far as I know, only once. When he asked "non musame utsukushi-ka?"—which girl is the prettiest?—I pointed out one that looked most Western. He threw up his hands in mild disgust and walked away. The schoolchildren appeared to be 12 or 13 years old. They showed mild curiosity, but no animosity.

I asked an old Japanese what was being done with the metal that was disappearing each night and he gestured to show that it was being buried. All this I reported to the occupation forces a few months later.

The next day we lined up for work without breakfast, about six o'clock. After a few minutes we were told to go back in the barracks, where Red Cross parcels were distributed, one to every four prisoners. We conducted a Dutch auction, as we called it. One turned his back while another picked up one of the major articles from the box. The one with his back turned named who got that item. This was repeated until each of the four had a major item. Then the last got his choice of what was left, then the next to last, then the third from last, then the first. Then the first started the process over again. After that the trading began, first within the group of four and then with other groups. Then we ate.

While we were eating, the guards came in with bread rolls and told us to gather up all our belongings and line up outside. By 8 a.m. we were marching to the train station. Around 10 a.m., perhaps 100 of us were in a passenger car with the shades drawn, traveling through an abomination of desolation. Within a few miles we were in a beautiful countryside untouched by war, as seen through the window shades. Several hours later, after numerous stops, we passed through Kyoto on our way to Notogawa on the eastern shore of Lake Biwa. The holy city Kyoto, in an expression of American piety toward a foreign god, had seen no war.

That evening, after walking several miles from the train station along a small river, the banks of which had been lined with stone perhaps centuries before, we arrived at a stockade. Notogawa would be our last home in Japan.

The stockade was a rectangle about 150 feet long and 100 feet wide. Sleeping quarters lined both sides and part of the back, where latrines and the wash area also were located. The front on both sides of the gate was set aside for guards and administrative personnel. The galley was in the center, along with the storerooms. There was a narrow area between the outside of the buildings and a seven-foot fence surrounding the compound. At the four corners of the compound, sentry posts containing machine guns looked down the corridors between the buildings and the fences.

Anyone trying to get out of the compound other than through the gate would have to break through the outer wall of a building and scale or break through the fence. This was the first time in Japan that we had experienced a serious menace of arms.

The two main topics of conversation soon became the progress of the war and how to avoid the four sentry posts that had the compound, but not the surrounding countryside, in their arc of fire.

I removed two boards from my bunk space and slipped through to investigate. There were several inches of loose, heavy dirt left over from construction days, but under that the earth was silt solidified into a clay that barely yielded to a spoon. A tunnel would take months and would lead into plain view in a farmer's garden. The word was passed that we would have to try to obstruct the firing ports in the sentry posts and break through the main gate, dash across the road a few yards to the river and run downstream to the lake. From there it would be every man for himself in getting to the heavily wooded hills some four or five miles away.

It was a bleak prospect, but many or even most of us could

make it if the guard contingent wasn't increased. Some of us agreed to make a break at the first sign of major guard reinforcement. We hadn't reckoned on another enemy—hunger.

The food ration was bad from the first day in camp, both in quality and quantity. The rice contained what appeared to be a millet or a grain sorghum, neither of which was fully cooked for the first few days. The soup was an almost clear daikon broth, lukewarm and tasteless.

We were put to work immediately building a dike across the mouth of a several-hundred-acre inlet of Lake Biwa. The plan was to close off the inlet with earth taken from a canal being dug to reroute a stream feeding into the inlet. Once completed, fine lake bottom would be added to the agricultural economy of the region.

We loaded rail cars with the heavy clay soil, pushed them out on a dike, extending and building up its sides, then pushed them back to load more material. We were worked unmercifully by most of the honshos, but received consideration from some when the military guards were at a distance.

The canal, our source of earth to build the dike, was emptied of stream water by a pump that may have saved my life. The pump was in a sump near the end of the canal. The track, running along the side of the canal before branching off to the dike, allowed several hundred feet of canal to be dug to its final dimensions so long as the water in it, which amounted to several hundred gallons a minute, was pumped out into a slough that emptied into Lake Biwa.

It was a grinding routine: digging inch-thick slices of clay from the canal, scraping it off the shovel into the rail car until it was full, pushing the car out on the dike, off-loading enough so that it could be tipped, emptying the car, lifting it back on the tracks and returning for more. There was no light work for anybody. It was almost impossible to work the shovels into the earth; it was also nearly impossible to break the clay loose from a full shovel. (Many broken shovels and beatings for breaking them occurred before we learned how.) Under pressure, water would ooze from each shovelful, forming a vacuum that had to be broken before the clay would release from the metal.

In one way, off-loading was even worse because the initial work had to be done at chest level, affording no leverage. We had little strength in our arms to begin with, and our strength lessened as the days of poor food intake mounted. Again I got lucky. My heart again enlarged so that it could be seen beating all over my chest. I was given two or three days of bed rest, then was assigned to tend the electric pump.

My heart was normal when I got up in the morning. I ate without difficulty so long as heart action was normal, but when it wasn't I could feel it throughout my upper chest, especially in my throat, and I had no appetite. So in the evening I normally ate my food cold an hour or so after it had been dished out.

I started out to work at the head of the column, gradually falling back and bringing up the rear by the time we arrived at the work site. The Japanese all came at one time or another to see my heart beating. It was mid-summer, so we wore only pants, or a G-string and shoes, those of us who had them. "Dami" (bad), the Japanese would say after observing my heart, then lower their heads and shake them in the Oriental way.

Their solicitude, however, didn't save me from a mild beating one day when the pump failed. I had been warning the honsho of a problem because of the electric shock—more of a strong tingle—I had been receiving when clearing the pump intake of debris. The motor was replaced several days later, and I got my job back.

I built a makeshift bench across a corner of the pumphouse and would sit and doze at the whine of the pump and awaken at the increase in sound frequency as the pump inlet became obstructed. But my weight, as it did with all of us, declined steadily, and sitting on a hard surface became increasingly painful. Thus both standing and sitting became a difficult task. When I could neither stand nor sit any longer, I would go down into the sump and lean against the side that was inclined from the vertical about 30 degrees. Once in a while I would hear "Korah!," but mostly I was left alone.

One day I and 20 or 25 of my fellow prisoners received the greatest treat of the entire prisoner-of-war experience. Nearly a score of girls about 16 years old had been working most of one day salvaging mussels from a section of the land being reclaimed from Lake Biwa. A guard said they normally unraveled silk-worm cocoons. About 3 p.m. they came single-file up to the pump house along the dry side of the new levee. Each carried a bundle of clothing on a stick they had used to keep it out of the water and off the mud while they worked. Several of them carried flat baskets filled with mussels. Most of the rail cars were out on the levee, but four or five and their crews were held up by a track problem.

As the girls approached, I could see they were covered with mud, especially their arms and legs; I could also see something else unusual: They were all stark naked.

One by one they descended into the slough that was carrying the stream water lifted by the pump into Lake Biwa. Completely without self-consciousness, they cleaned off the mud and helped each other up the bank. They dressed, waited for the last to come up and out of the water and filed away across the levee along a previously reclaimed section of the lake.

The beauty of their young bodies and the simplicity and inno-cence of the moment left me, and those who had viewed from a distance, in a state of wordless awe. I never heard a coarse word about the incident nor talked with anyone who saw it who did not feel it was a rare and privileged moment. They were no longer the marines I knew in China and the Philippines. It also emphasized how profoundly different our cultures were. More than anything else, however, it reawakened us to a beauty we had nearly forgotten and one we were in jeopardy of never seeing again.

We watched Japanese aircraft practice dropping aerial torpe-does into the lake; we watched crops grow, burst into maturity and disappear; we saw large fish come out of the lake and disap-pear into villages and wondered if the obligatory fee were paid the emperor for taking from his waters; we heard and saw the United States come to dominate the sky and the Japanese recognize that the Americans flew where they would and when they would. We knew something of the beating Japan was taking by the times all prisoners (except me) were required to stand at attention after work, or made to double-time in place, or when the blond-haired or exceptionally tall were singled out for their own beatings.

As the frequency of the signs in the sky and signs on the ground increased, we knew our situation was becoming critical and that perhaps we had not yet paid the full price. We ate what we got and drank the broth in the hope that it held hidden nutrients. We husbanded our energy by a show of work and a daily change of signals that warned of the military approaching along the levee or a honsho getting anxious about not making his quota. The lead rail car of a group usually managed to be the last one filled, giving the others a rest; the last to be emptied often was the one that led the return trip. To give credit where it is due, most of the guards understood our condition and were reasonable in what they demanded of us. An unspoken agreement developed in which the prisoners made a strong show of work when certain officials, civilian and military, were around.

We had arrived in Notogawa sometime after the second week of May. June came and went. In July the number who were unable to work went up dramatically as a wave of diarrhea swept through the camp. The result was even less food, as those who did not work were supposed to be put on half rations. In practice, the weak and the strong got weaker together. I was unaffected by either the diarrhea, the dysentery it turned into for some, or the summer flu that followed, but I was now down to 50 kilos (110 pounds) on the galley scale for the first time in two years. It was not so much the weight itself but the speed of the loss that was the worry. We couldn't understand why, in the midst of harvest, we could have nothing more than radish or eggplant broth and doubted the nutritional value of both. We wanted an end to it.

But the end did not come. It was announced that there would be only two partial rest days a month. It was futile to get worked up about it, even to ourselves. After about a week, some of the military guards that had been with us from the beginning were replaced. One day they were there; the next day they were not. The new guards were both younger and older. Two appeared to be about 19 or 20 and very green. One was crippled. The other two were well along toward 60 and did not appear to be military men. We waited to see what they would be like. It didn't take long to find out. When a prisoner came near, they were motioned away. I knew of only one exception.

The crippled guard had brought a baby goat into the compound. It was very young and very much in need of its mother. Its bleating aroused a strain of sympathy in the prisoners, especially at night. Its coat was sparse and the mosquitoes from the paddies descended on it in a cloud. Some of us would go out before curfew and let it suckle a finger while we kept the mosquitoes off it.

Late one evening I was tending the kid by keeping the voracious insects in flight with a towel when one of the new young guards came up to me, looked around and said in a low voice in American-tainted English: "If the Americans land on Japan, you will be killed." Startled, I asked him where he had learned English. He told me he had worked in an American diplomat's house and had gone to a Catholic seminary. I thanked him and, as he left, I noticed that he had been observing the rosary I wore around my neck—half as a reminder of my heart condition, half as an amulet. I never was close enough to him to speak again, but I wondered how he would behave if the Americans landed: as a Japanese or as a Christian?

12

Never Again, Never Again

On August 13, 1945, I began again to keep a journal. I had done so three previous times during my captivity, but had lost or destroyed all my notes—including the set that became a casualty of dysentery in the Philippines. This time, on a sheaf of note paper left by maintenance personnel in the pump house, I recorded the events of my last days in captivity.

Everything you have read to this point is the product of a not-infallible memory. And the entire volume is a single marine's story; it is not a product of research. But one day in 1988, after I already had written a draft covering the events of 1945, I stumbled across my old olive drab, Corps-issue field scarf. The journal pages I began in Notogawa had lain in the field scarf unopened, and almost forgotten, for more than 40 years.

The bad news was the pain of holding in my hands not just words that told the tale, but the pieces of paper themselves, something physical that had been there with me. The good news was that memory had served me well. The old journal pages revealed some minor skewing of chronology, but events themselves were almost entirely intact and accurate. The degree of correlation was astounding. A journalist once told me he did not bother tape recording interviews on grounds that "if you can't remember it, it's probably not worth writing." My memory passed a serious test; someone else will have to judge whether these words have been worth writing.

Journal in hand, I returned to this manuscript, able to apply precise dates, to flesh out distant thoughts, to recount small but telling facts that had slipped from recall, to put my exact feelings in an exact time and place. Just as the old Navy hospital towel had served me well beyond its assigned duty, the old field scarf had yielded a sorely needed measure of confidence in my task.

The remainder of Part Two, then, is a personal adventure from a significant period in world history, adapted from my daily notes written in longhand on Lake Biwa pump-house paper. More than anything else, you will see the folly in assigning a date to the end of the war, at least as far as those who were there are concerned.

AUGUST 13, 1945: Dive bombers have returned, the first we have seen in many days. This tells us we have carriers within a few hundred miles, relatively secure from attack. Maybe they aren't dive bombers but long-range, land-based, two-engined bombers. That tells us we have secure bases much closer than the Philippines or even Formosa. Maybe they come from Russia or China. Maybe we even have carriers that will accommodate long-range bombers. The consensus is still dive bombers.

Today there was also a large flight of B-29s. They glistened, disappeared in the southern sky and reappeared again. A lone Japanese fighter rose to meet them. It peeled off as it came near them, seemed to come within a couple of hundred feet and then start a long dive. There was no sound and no smoke. It crashed without the slightest change in trajectory, several miles south of our camp. It was the first Japanese plane I have seen shot down. The guards thought it was an American plane at first, but soon learned of their mistake. It was double-time after the work party, but it didn't last long. The war is again coming near.

AUGUST 14: It was out to work as usual, but there was no banter between guards and prisoners. At 11:00 all prisoners were told to drop their shovels and return to camp. The Japanese never leave a tool uncleaned, so this is really an occasion to think about. We were told to rest until 2 p.m., and at noon all the sentries but two left the camp. Some said it was for a lecture (hand opening and closing in front of the mouth); others said it was for a radio broadcast (hand cupped over the ear).

At two o'clock we returned to work, with no explanation from the Japs. At 3:30 we were ordered to clean our tools, and at 4 p.m. we were back at camp. No planes were seen or heard after about 11 a.m. No one knew what to make of that. There were no annoyances from the Japs. No one knew what to make of that, either.

AUGUST 15: A rest day was announced at reveille. Many, included me, plan to rest all day. I feel completely normal when I'm not tired. But exhaustion breeds a vagueness, like a curtain drawn between me and reality. I don't like to feel that way. It's hard to think and I get afraid that things happen that I don't remember or can't react to.

There were no annoyances from the Nips last night. No bed check. No one absent to the benjo that had to be accounted for. No air raid alarms, just mosquitoes and sore hips, tail bone and shoulder blades. No alarm all day and no sign of aircraft. Maybe talks are being held. I hope they take into account what has been done to us. It was announced after the evening meal that there will be no work tomorrow. Some of us got together for a serious talk about the possibilities. One sobering thought was that the Jap civilians may be getting hostile, but that doesn't explain the absence of aircraft. If only we could go to sleep with a full stomach! Just once!

AUGUST 16: No alarm night or day. There is open conjecture about a cessation of hostilities. We have begun to test the Japanese more seriously, at least some of us have. I declined to bow and yell "attention" as a sentry came through on patrol in mid-morning. I didn't challenge him, just followed him with my eyes. I was already standing, and don't know whether I would have stood up or not if I had been sitting. We made eye contact. He looked uncomfortable but didn't say a word.

I've suddenly realized the guards don't come into the compound nearly as often. It used to be that on rest days a guard was nearly always patrolling. Someone was always asking them for cigarettes, so they began leaving them in their dormitory. But they still don't like to be asked, and asking sometimes keeps them away from groups of prisoners or even restricts them to patrolling the open space between the prisoners' quarters and the service island in the center. Like most Americans, many have been surprisingly generous with their scarce cigarettes.

This morning there were both potatoes and eggplant in the broth and a full ration of rice and barley mix. We also got a full ration of rice at noon and a small salad of cucumbers and soy sauce. Usually on rest days the morning and evening rations have been spread out over three meals. The word was passed today that there would be three full rations. The evening meal was very late, which caused considerable anxiety. The Japs said they were waiting for meat. It didn't come. No one believed the story about meat anyway, and we all wondered what was going on. Just before dark we were fed a standard rice meal with eggplant broth and told we would not work tomorrow. The reason for no work was that there are epidemics in the area (hara biyoki— stomach problems).

We are all afraid talks will fail and the war will start up again. Morrie, the Englishman from Singapore, tried again to teach some of us contract bridge. We thought auction bridge was bridge. I was dealt 12 spades—all but the ace—bid six spades and went down one and couldn't figure what happened. Morrie thought someone had stacked the deck, but it was shuffled and dealt in front of all of us. I was dealt all but the death card, and didn't fail to take note. I think my 13th card was the six of hearts.

AUGUST 17: I woke early in the morning to the smell of meat being boiled in water. It haunted me for an hour. I finally got up and walked over to the kitchen and there it was, under a white scum in a large black cauldron. Just under 300 men had been allotted seven kilos of beef. I stood downwind of the cooking activities as the rice pots were being filled with water; then, still wary of the Japanese guards, I went back and sat on the edge of my space with a blanket over my shoulders. I have seen fresh meat for the first time in 2$^1/2$ years—since they started fattening us up for the march from Camp 3 to Camp 1 near Cabanatuan.

Breakfast-time finally came. I had a large spot of grease and a small one in my cup of broth. I couldn't decide whether to flavor the rice with the broth or to sip the broth to get the full flavor bit by bit. Finally, I did both. When I got to the bottom of the cup I found a half dozen shreds of meat and a bone chip. It probably took me five minutes to finish those shreds and a half hour to suck the flavor out of that bone chip. Then I couldn't decide what to do with the flavor-depleted chip. I decided to chew it and swallow it for the calcium, but it splintered and I spit it out.

It has struck me what is so different about Japanese farms: There are no animals. I've never seen a horse, a cow, a pig or a sheep on a Japanese farm and a goat only in the compound. They do have chickens, but I've never seen a duck, goose or turkey here.

The kitchen made an attempt at bread at noon. They were supposed to be small round loaves, but they failed to rise and turned out to be about four to five inches in diameter and an inch and a half high in the center. They were very tough, pretty bitter and very heavy, but very good. I don't know how long it's been since I've had something to chew on. They varied in size, so our group had a Dutch auction. I probably got the biggest one in the rice bucket.

No one has been out of the camp since the 14th. The guards almost never enter camp anymore. For the first time, the prisoners didn't empty the benjo this week. Some Koreans did it.

AUGUST 18: Fewer than 50 to sick call this morning. Some don't go when they know they don't have to work. I still go every day even though I haven't had any symptoms for nearly a week, when we double-timed back from work.

I climbed into the upper tier today and watched the Japs dump what looks like scrap iron into the lake. We know the fighting has stopped but are afraid to believe it's over. The view is pretty much limited to the west. We look out between the siding past the wood they put outside our windows so air could get in but we couldn't see out. We can see an arc of about 40 degrees, but it's the same arc from all the viewing places.

They cooked up more bones for the soup tonight. It had onions and carrot tops in it and was thickened with rice flour. Very good!

There was a bad fight between a half-black, half-Indonesian and a Dutchman today. It was about the Dutch getting out of Sumatra after the war. There was another half-hearted fight between two Americans. The doctor made a speech about acting like Americans, but most just walked away.

We've been hearing train whistles again at night. Either they had stopped running or the wind had shifted. Or maybe I am awake more at night to hear them.

AUGUST 19: This is the first Sunday in months with no work scheduled. We've had two or three Sundays off since the bombing of Osaka but they were last-minute rest days, normally because the contractors changed their plans and let their Japanese workers have the day off.

There was no grain in the rice today. We always thought it was part of our diarrhea problem, but some say the grain has vitamins that the rice doesn't. It doesn't have vitamins if you can't digest it!

Everyone is cleaning and repairing clothes and shoes. It got started on our side and our tier, and soon everyone was washing and sewing and trying to find someplace to dry their clothes. Most of us are walking around in G-strings while our clothes dry, but we will have to wear wet clothes to keep off the mosquitoes tonight if they don't dry. Only one in eight or 10 has a change. Most of us have Japanese fatigues that are far too small. Maybe one in 20 has shoes; the rest of us either have clogs or no shoes at all.

The sick bay is beginning to fill up with men with intestinal flu. The doctor is trying to get a fly-killing campaign going, but it seems a lost cause. The benjos are the main problem; there's no way to seal them. The problem is letting all the food sit out until everybody's bowl has been served.

There are also a half-dozen cases of malaria and some asthma, but no medicine. Some of the "asthma" is probably TB.

I'm feeling well and trying out my memory by copying "The Raven," but I can't force the words into my memory. There has been no cigarette ration for about two weeks, but the Japs have become more free with their own. There has been almost no aircraft activity; we can't see much from the camp anyway. The B-29s have a characteristic drone that we can't mistake, at least when they come in numbers, but we haven't seen or heard them in days. No one believes the epidemic story anymore. War has taken a holiday. I wonder how we will take it if the war starts up again.

AUGUST 20: Strange activities. No more need of toban (counting off while in ranks). There is still no contact with Japanese outside the camp, and the guard staff is now bringing in vegetables. Prisoners are emptying night soil into carts left by the Japanese. They ferment it or something, and then use it on their crops.

Someone swears there has been no flag flown since the 14th. I don't remember seeing one or not seeing one over the last few days, but it isn't there today.

There was a lot of revelry in the prisoners' administration office. The guards came to see what was going on and got a crowd asking for cigarettes. Their answer was that they soon would be asking us for cigarettes, or so the rumor went. Nobody has found out yet who heard it.

Today I got men from each group of about 40 together to discuss what we knew or what was rumored. One from the Aussie-English group said no one had been struck since the 14th. We decided we had a lot of signs—no one struck, no work, better food, meat for the first time, no flag, fewer patrols in camp, almost no overflights, dumping metal in the lake, no contact with anyone outside the camp, and some rumors no one could trace down.

But if the war is over, why are we still prisoners? The answer to that was to protect us from the Japs, or that the terms aren't finalized, or that prisoners in the big cities will be repatriated first. Everyone was waiting for us to get back from our "peace conference," but we didn't have anything that they didn't already know. Schoolboys were seen marching out to do our work on the dike. That sort of looks like it's permanent, and we won't be going back.

More of the men are down with the stomach problem. It's more like dysentery than flu, as most don't have fever and aching bones. I haven't had any signs of it yet. A big worry is that those who got it first aren't getting better. Some of the worst ones can hardly walk. No one has died yet in this camp, but some look like we did at Tanagawa when things started going bad fast.

One of the Aussies, Arthur Volks, has an incredible tale, except that he looked me in the eye when he told it and I have no doubt that it's true. He was on Java when the Aussies surrendered—but he and three other men out on patrol didn't know about it. A truckload of Japanese came down the road, and Arthur and his friends killed them all. The Japanese captured the patrol, forced them to dig their graves, and shot them. All four men fell into the graves, but only three of them were dead. The Japs moved on without filling the graves. Volks came to, crawled out and made his way into the hills. He didn't get captured again for a week or more, and the Japs who recaptured him didn't realize he was supposed to have been executed. He has appropriate bullet hole scars on his chest and back.

AUGUST 21: We've started to have a late reveille. Morning chow wasn't served until about eight o'clock. We are supposed to be getting bread and broth at noon from now on. It's great to have something to chew on even though our jaws ache for quite a while afterward.

The doctor who came in with the Aussie-English group and the American dentist who came from another camp in Osaka are both claiming seniority and claim to be the group commander.

The dentist is cautioning everybody through the barracks leaders not to do anything to incite trouble within the camp or with the Jap guards. Someone started to form a prisoner-of-war group and the dentist "refused permission." Everyone laughed and exchanged addresses. *(Forty-six years later I still have a little address book I found on a work party during the cleanup of a bombed-out waterfront. I had saved it blank except for a few attempts at poetry, then I pretty much filled it up in a day or two with addresses from all over the world.)*

The dentist's military cap was returned to him by the Japanese. It's the only piece of regulation military uniform he has. Everybody is wondering what's behind that. They also officially have let us keep razor blades.

A guard was reported as saying: "Britain, Japan, America kusen" (armistice). The camp is of one mind in refusing to accept anything but a complete victory after so much suffering. We can't have been losing enough men to compromise, not with the way our planes have dominated the sky. We didn't negotiate with Germany. Why should we negotiate with their pupil? Faith! Hope! No charity!

AUGUST 22: Reveille the same, food the same. An assembly was called for 11:40 and a letter from the Japanese camp commandant was read:

> The day for which you have so earnestly waited and so ardently prayed has at last become a reality. The war is over! An armistice between America, Britain and Japan was agreed upon on the 16th of this month. However, hostilities will be resumed if peace is not reached. You will be protected by Nipponese soldiers until you are turned over to your country.
>
> You have suffered much in Japan and soon you will return to your loving homes; so let us forget and return to our loving homes.
>
> —Nakanishi Shoko

The announcement was read by an inadequate new interpreter with the second-in-command present. There was mild cheering and then a general silence followed by quiet conversations.

The noon meal was a level bowl of plain rice with a salad. Some salads or cigarettes were traded with the sick for rice. I'm afraid their mess kits are dirty. Speculation seems to have stopped.

A wave of anxiety as to how I will cope with a complex world after such a simple one has come over me. I wonder how it would be to stay in Japan as a victor after being a slave. There will be a lot of furious POWs if we accept anything but total surrender.

Evening rice. Same level bowl but a generous serving of bean, potato, eggplant and cucumber soup. One of the best in years except for the one with meat.

Everybody seems to be on a rumor hunt, wandering from group to group, talking in subdued voices about food, repatriation, home, money, being quarantined before being let back into the States, about the future as civilians or in the military. Where will they hold us if they don't let people with chronic dysentery in the States? Here in Japan? In the Philippines? Will they worry about leprosy after six years in the Orient, much of it in filth? I'm now over 24 years old. I haven't talked to an American girl in six years, or any girl in four years. How will I know how to act? If I stay in the Orient, I won't have a language problem, at least; Oriental women don't need to talk with their men, nor their men with them.

AUGUST 23: I've had the wrong day of the week. I thought this was Friday, but it's Thursday. There was no reveille today. We got up about 7:15 to overboiled potatoes, squash and eggplant cooked in grease until they were unrecognizable, and the first white rice I've had in Japan—all I wanted. The Japs are promising "every consideration: cigarettes, protection, better food."

Chief Saunders, the American camp commander, is still saluting every Jap he sees. Mouse! The officers and others who didn't go out of the camp to work—like cooks and dispensary people, American and otherwise—are much more fearful than the rest of us. They never tested the limits to which they could go and never gave any opposition at all. We who went out always looked for, and usually found, a weakness in the guards or honshos. Mostly it was fear of their own superiors.

They promised us the best day of food in Japan. It wasn't as good as the day we had meat in the broth, but they tried. The cook crew is being depleted by stomach flu and they are looking for subs to take their places. A week ago everyone in the compound would have jumped at the chance. Now they barely are able to recruit replacements.

AUGUST 24: Everybody is cleaning house, getting rid of clothes they would have needed, and may still need, for the winter. I still can't part with my Navy hospital towel, the gray one with the blue stripes at each end and "USA" stamped on it. It's still in good shape after serving as a belly band for three winters. The rest of my inventory is meager: A dirty rice-husk pillow, two synthetic blankets, an almost empty bottle of Vaseline hair oil I've smelled occasionally but never used, a Gillette razor with half a blade I hid in a copy of *Think and Grow Rich* that belongs to Corporal Cook from Houghton Lake, Michigan. Until recently, I had four blades left. Now I have only a big half of one left; the others all have broken into pieces too small to hold in the razor.

I still have the Protestant New Testament that I read sporadically. It reminds me that after all these years of praying, it took me hours to form a prayer of thanksgiving for the news of an armistice—"Though a mother abandon her child, I will never abandon you," sayeth the Lord!

I also have an American toothbrush, some Japanese tooth powder, a piece of soap I stole from a waterfront warehouse and an olive-colored turtleneck sweater knitted by an 83-year-old sweetheart from Lorain, Ohio. It was a "Christmas present" from the Japanese, who had it in the storeroom for nearly a year before it was issued. The sweater was one of my best Dutch auction prizes. I couldn't get my head through the neck, so I had to cut it out and sew a hem in it to keep it from unraveling. I still have three needles and the Marine Corps card with white, red and olive drab thread on it. But best of all, I now have two notebooks of names and addresses and about 50 sheets of Japanese note paper that I'm writing this on.

That is my treasure. All but the clothing I have wrapped in a Marine Corps field scarf.

Somebody has started a rumor about planes dropping food. No one takes this seriously. How would they know where we are?

A former bugler who had gotten hold of a bugle or trumpet sounded taps last night. It was a moment too charged with emotion for words.

Suddenly I got up, told Mario Simo, whom I knew in China, that I was going for a walk, waited for him half a minute, and walked out to the front gate, Mario at my heels. A guard 10 or 15 yards away said: "Abunai"—be careful.

We walked along the river to the lake about 300 yards away, stripped and went for a swim where we had several times been allowed to stop to bathe on our way in from a work party. That's the way it was. No thinking was involved. One minute I was a prisoner and a slave, the next I was a free man on an evening stroll.

We went back after about an hour of floating nose out of the water to avoid mosquitoes. We stood outside the gate for a while, looking in. Several others joined us and went back in to tell the others. It was now about 10 p.m. Soon maybe 20 or 30 prisoners came out and stood in the road talking. We didn't know what to do with our freedom. I went back into the compound, not as a prisoner, but as one with a savage determination never to allow anyone or anything ever to hold me captive in any way ever again.

AUGUST 25: I rushed to the benjo around midnight and spent much of the night there. In the morning I was too weak to think of leaving camp. A number of others went out shortly after breakfast.

By noon I felt better and headed out, going east away from the lake. After maybe half a mile, I came to a building on the river with many windows. I could see a large number of people working with their heads lowered. I went in and found about 40 girls unraveling silk from silkworm cocoons. A little Japanese woman came over, bowed and spoke. I could understand only a few words. Maybe she was Korean. I didn't ask.

I knew the girls were aware of my presence because they kept their backs to me as much as possible and never looked up. It was the apprehension of all girls to a foreign soldier in their land. I watched one little girl with delicate hands find the end of a silk strand and attach it to a wooden instrument like a kite spool, the first step in a major Oriental industry. Then I made a hurried return to the camp. The intestinal problem had returned.

When I got back, a Japanese guard was loading a sack of rice flour on a bicycle. I pointed at the sack and said: "Dokoka?"— Where? He made some confused gestures and I pointed to the sack and then to the storeroom. He took it back. I closed the door and said: "No more." He went to his bicycle. I went to the latrine.

AUGUST 26: I was awake with cramps most of the night. I reek like the benjo. Neighbors asked why I didn't go to the dispensary. I tried, but it accommodates 30, and nearly 150 had the stomach problem.

Some of the men have been into Notogawa. No trouble with the Japs. Several came back with bicycles, and other prisoners took them as soon as the first got off them.

No breakfast, lunch or dinner for me. I don't even know what was served. No one knows what to do with their freedom. We don't know how to get news.

The Japanese guards are taking all the clothing that is thrown away. Another recovered a broken bicycle a prisoner—an ex-prisoner—threw in the canal. A Japanese sergeant has been left in charge of three subordinates. He is a gentleman. He says he is "mostly Christian," if I understand him correctly. Another ex-prisoner said he was told by the sergeant that Pope Pius in Rome was sending us clothes.

Several of us went to Chief Saunders and asked him to tell the Japanese that we want everything in the storeroom issued at once. (He is still saluting the guards, while they are saluting us!) Finally, he said: "Do it yourself." The Japs didn't know what to do. They can't function without instructions. Finally they opened the storeroom. The beer, as has been rumored, was there. So were several hundred cans of salmon. I took a quart bottle of beer and a can of fish. There was no great rush. Half the camp was sick and the other half had the sick prisoners' food as well as their own. Saunders was very unhappy about the storeroom being opened. He said there were going to be some courts-martial. We told him he would be at the head of the list. He whined and said he only had done his job. We said he had done the Japs' job.

I shared the beer and the salmon with Simo and felt better. Both were of excellent quality, especially the salmon. I feel weak but not too sick. No recurrence of the heart problem.

Taps again. A link with the past and with America. Strongly reassuring. The galley steward told another American to "get out," which almost started a battle with utensils as weapons. It was a standoff between a strong, well and intimidated cook and a sick, weak, unintimidated outside worker. For years we resisted the Nips, now we have to stand up to our own people. The steward has been king of the galley for years. He thinks it's his.

The Nip guards don't know what their role is. The allied camp administration people want to continue as usual and wait. The workers want out but don't know where to go or how to get there. I don't remember seeing any of the "camp people" out of the compound yet.

A Jap came in with something in his hat and gave it to Saunders and the two doctors. I had the feeling it was eggs. The thought of poached eggs on toast like my mother made when we were sick but on the mend brought a wave of longing. Funny, I haven't thought of home since I started to take notes. It's been 7½ years since I've been "home." I wonder where "home" is now and where it will be. If I consider home to be what I am most familiar with, then Tientsin would probably head the list.

Osaka—where I was a prisoner!—would probably come next. As much as I hated it there, I could handle it.

The doctors and Chief Saunders getting eggs shows why they have been so reluctant to stand up to the Japs. The Japs have built a buffer between themselves and us and have been keeping the buffer happy. Let the Nips loot the warehouse as long as they are getting theirs! I'm going to report Saunders as soon as I get out.

Some of the prisoners are eating fresh vegetables out of local gardens—tomatoes, onions and beans. I'm sick enough as it is. Four to six years in the Orient hasn't taught some of us very much.

An Army staff sergeant made a dramatic appeal, of the soapbox type, for discipline and respect for superiors. He had attention at first, then almost everyone walked away or waved him off.

The prisoners have been very well behaved, except for the bicycles. And what does the sergeant want for the doctors and Chief Petty Officer Saunders in the way of respect? What are they going to do, issue liberty passes and start work details? It looks like they want to give the impression they have run a tight ship when our forces come in. The truth is they have been the worst representatives of the Americans in the whole affair by refusing to stand up for the men. They have put their friends on the sick list when dying men were forced to go to work. They also appointed their friends to kitchen details instead of having the job elected or rotated. And they got their favorites on the easier details. Now they want "respect and discipline." What they really want is to regain some of the self-respect they've lost, and some undeserved respect from others. Then they want to represent themselves to our forces as the ones who have held our men together. Especially the Aussies feel the same way. I'm going to file complaints against Chief Saunders, Lieutenant Leone and Lieutenant Hagan as soon as I get back.

Thickened potato soup for breakfast and bean soup this evening. I still can't eat rice or salad. I have the feeling that it's the salad that has made the camp sick. It's useless to go to sick call.

They give you a little packet of powder and nobody knows what it is. Those of us who are sick are terribly bloated and have extremely sour stomachs. Maybe it's the white rice. I don't think we had whatever the disease is before we started getting white rice. Maybe the Nips were right about an epidemic.

AUGUST 27: It's been 11 days since the armistice and all we know is that there isn't any evidence of hostilities. Maybe if they won't come to us we should look for them.

Awoke to English reveille this morning and got a piece of eggplant fried in batter. After eating, I walked down to the canal toward the lake and stopped off at the Koreans' shack. The squalor was equaled only by what I saw in China. Fifty people live in an area that seven or eight would occupy in the U.S. The rooms have a common roof and are separated by partitions without doors. The house has a grass roof and mat floor, over dirt, I guess. They have been in Japan 10 years as workers but can get only the lowest type jobs. Many of the children are covered with sores. They have little color and it looks like there isn't a healthy one in the 12 or 15 I've seen. The women are naked to the waist and it's hard to believe that the girls we've seen go by neat and clean will look like them in six or eight years. A woman asked if I wanted "ocha"—green tea. I said no. Then I was offered a chicken. I accepted some green onions. Maybe they were leeks. I said I would be back with some clothes.

When I got back to camp nearly all the American prisoners were gathered around the POW office. Chief Saunders was demanding attention. Captain Burge, MD, U.S. Army, made as caustic and derogatory a statement as could possibly be made to a group of men who have gone through so much and handled themselves so well. He gave no specifics except "disrespect" and "discipline" related to "his staff." Then he threatened us with courts-martial if we didn't submit and accept him as camp commander.

When Burge was through, I yelled that he and Saunders would be the first ones court-martialed, and that we had a catalog a mile long about both of them. Someone else yelled that if we weren't good soldiers, he was puke as an officer. That brought on some profanity and obscenity, and Burge stood there on the inverted daikon cask for a minute or two and then went back into his office.

There has been no stealing in the camp and no significant violence. Burge was never in charge. Chief Saunders was. The Japs wouldn't let the officers take command. The Japs always went through the highest-ranking non-com. Nobody knew what Burge was talking about, unless it happened in the camp he was in before he was brought to Notogawa. Maybe he was like the English merchant marine captain who refused to scuttle his ship and was given the silent treatment by his own men, started seeing things, and then cut his own throat one night in the benjo. No one I talked to took it as seriously as I did. They planned to ignore him, so I did, too.

About 2 p.m. the captain announced that no one was to leave the camp. Hall and Davis and I decided to go for a walk. Saunders was standing at the gate looking at a group of about six walking east toward Notogawa. He was furious but said nothing. We came back in about an hour and a half. I was half asleep when I became aware of a commotion in front of the camp near the gate.

Four U.S. soldiers, the first of the occupation forces, had arrived from Osaka. The leader stood on the daikon bucket and shouted the news. Total capitulation! Philippines recovered! U.S. battleship Missouri to host the surrender ceremony! Atom bomb! Jet aircraft! Prisoners to recuperate in Manila! Nagasaki and Hiroshima destroyed! Land poisoned for 100 years! MacArthur comes to Japan tomorrow! Questions and answers— I couldn't keep up. My mind jumped from fact to fact. Prisoners talked and drowned out the visitor's voice. I had to sit down and think things over.

Captain Burge made a plea for moderation and patience, then went into the office with the head of the delegation. The POWs surrounded the other three from the advance invasion force and bombarded them with questions. My head whirled with the significance of the moment. Our visitors said there would be air drops. We were told to stay put. Some Japs might not accept the surrender. We could be here another two weeks. I didn't realize how much I had feared the armistice would fail.

About 40 of us, those who were well enough, maybe more, took off for town. Holt and I and two others went to the mayor and told him we wanted 12 cases of salmon delivered to the camp. We signed a chit for 15; I don't know why, unless it was to look generous. We also asked him for, and got, a radio. Then we started to leave but went back and asked for beer and sake—all he could get. The mayor agreed, as though he were a salesman taking an order. I left feeling as I had in China—fully in command of the situation.

We moved on to the train station where we learned how often trains left for Kyoto and Osaka. A full passenger train was in the station when we arrived and another pulled in while we were there. The cars I saw were overflowing with very young men in uniforms that were not familiar to me. They looked like the dress of a low-budget military school.

Holt and the other two wanted to explore the town. I was eager to get back to the camp and learn more about how the U.S. had retaken the Pacific, and what changes had taken place in the last 41 months.

I started back. Passing what looked like an alley, I saw a bicycle repair shop and went in. As I was looking around, someone said, "Good evening." I said, "Good afternoon," after I spotted a frail man of about 50 in a homemade wheelchair. It took a few minutes to become familiar with his English and his very weak voice. He lived for several years in British Columbia, where he worked as a railroad laborer and developed a chronic kidney disease. He returned to Japan to die and has alternately improved and worsened. He says it will not be long, but he is glad to have lived to see the end of the war. "Japan did not know America or they would not have gone to war," he said.

I told him I had many questions but was very tired. I would come back later. He said he, too, had many questions, and asked me to return for dinner tomorrow night. "Where is your house?"

I asked. "This is it," he said, " I live behind the shop." He apologized for the food he had to offer. I told him anything would be an improvement.

For some reason, I went back to the train station, maybe because I saw some prisoners heading there with their possessions tied in bundles. "Where to?" I asked. "Osaka ... Tokyo ... Kyoto," they replied. "Why?" "To greet MacArthur ... to see something of Japan while I can ... to get a good hot bath." An old man offered his seat on a waiting train. We all refused. It felt good. The Japanese looted; we didn't. The Japanese took revenge on the innocent; we didn't.

A train stopped and a number of armed Japanese soldiers got off. The U.S. soldiers who visited our camp said they were not allowed to keep any arms. The armed Japanese became confused, realizing we were Americans but not in uniform. We ignored the rifles they carried and waved them on; they hurriedly left. Some ex-prisoners started to get on the train and found out it was continuing north, so they got back off. After a few words with a conductor and a glance at his watch, they came over and said the Tokyo train was at 7:30 that night but trains were leaving for Kyoto and Osaka in two hours. I said, "Good luck," and left.

Outside the train station a store displayed fans, lampshades, mirrors, cigarette holders, vases, glasses, notebooks and pads of paper. I picked up a notebook and a pad and turned around to see a tiny old proprietress, arms crossed, bowing repeatedly. She was saying: "Sumi ma sen, sumi ma sen"— words of deference. "Ikura deska?" I asked. The items came to 30 sen, she said, about a cent and a half. I suddenly realized I had no money. "Kani nai, oba san," I said. She indicated I should take the articles anyway, which I did. She began to bow again and apologize, repeating, "Sumi ma sen." I thanked her and left, returning her bow inadequately. Taking the articles bothers me.

On the way back I felt freer than I could remember. I had left the camp before, but with one eye over my shoulder. Today it was with the assurance that the Japanese had accepted defeat and were not a danger. I felt intensely alive—arms freer, feet lighter, eyes, ears, nose, skin infinitely more sensitive than ever before. What an incredible treasure freedom is.

I found my mind filling with resolutions. Never again would anyone take from me my freedom. Never again would I be hungry or cold. Never again would I eat food with rodent droppings or any other filth in it. Never again would I live in filth. Never again would I work to exhaustion. Never again would I be the victim of an injustice. Never would I submit to a military authority. And never would I allow these things to happen to anyone else.

Amid all this thought, I realized I was weak, tired, chilled and hungry. I moved on, worrying again about my heart. A strong wind came up from across the eastern part of the lake. I sat on an ancient stone bridge for a long time, then lay on some gravel at the entrance to a shrine until the moon rose. It was two days past full and incredibly bright.

I got up and continued on past long, reaching arms of conifer trees. Roof lines were black against the silver of the southeast. Small clouds blacked out the moon for brief periods, but it reappeared in new shapes, new textures, new patterns. It was incredibly beautiful and I felt incredibly bad. That a country that has caused so much pain can be so beautiful disturbs me beyond description. It must be a false beauty; at the same time it is very real. I tried for a while not to look, but was drawn to see the moon appear and disappear between roofs and trees and black clouds fringed with pure silver. It has been a long time since I have really looked at the night sky.

The moon was still low and casting long shadows when I arrived at the compound. More have taken their belongings and left for Tokyo. I must have missed them while sleeping along the road.

Red Johnson left for Tokyo earlier today. I refused to go because of my stomach problems. He was unhappy, because he hadn't picked up much Japanese. I told him to come back if he finds something we would like. He left without saying a word.

I've probably talked to him more than anybody else since I arrived at Chikko in the spring of 1943.

The first day of freedom is now over. I am proud of myself, my fellow ex-prisoners and my homeland. I haven't responded in kind, and neither has my country. We have exhibited the superior culture.

I thank God that right has finally prevailed. How did He decide to bring me through when He allowed so many fine young men to die? He must have a plan for me. How do I find out what it is? An empire, a feudalism, a culture and a god have died. What will take their places? In three years of beatings, starvation, hard labor and exposure, we prisoners have refused to yield. The Japanese have yielded overnight.

Our advance occupation forces tell us to requisition what we need from the local authorities and the authorities accept that without question. We also are told to remain in the Notogawa camp for "repatriation."

Too much for one day. I can't fit my mind around it.

Camp supply here has been put in the hands of a military quartermaster who, with the mayor, rations food for the area. He promises to provide all we want if it's available.

The beer I ordered from the mayor this morning arrived while I was gone and already was mostly consumed when I got back. The salmon was there in good supply. I took two bottles of beer and three cans of salmon, rolled them in my blanket, and spent a long time in the benjo. I'm going to bed without eating.

13

Roaming a Vanquished Land

AUGUST 28: It was a bad night. Abdomen very distended and painful. After one trip to the latrine I went to the galley for some soda and found several prisoners sitting around a cauldron of hot water, which is to be available 24 hours a day. What I wouldn't give for a cup of rich coffee with cream and sugar. My last coffee was in May 1942 at the 92nd Garage on Corregidor. It was powdered C-ration coffee that had solidified and it tasted like anything but coffee, if you could get it to dissolve in water heated by burning grass, twigs and roots.

I had a brief talk with the galley steward. He hasn't been away from the camp yet. He's "a soldier and takes orders." After three years he can't shake it off. What could happen to him that would matter if he went out? He needs sugar, oil, potatoes and milk, and eggs if I can get them. I agreed to tell the mayor.

Fleas, mosquitoes, conversations and uncovered lights gave me a fitful sleep. I overheard "all to Manila for reorganization and rejuvenation, and to be put on display." More words came in snatches—"freedom, easy life, ice cream, milk, clean new clothes, beds, girls, banquets, parades, medals, money." I fear my family seeing me like this: 110 pounds, covered with well-scratched vermin bites, scale up the back of ankles and on wrists, lifeless hair on head and small eruptions where it has broken off on arms and legs, cracks to the point of bleeding in my heels, filthy Japanese Army trousers, smelling like a latrine.

How could any human being be let to look as I look? More than anything I want to be able to cope with sympathy. If they let me lean, I may never be able to stand upright by myself again. I don't want to go home—not to Michigan, not to the United States, not to Manila. The only place I could stand to be seen is in Japan, which I hate all the more because it is beautiful.

I ate a salmon patty for breakfast, along with three tough sugar cookies. There was lots of bread at the galley—all you wanted—and I didn't want any.

I rested or hunted rumors, then talked with a Japanese man of about 50 who came to the camp. He had lived for 20 years in the States and had two sons in Ogden, Utah. He came to Japan to visit days before the war started. He told us that he had said 100,000 times that America would win the war. He told them: "I know America." We talked for two hours. He has a clerical job with the railroad and is used as an interpreter and translator. He is very concerned about not being let back into the U.S. I gave him my home address in Michigan and said I would help him, but that he probably would be very closely investigated. I told him about Tani, the young American of Japanese parents who helped us in the military hospital.

We talked about the defense of the Philippines and about the war as the ex-Utah resident had seen it through the sanitized Japanese press. I summarized what the prisoners had gone through, and he kept repeating: "Those bastards!" He sure sounds like an American. He made an invitation to visit him sometime. After a few minutes of indecision, I decided to go into town with him on the spot.

A street vendor passed with flavored ice on a stick. "Aren't they afraid they are selling for useless money?" I asked. He said that couldn't happen in Japan. He took me to a clothing factory that had been hit by a single American bomb. It hit in the creel room, destroying 60 to 80 creel machines.

From the creel room we entered a room filled at one end with bales of cotton. I wondered if they were the same bales from China we had handled on the waterfront. About a dozen girls recoiled to the other end of the room. After we passed through, they rushed to the door and windows, watching as we talked about them. He told me that nearly a hundred girls aged 16 to 22 worked there. They looked to be from 10 to 18. They live in dormitories and work eight hours a day, five days a week. The girls are regimented through formations and regulations aimed to achieve compliance and uniformity. "Japanese girls are dull," my escort said, "clean, naive and dull." Most of them work one or two years until marriages are arranged.

He stopped in a shop—maybe it was a post office—and brought out a copy of Mianichi Shimbun in English. I looked at the headlines, which announced that the American fleet was headed for Tokyo Bay. He went his way, and I kept my dinner date with the Nipponese from British Columbia.

The ailing old man's wife served a chicken, potato, onion and curry stew, with rice, salt, cucumbers, cow's milk and green tea. She served and did not eat with us. She seemed resentful. Before I left I gave her three cans of salmon and a homemade bag containing several pounds of sugar. She seemed to soften a little.

He and I talked about the war. He had thought Japan was winning until word of the major cities being bombed was received, and it became clear that U.S. bomber formations were undisturbed by Japanese planes. He didn't have much information on how Japan had lost what they won early in the war. He didn't seem too much disturbed about how the war has turned out, but he was very bitter about prisoners taking bicycles. He called it looting. I remembered the notebook and the paper I accepted from the little old woman; I had a can of salmon with me to repay her, but it was still bothering me. I asked him if there was any other "looting." He didn't know of any. I told him of how we had been stripped of everything valuable by Japanese soldiers. I told him about Cabanatuan, the voyage in the hold of the ship, all the prisoners lost in Tanagawa, beatings and overwork and poor food, of being 60 pounds underweight while none of our captors lost weight.

He said soldiers had done that to us and we were taking from civilians. I told him that Japanese civilians in uniform had done all that, and that the bicycles were borrowed, not stolen. We couldn't take them back with us. He felt better after that, and I realized that this was a sick man who repaired bicycles for a living. After that, we didn't have much to talk about. He showed me his garden, an area of eight by 10 feet or so, which suffered much from neglect. I thanked him and his wife, which seemed to surprise her, and left about 9 p.m. I went past the what-not shop with the last can of salmon, but the shop was closed. I left the can partially hidden in a bush.

After I returned to the compound, a Japanese girl of about 15 came by asking questions no one understood. Someone came to get me to see if I could translate. What she wanted was to borrow back her bicycle, which she needed for her "shigoto"— work. I had her find it among about 20 bikes. I should have told her not to bring it back, but it didn't occur to me. I probably couldn't have made that clear, anyway.

Of the 301 men in the camp, not one has claimed an adventure with a Japanese girl, which says more about our physical condition than our restraint. The fear of never being able to express our manhood has faded into the background since the armistice.

Two men thought to be dead in a Japanese prison where they were sentenced for stealing were seen in Osaka. They went 26 days less than a year without speaking. Their food had been better than ours, but they sat alone in their cells making brooms and baskets the entire time. I hope I get to talk to them, though I hear they can barely speak. A prisoner said he had returned from Osaka because all POWs were ordered to stay near their camps for repatriation. He also brought back word that two officers, who had tried to escape and were tied in a kneeling position and then placed in front of a guardshack for two weeks, were released and were now in charge of their former captors.

Some prisoners demanded a no-rice diet, at which the Japs were aghast. Relief parcels have been dropped in Osaka and can be expected at our camp as soon as airmen find it.

AUGUST 29: I awoke at 3 a.m., hurried from under the net, and returned at 4:00, weak from retching. Slept heavily until 7 a.m. Many were sitting up listening for the promised aircraft. I rushed to the street and crossed the old stone bridge on the route to the work site. From there we had a clear view except to the north. A million thoughts crowded in, mostly: "They remember!" Remember Bataan and Corregidor? Wake and Guam? China's Tientsin, Peiping and Shanghai marines? Planes appeared and circled low over the lake and headed for the camp, where a large makeshift Stars and Stripes was spread out on the cookhouse. We had mirrors to signal them, but last night's storm filled the sky with high-level cloud cover. The planes turned sharply to our left and dived toward a distant village to the south. Three years of hope for relief from the sky dissolved into disappointment.

All of us were orphaned from the beginning and still are orphans. We feel stigmatized for not fighting to the death, even though we could not have inflicted significant damage on the enemy—even though the skeletons on Corregidor had done more than their share of that. We need a gesture that says the country cares, not just that we are going to be repatriated. All those valiant men on Bataan and Corregidor, at Cabanatuan, at the bottom of the Philippine or South or North China seas, all those who died in dozens of camps—and still it is not over.

Most said nothing—just walked back into the compound. We knew each other's thoughts; soldiers aren't good with words at times like this. We need the country to reach out to us, but it didn't; it hasn't in 3½ years. We have no poets to voice our feelings.

It isn't that we are convinced we are abandoned or stigmatized, but we need a token. We need to know how they feel out there and back there. We'll make it anyway, even if we don't get a signal!

Back to the train station. I needed a walk to ease the fire in my stomach. I alternately sat and walked for a long time, maybe two hours. The traffic seemed to be much reduced. A train pulled in from the north headed for Osaka. When I found out where it was going, I got aboard, entered a dimly lighted passenger car and, as soon as my eyes became accustomed, saw it was full of soldiers being disbanded. They looked weary of travel, not hostile, not friendly. One of the tallest, thinnest Japanese I ever saw appeared to be discussing my freedom, my queer clothing, my whiteness. A drunk soldier standing three seats away started making trouble with some other soldiers crowded in a bench seat, but he looked mostly at me. He staggered and stepped on the feet of a little girl sitting on some luggage on the floor. She looked at what was probably her father with helpless eyes but said nothing. I caught the drunk soldier's eye and pointed to the little girl. He looked at her and moved away a few inches and never looked at me again. After a little while, he also fell silent.

I realized these soldiers were not speaking Japanese. It was more like what I was familiar with in China. Their officers had swords, the enlisted men were unarmed. They were clean, but with several days' growth of beard. After about an hour, a small, uniformed girl announced: "Kyoto! Kyoto!"

Many of the passengers got off, but none of the soldiers with the strange language. I wondered if they were from Mongolia or Manchukuo but didn't try to talk with them. Some, but not many, passengers got on the train. I took a vacated seat and a new passenger in uniform but without insignia looked at me, stood up, bowed and sat down beside me. Within five minutes he was dozing. He seemed to be alone, was very young and seemed very lost. Within a few more minutes he was sound asleep, his head against first my arm and then the man's at the window.

I also fell asleep, and awoke to another young lady in uniform calling out: "Osaka!" The station was familiar, but I couldn't remember which way I had approached it from Chikko. I struck out to the south hoping to see the Sumitomo building if it were still standing and dominating the skyline near the camp. As I met people I asked them where the camp was—"Chikko doko des'ka?" I never got far without having to ask again. Left, left again, then right, then straight. The walking was good; my stomach was on fire. The half moon in the southeastern sky, at about 10:30, showed the extent and nature of the destruction. The entire city, in the colorless moonlight, looked as though it first had been burned and then covered with a uniform coat of ash.

AUGUST 30: I finally saw something I recognized: the Osaka gas works. It looked undamaged by the firebombs. In an hour and a half of walking I had seen one truck, one Caterpillar-type tractor and five or six groups of people. I wondered what they were doing out among the ruins and decided they were salvaging what they could in the way of metal or pottery. They were too terrified to speak. I must have looked like some foreign devil appearing out of the ruins.

I passed a two-storied warehouse I recognized, then a cross street with a monument in the center that I had passed on work parties. About 3 a.m. I aroused some Japanese workers sleeping in a small clearing under a lean-to. They pointed down the street. I thanked them and walked a few more blocks. The Chikko camp I was looking for had disappeared from the waterfront in a bombing that took place after I was transferred to Notogawa.

Confusion, and a waste of time. I should have headed straight for the waterfront, and then gone east until I found what had been my home for two years. My zig-zag circular route cost me more than an hour of walking. I continued along and soon I smelled the camp; then I heard it; then I saw it. The ex-POWS have taken up residence in a three-storied warehouse. First I saw a prisoner from Notogawa. He had a mess kit full of ham and beans warmed over an open fire. Bread, canned peaches and canned ham sat on a makeshift table. I ate a few mouthfuls of bread and ham, found the latrine, and went to sleep on a pad of fiber packing material I pulled partially over me to ward off the cold and damp of Japan's inland sea.

I woke up about 6 a.m. to the aroma of fried ham and hotcakes. Again I ate what I could—a few mouthfuls—and drank two large cups of hot chocolate. I had landed in heaven! All this was served up by a friend I left dying, I thought, in Osaka Camp 1, Carlos Roybol.

"Carlos," I said, "you were supposed to be dead from TB by now."

"I had pleurisy and a collapsed lung," he replied, "and it's 100 percent better now."

He poured me a peach can half full of grapefruit juice. I told him of my trip from Notogawa and how worn out I was.

"Take my bunk," he said, and led me down a dark aisle. "Have some chocolate," he insisted as I lay down on the first bed I had seen since Kanaoka Hospital. He had a carton of Hershey chocolate bars on a shelf along the bed row. I ate one before he left, and another before I dozed off in his blankets. My head was beginning to feel like I had been doped. I would get "an issue" later in the morning, Carlos said.

I awoke about 10 a.m. to a great commotion and the sound of planes. Everyone was heading for the warehouse door yelling, "Take cover," just as I was trying to go out to see what was going on. Someone grabbed my arm and pulled me back inside a second before an "explosion" occurred several feet from where my head had been. When the roar of planes subsided, I went out to discover that our Navy dive bombers had sprayed us with food. The explosion by my head was a canned ham, now a millimeter thick and an acre wide on the side of the building. Its parachute failed to open. A cloth envelope was tied to the lower end of the parachute strings. I opened it and found a page of writing paper scrawled with 20 or 30 messages. One said: "We'll take over now, men! Welcome home! Thanks for a job well done! It won't be long now! Let me know if you receive our package— Lieutenant Robert Daly, Portland, Oregon."

There were others. "Sorry we took so long." "You've done your job, now let us do ours." "Vacation's over—back to work." On and on they went. It was all I needed to know.

My eyes filled with tears. I sat down. My chest and shoulders shook convulsively. I handed the note to someone. It was passed around, and it disappeared. I lost a treasure.

The last time I remember crying I was a junior in high school, about to head west (and, unknowingly, to where I am now), and had just said goodbye to a beautiful girl I met only weeks before and probably would never see again. It was a rare pleasant Michigan day in the middle of March 1938. She cried, too. Two days earlier, I had taken her to a St. Patrick's dance at her school, St. Mary's. Like all of us, she was poor. She wore a deep blue dress that was too warm for the dance and too tight for her beautiful body. She asked me to unfasten a few buttons as we sat parked in the car at the end of a farm road. She wore nothing underneath. Before either of us knew it, her dress was down to her waist. She gave me that much of herself and no more. I was completely awed by her perfection. I took her home at 1 o'clock. She went in the house and came back out after telling her mother she was home. We were in each other's arms until after 3 a.m. It was an innocent time, one by which I would always be able to distinguish the sacred from the profane.

The planes came again. The sky rained peaches and chocolate, cigarettes and matches, magazines and ham. At times it seemed dozens of parachutes were floating from the sky. The Japanese stood a quarter mile away in disbelief. Terror in the sky had become a cornucopia of gifts for people who a week before would have rejoiced over an extra half bowl of rice. We waited until the "raid" ended, then charged en masse into the streets and acres of razed kitchen factories to retrieve our manna from the desert.

All afternoon I met old friends and soaked up news, both good and horrible. Many had fared far worse than I. Another camp in Osaka had lost one-third of its men in two years.

A friend from China invited me to stay the night in a Red Cross hospital. It took an hour to make up my mind and half an hour to get there through a steady rain. We arrived shortly before dark. Inside, it was well-lighted and clean. Despite low water pressure I had a hot shower and a clean shave with a new Gillette razor blade. I spent a half hour washing my hair to be sure I got the lice, fleas and bedbugs out. My clothes were dipped in boiling water, then washed by a Japanese girl while I walked around barefoot in a hospital gown with a blanket over my shoulders. Two men have been brought in from Notogawa with severe malnutrition and the stomach disorder I'm just now getting over.

I had my first meal at a table in three years and nine months—since December 7, 1941. Japanese nurses ate with us, then joined us as we talked about our separate experiences. They spoke well but didn't seem to understand much. They answered questions, but there was no give-and-take conversation as there is with Western girls. It was still my first real conversation with a woman since I left China. Someone brought out a guitar, and we sang "Roll Out the Barrel" and "Red Sails in the Sunset" and some Bing Crosby tunes. My throat quickly tightened and I was content to listen. Except for a Japanese guard at Tanagawa and a few lame attempts with Tani at Kanaoka, I hadn't heard a song since a few bars of "Blueberry Hill" came over the Voice of America while we waited for the Japanese invasion of the fortified islands. Too much too fast!

I went to sleep naked in a real bed with real sheets and a Western-style pillow, a full stomach, a song in my ears and head and heart. I have all I can ask for.

AUGUST 31: It was a long, cool, refreshing sleep. I awoke with the odor of a cup of coffee at my head and a kangasan holding a basin of warm water for me to wash with.

I roamed the halls and rooms looking for I didn't know what. In one I found large numbers of recent American magazines and selected a few to read later. One article caught my eye: The Detroit Tigers, led by someone named Newhouser, are leading the American League. There was a choice of ham, roast beef, rolls, bread and jam for breakfast. I asked for eggs, which they didn't have, so I had my first roast beef since leaving China.

I was eating bread and jam when an English doctor came in and demanded to know what right my host had inviting anyone to the hospital. I was instantly furious. "Who the hell are you," I demanded, "to deny American food and shelter to Americans who have been deprived of both for years?" He stood his ground. I gathered my clothes and clogs and went back to the warehouse. Before I left, they told me the doctor had only four real patients and a staff of 46, to whom he was diverting food.

More stories. More faces to recognize. Each has a nauseating tale to tell. The worst so far is 1,200 men put in a hold next to the boiler room of a ship headed for Japan. They went days without food or water. They soon began dying of suffocation, then of dehydration. The heat from the boiler was intense. The Japs wouldn't erect a wind scoop. Soon they were going crazy by the dozen. They drank each other's urine. Others were murdered and their blood drunk. An officer who said he "would return to the States at the expense of every soldier in this ship" was hung in the hold by his own belt. The prisoner I talked to said only 117 survived to reach Japan. He kept shaking his lowered head and looking away. What a price he already has paid for life, and what a price he has yet to pay.

Another 1,800 were in the holds of a ship in a convoy when the ship was sunk off Formosa. The Japanese picked up their own but refused to rescue prisoners, except four men picked up by a destroyer.

If we only could lower ourselves to their level, we could kill them all! What possible right do they have to live in this beautiful land? I have great difficulty sorting out these thoughts. I have experienced much suffering at the hands of individual Japanese—many individual Japanese. Some others have been friendly, even kind. But what is it about the Japanese? Do I loathe the entire race? I don't think so. Their culture, yes.

Someone knows of a Japanese "hotel." The girls accept any kind of food. I looked at my body: cheekbones and collarbone poking through my skin, my head teetering on an unlikely neck, hair uncut and unkempt—how could any girl want to be with me? I said I was saving myself for an American girl. I was really hiding self-contempt and inadequacy. They went off with their canned goods and cigarettes.

SEPTEMBER 1: Feeling better, I decided to see the city. Some streetcars are back in operation connecting the fringes. The city center is a wasteland. I caught a car and continued to the end of the line. I made a leisurely return, partly on foot following the car line. Mostly I got off, looked around and caught the next car. There were five or six people in every block, frightened but eager to assist. People are living in foxholes and lean-tos. They were sifting through the debris, piling usable articles in one place, recyclable metal in another, and debris to be hauled away in another. The girls now gather close to hear conversation rather than hanging back as we have been accustomed to seeing them. They cook in the open and catch water bubbling from broken lines in the gutters. The people are busy but full of indecision. Babies and small children are energetic and healthy. Every indication is that the rebuilding of Osaka began soon after its destruction. It's amazing how clean they are. I wonder if I ever have seen a filthy Japanese—dirty, but never filthy.

One of them said the war was too long, which I guess means it should have been stopped before it came to Japan proper. Shintoism appears doomed, at least that part that holds the emperor to be a god. Even during the war the Japs showed great interest in things American—cars, clothes, leather, glasses, false teeth, Deanna Durbin, Shirley Temple, Western songs—anything American. When they stole the pictures of our mothers, sisters and girlfriends, their interest seemed to be more in the backgrounds than in the women. The Japanese soldiers' hatred of Americans did not extend to *things* American.

Back at the warehouse I learned that more bundles had come from heaven. One can from an unopened parachute ricocheted around a corner and hit a prisoner in the shoulder, probably breaking it in several places.

SEPTEMBER 2: More tales of atrocities. Prisoners in one camp are too weak to walk. A search is reported to be on for the Japanese colonel who was in charge. There are no details on how many or what percentage have died there. Someone has left for the camp. The more we hear things, the more we are convinced that their culture has discredited them more than their defeat in the field.

Many prisoners are eating little but chocolate. I've resolved to eat only nourishing food until I am repatriated. I borrowed someone's bunk. He came in late and I borrowed someone else's.

I had a long, deep sleep despite reinfestation with "migratory dandruff" and "seam squirrels."

There was an incredible food drop today. Much is being given to nearby Japanese, especially those with children. A lot is also being traded for souvenirs. Everything damaged is given away by leaving it on the streets.

More rain. Talk of a typhoon in the Philippine Sea. We could have used this weather when we were working on the dike. The occupation forces have been held off. The whole camp expects moving orders. I better get out soon. I don't want to be in a position of having to obey a direct order. My gear is still in Notogawa. Four thousand men reportedly have been flown from Tokyo to Okinawa. We are warned to return to home camp or be listed as deserters. What could they do now? What would they do? There's always an adversary. Rain, rain, rain. I'll leave tomorrow.

SEPTEMBER 3: More rain. I waited until noon, then left. The streetcar went right to the station. A train to Lake Biwa was waiting for me. It was a good trip. I took a can of meat and something like an egg hash. I still had the can of meat when I arrived in Notogawa about an hour before dark. I stopped at the bicycle shop, where a number of Notogawa prisoners were talking to the invalid from British Columbia. They were discussing a fairly honest way of retaliating against the Japs by some moneymaking scheme I didn't try to understand.

While there, I sighted an officer friend I knew in Chikko. He asked where I had been. I told him about Chikko Camp and where it had moved. He had almost never been out of Chikko in his two years there and didn't know the city or the waterfront. The new quarters in the warehouse was news to him. He said he was being sent to contact the occupation authorities and get some orders for the Notogawa camp. I agreed to take him to Osaka. Again we made almost immediate connections and arrived in time for the last streetcar. It was 12:30 when we arrived wet at the Chikko Camp. It rained all the way. Even without rain, he would have seen nothing except an occasional light, even in Kyoto or Osaka. Half a dozen prisoners were sitting around talking quietly and drinking coffee. I found a bed for the lieutenant and another for myself and went to bed wet and cold.

SEPTEMBER 4: I got up at 6:30 and prepared my own breakfast for the first time since I was herded together with 12,000 others at the 92nd Garage on Corregidor. It was Spam heated in a mess kit. I put slices of bread over it to absorb the flavor and aroma, and ate it with hot chocolate and coffee and canned peaches.

A second lieutenant came in inquiring for me. He had been talking with the officer I brought to Osaka from Notogawa, to whom I had mentioned working at Osaka Seiko between Osaka and Kobe. The lieutenant wanted me to take him to a prison camp in Kobe. He knew I spoke enough Japanese to keep out of trouble. I agreed, assuming I didn't have to walk too much. He needed to carry a message from the camp commander and medical officer to the commander of the No. 1 Kobe camp. He had the address but no directions.

We walked to the car line and got a car to the inter-urban station in a matter of minutes. The inter-urban was so crowded it was impossible to move. Much of the way I was pressed by a young woman as the car lurched on, starting up and stopping. I held the overhead rail, which she couldn't get to. She murmured "Sumi-ma-sen" several times, then settled down to enjoying the trip—or enduring it—until she got off near a factory. She was the first girl I had touched or who had touched me in nearly four years.

We got off at the proper station, with the lieutenant ribbing me about my traveling companion. The first persons we encountered when the crowd dispersed were two Americans who had just been released from military prison, also for breaking into a storeroom in their own camp. They didn't know where they were or how to get back to their camp in Kobe. We told them we were looking for the same camp and to stay with us. They had done hard labor and looked in good shape.

I addressed a Japanese girl with "Horio no uchi doko desuka?"

She replied in English that it was about a half-hour walk from the station toward the waterfront. She had been educated in Nagasaki and was away when the atom bomb was dropped. She was a Christian, she said, and added: "Most of us were killed." I asked her what she was doing here and she said: "Selling English-language newspapers." We talked a bit and were told that the Japanese thought the atom bomb was part of the war; they would have used it themselves if they had it. As we were leaving, her father materialized and repeated his daughter's directions, also in excellent English. We asked if they would be okay. He shrugged a universal shrug. We wished them luck and started for the POW camp.

We hadn't gone more than 50 paces when two strange-looking Caucasians caught up with us. They had been watching from a distance. One was wearing a marine overseas cap with a crest that I recognized. We had once played a group of Italian marines water polo in the swimming pool of their legation at Tientsin, where they nearly drowned us, then treated us to a three-hour banquet and seats at the jai-alai forum. Two years ago they were transferred to a legation at Kobe. I knew some book Italian, and they knew less English, but we communicated well enough to learn that they would like some clothes and some food.

Both were nearly six feet tall, in their mid-20s, blue-eyed and blond. They were from Piedmont, they said, the source of most Italian marines. Both were almost barefoot and very glad to see the end of the war. They had received American medicine and treatment for burns suffered in the bombing of Kobe. I asked if they knew what happened to Yolanda Martinella, the Italian legate's daughter in Tientsin. They know of her, but not where she has gone. We left them at the Kobe camp with Mario Simontacci, an Italian-American who also had been in Tientsin and had helped me with Italian vocabulary and pronunciation.

I had a fried egg for lunch. I forgot how good eggs are. The yolk was almost orange, indicating a hen that had to scrounge for a living.

I was invited to a sake and beer party by some old acquaintances to swap stories and find out who died and how, and who survived and how. I promised to return to Kobe with food, which is being rationed there, if they supplied the beer and sake. The lieutenant and I rode to the station on a truck that ran on the fumes of smoldering fuel burned in a tank that looked like a farm wood-burning water heater. It's something the Swedes taught the Japanese to get around the shortage of oil and gasoline.

Connections were bad, and the inter-urban was slow in both directions. I got the lieutenant back to Chikko Camp about 6 p.m. and gathered up some food, but I couldn't get anyone to give me any sake—and I didn't have anything to trade for it.

It was very dark when I got back to Kobe. I followed some detailed instructions that didn't say anything about the street being pocked with shell holes. There were no lights, and the night was so dark that the water-filled shell holes looked like wet spots in a smooth street. I learned the hard way and finished the long walk wet to my knees. I heard the party as I stumbled along. About 20 Americans were there, mostly marines. I knew five or six. I brought powdered chocolate drink and powdered milk. I hadn't eaten since noon but soon found out that the food was not for eating but for drinking. One American took the food and came back in a half hour with two magnums of sake.

In an hour, on an empty stomach, I was beyond hunger and beyond memory. If I heard any stories of what happened in other camps or the fate of my friends from North China, Shanghai, the Philippines, Cabanatuan, Tanagawa or Chikko, they made no impression on my memory. So much for a party in a building I never saw, in a dimly lit room with boxes and kegs for furniture, and a charcoal brazier for heating tea water.

SEPTEMBER 5: I awoke very cold and not at all hungry. A truck was going to Chikko Camp in Osaka and then on to Notogawa. I decided to go at least as far as Osaka, where we arrived before noon. The camp was in a turmoil. Everybody has again been "ordered to return to their home camps." The 6th Army is expected in a day or two. No one knows why it is important to be repatriated from a home camp rather than one our occupation forces get to first.

I walked through the ground floor and compound and saw a number of marines who had been given rifles and assigned to a beach patrol. I also met some civilians I had not seen for years: a Lebanese who worked as a foreman on a construction crew in Mariveles; an Indonesian from a Dutch merchant ship; a South African colored from Durban; a Muslim from Yemen, and a blue-eyed Pakistani who was an oiler on an English merchant vessel. I met no one from Tanagawa and learned nothing of what happened to those I left in a camp where I hear one-fourth died in three months.

I was given a number of messages and notes to deliver to Chikko prisoners' friends in Notogawa—mostly addresses and brief statements of well wishes, comments on health and intentions.

I got back on the truck, and we picked our way through burned-out Osaka. It was a matter of going northeast, landmark to landmark, by dead reckoning. We entered a street where the trees had returned to full, dense leaf. It was an arcade of green, a tunnel of life between two regions of hell. Ahead an avenue of life and beauty, but to the sides desolation framed by arches of green—mockery by the gods of war.

There is no migration. The occasional cart on the streets is local. Likewise on the main road to Kyoto.

At first the sight of the burned-out city gave me a savage satisfaction. Maybe it wasn't the right ones who paid, but at least someone had paid and was paying. The feeling is becoming one of loss such as you experience when you lose something you value and know it cannot be replaced.

The road went along a dike, and girls and women were working in the riverbottom wearing only a bloomer-type garment. They turned and stared and some covered their breasts when they saw us staring back. As we neared Kyoto, we saw five or six Japanese men apparently stealing government horses. They seemed confused as we threaded by them and then waved them on. We passed a woman apparently lying dead beside the road. We didn't stop.

Kyoto, as far as we can see, has not been touched by the war. The people in the country seem very surprised to see Americans among them, but in Kyoto we were paid little attention.

We passed a small, white Protestant church, like those in paintings of stark New England landscapes, almost profane sitting in front of a magnificent temple and its grounds. The road continued about a quarter mile, then passed between two hills. The hill on the east is heavily wooded. A Western-type hotel sits on its lower reaches. Unexpectedly, a group of prisoners waved us down. They wanted the truck, and hadn't realized we were also Americans until they stopped us.

It turned out that the city quartermaster will supply them with anything in his stores, but there is no way to get it to the hotel. The lieutenant I was escorting back to Notogawa hesitated a few minutes and then told me to take a break while he and someone he knew got a supply of food for the hotel. The truck left and I went into the hotel.

It is the Miyako, first-class all the way. Most of the prisoners have been there a week; some as long as two weeks. I saw hotel staff everywhere, some speaking good English. The hotel catered to Westerners before the war and to Japanese who were attracted to Western customs or who conducted business with Westerners.

I soon discovered that the food and supplies the truck had gone for were not for the hotel, which has plenty in fairly good variety. The food was for women and the black market. The scheme I had heard about in Notogawa is in full sway here. The prisoners sign for food or supplies with the quartermaster using real names, or false ones as it suits the individual. The food is then sold or traded on the black market.

The hotel is amply supplied with beautiful girls— Eurasians, Russians, Chinese and Japanese—who barter themselves to the highest bidders. The Miyako probably hasn't changed, but it certainly has lost its pretense. Food brought in from camps is in high demand for its barter value. The prisoners seem increasingly wary about going back to the camps for fear they'll be prevented from coming back or will be court-martialed if they do.

The lieutenant came back in about two hours with a bottle of Canadian Club and announced he would stay the night at the Miyako. Americans continued to show up into the night, and Japanese were moved out to make way for them. The Japs showed irritation but gave little resistance. The Americans are requisitioning rice at 40 yen a bag and selling it at 2,400 yen. The girls take the money but prefer clothing, food and other tangibles.

It was a long day in the truck, and I was short on rest. Beer and sake together with a bowl of vegetables with strips of meat that was much like Filipino pancit made me ready to sleep. But, "hotel" or not, there was no place to do so. I went from group to group listening to the inevitable stories of privation and coolie labor, numbers of dead, and names of those who had made it through.

About 10:30 p.m. the lieutenant found me and announced he was ready to leave. He never said what changed his mind, but again and again he talked about the girls back at the hotel.

We got to Notogawa about 2 a.m. after having headlamp problems all the way. I turned on the light in the room and saw that my blankets were gone, along with all the clothes I had not taken with me to Osaka. The mosquito bar I got from Lieutenant Pitkins' belongings when he died at Tanagawa was still there, as was my olive drab field scarf with all my personal effects and many of my notes, and my Spanish and Japanese word lists. There was no sign of the Navy hospital towel. That multi-purpose garment survived the war but disappeared with the peace.

I crawled under the net and went to sleep.

SEPTEMBER 6: Steak, gravy and bread and a hard-boiled egg for breakfast. I got very tired chewing. Our planes have dropped everything conceivable. There are many requests for letters giving details about prison life. I copied down a dozen or more addresses from Michigan and nearby states. Suddenly I realized I intend to go back to Big Beaver, Michigan.

The Japanese are now doing all camp work in exchange for clothing, blankets and food. Several honshos who have come back regret it. One was beaten by a tall, blond soldier the honsho had beaten and he was thrown into the canal, too injured to crawl back out. Other honshos were accepted as part of the work force. The one who searched the lake half an hour for an Indonesian's wedding ring, and who showed many other considerations, was welcomed back but not allowed to work.

The Japanese staff is lucky no one died in the camp in the 3½ months we have been here. Of the 80 or so at the last sick call, only about 20 were suffering deficiency diseases; the rest were sick with the intestinal problem.

SEPTEMBER 7: I slept poorly without blankets to lie on. I got chilled before dawn and got up to warm by the galley fires. Prisoners are doing most of the galley work. Japanese are doing the heavy work without hesitation.

The Aussie lieutenant called an assembly, claimed he was the senior line officer and formally "took over the camp." The British and Aussies accepted it eagerly, but the Americans drifted away as soon as they found out what was going on. Others stayed milling around and talking among themselves. Several made catcalls in strong British accents. Someone yelled: "Where's your brass buttons?" The Aussie made some remarks about "being soldiers," which brought retorts that we didn't need lessons.

A lone B-17 flew over and then around and everyone lost interest. No drop was made. The lieutenant continued for about 30 minutes, yet never made clear what he intends to do with his "new command." I rested, walked about for a while, and rested again. I'm getting to the point where food looks good but I can only eat a few mouthfuls.

I couldn't sleep tonight so I walked toward town. I think only about 30 or 40 of the prisoners, all of them Americans, have been in Notogawa. The word came again, this time from the Swedish embassy, that we are to stay in camp until our occupation force comes, but no one knows when that will be. I thought of going back to Kyoto, but I have no money and nothing to trade. I came back to camp tired enough to sleep.

SEPTEMBER 8: Today we had an airplane reveille. I have a slight heat rash, especially in my groin, waist and armpits. I went down to the lake for a bath and stayed there two hours. The Japanese resent our soaping up in the lake and rinsing off. They soap up ashore and rinse off with a little wooden half-bucket, then they soak in the lake. I'm beginning to think they're right. They have a saying that they seem to generalize into a philosophy that I can't find fault with: "Never dirty the water for the person downstream." I guess it's their version of "Do unto others ..." I find myself wishing it were an American saying, not Japanese.

More parcels were dropped today by Navy aircraft. Mostly they were seabags with clothing, newspapers, magazines and candy. Again there were addresses and requests for us to write. I got a sea bag with the name O'Dowd stenciled on it. It will keep me warm tonight.

Today I told a pretty large group what it was like in Kyoto, Osaka and Kobe. Only 20 or 25 have left camp except for trips to Notogawa or the lake. About 15 are still gone, but two or three come back every day. I wish I had not come back. The talk is that America will investigate our treatment in each camp and will want all the information together. I've been in three camps and a Jap hospital. Some have been in more camps than that.

I tried chewing some tobacco today. It smelled great, but I can't see why anyone would chew it.

SEPTEMBER 9: Reveille again to the music of carrier planes. Men in from Kyoto full of stories and news. Call to quarters. Colonel Murota, head of the Osaka system, said to have been executed. Tremendous cheering. All U.S. soldiers said to have been promoted one pay grade. More tremendous cheering. Prisoners of Miyako Hotel held a banquet for two war correspondents. Cheers and laughter. One of the correspondents made a speech at the hotel: He was glad to see the prisoners had Japan so well under control. He thanked the prisoners for getting them food and rooms. When the correspondents couldn't get taxis, the prisoners got them taxis. When two colonels asked for accommodations, the maitre d' told them he would have to get approval from the prisoners. It's beginning to be fun!

A new officer, a naval commander, has come to camp. He seems to have taken over from the Aussie. He said we are to have all information the minute it is received. "Come to the office if you want to know the truth about a rumor," he said. "Be ready to move. Travel light. Be ready to give all food to Japs who treated us well. Take a change of clothes and toilet articles."

Today the Japs brought in electric fans, new tatami mats, mosquito netting, a side of beef and a case of eggs. I wanted some three-minute eggs but didn't have a watch and they turned out pretty hard. I mashed them with a large spoon of butter and salt and pepper. What a treat!

14

Free and Bewildered

SEPTEMBER 10: Planes circled most of the morning, flying so low we could see the pilots when the sun was to our backs, but they didn't drop anything. The camp has been surrounded all day by Japanese wanting anything we are willing to get rid of. What a change. Three weeks ago we wanted anything they would get rid of, even cigarette butts. Now they are scavenging soap, matches, Nip shoes, damaged food.

Word of a noon departure. Men start handing blankets out the second-tier windows and over the fence. The shutters are long gone. Prisoners are grabbing hands of girls as they pass them things. Girls seem interested when they are away from their menfolk, probably fathers or grandfathers. There are almost no men between ages 17 and 45 in the group. I have given away all my effects except my hobo bundle. The good food has been shut away in case departure plans are changed. I go out in the street to try to talk to a pretty Jap girl whose eye I caught several times.

Planes up! All the food we will need for the next day or so has been packed and ready to go to the station. We try to wave off the planes as they make their initial pass. There are two B-17s. Back they come. Every parachute opens. Tons of food float down, some of it within 20 or 30 yards of camp. This is the most beautiful drop yet. Chutes of many colors float together, then drift apart. We tell the Japanese—several hundred of them—that they can have the drop.

The prisoners didn't even get up to see what was in it. I last saw the pretty Jap girl loading an apron from a canvas bag near the canal.

I made a last tour around the camp a few minutes after we were given the word to assemble in the road outside the main gate. The galley was deserted, leaving a pot steaming slightly. The storeroom was open and the rice, flour and oil that had fallen into disuse in the last few days had been given to the galley crew or had been dragged in open and partly filled containers to the front gate, where the Japanese galley honsho stood over them. Scraps of clothing were scattered around and empty tins of meat and fruit populated the mats that had been bed, dining room and gathering place, 15 square feet per man. I have the feeling the Japanese would have left it in much better order. I resent that.

As I went out the gate with the last of the stragglers, the camp commander went in and made the same rounds. He came out, lined us up by nationality groups and waved us on. Chief Saunders tried to force Angelo, the Spaniard who was a deckhand on an American merchant marine ship that was sunk, to line up with the Chinese, Filipinos and Indonesians. I told Angelo not to pay any attention to Saunders, that Saunders was going to have a lot to answer for as soon as I got someplace where I could file a report. Angelo had taught me Spanish well enough that we could converse in it, rarely resorting to English or Japanese. I told Saunders that Angelo had a pile of money coming from the owner of the ship and I was going to see that he got to America to get it. Saunders either couldn't or wouldn't argue with that.

The Japanese lined the street on both sides as we left, some waving but most with uncomprehending faces. I looked back on the camp where the sentry towers were visible on three corners and wondered how close I was to being killed, along with more than 300 other prisoners, if the atom bomb had not been dropped.

I thought I might die during the defense of the fortified islands, during the surrender, at Cabanatuan, on the voyage to Japan, at Tanagawa, during the destruction of Osaka and at this camp on the whispered speculation of a Japanese Christian seminarian. Now it is over. I am going home, wherever that is.

The walk to the Notogawa station was neither quick nor easy. Perhaps 20 prisoners were very drunk. Three were unable to navigate alone. One of these was Private Kevin Ryan, a soldier from Toledo, Ohio. He quickly fell to the end of the line, as did the other two. Ryan was nasty drunk, belligerent and stupefied. I prodded him and then slapped him, but it was when I called him a mick that he got violent and sobered up enough to stagger onward. When we finally arrived, he and the other two were laid out along a side of the station house. After we fell out of our interpretation of a formation, the bugler came by and played taps over them. Three hundred men stood around observing the ceremony, along with a number of curious Japanese. I'm sure they understood completely. I laughed until my sides ached, as did everyone else, including the Japanese. I tried to remember when I last laughed like that. It has been a long, long time.

The Japanese-American from Utah was at the station, but the one from British Columbia was not. I said goodbye and told him I would be glad to help if there was anything I could do. He was evasive and I got the feeling he no longer wants to go back to the States.

The commander had the bugler get our attention. When we were quiet, he announced that we would be leaving in a little over an hour.

When the train came in we saw GIs who had not been prisoners. They looked trim, hard and able—and too young for the responsibility. They were equipped with battle gear that was completely new to us. We boarded. In minutes we were under way. It was a bewildering moment.

We were heading home after so many years and so much pain. The moment we had so long awaited was upon us.

Instead of being attended by a great fanfare, this moment was marked by an escape of steam, a clank of couplings and a slap of wheels over rail separations. It was real but had an aura of unreality. Instead of a flourish or ceremony or parade to mark the passage of one life and the inception of another, it was more like closing a door quietly on something intensely interesting but incredibly disagreeable and opening another door to a long, dark tunnel. It was oddly similar to what I felt when the last strains of "Aloha" faded away as the Henderson edged from the dock in Honolulu and headed west to the Orient just under six years ago. I am heading east into the unknown now just as I headed west into the unknown then. The gates of a prison have been opened, and I have been pushed out into the dark.

I wonder why I have such misgivings about returning to my former life. I found out when I tried to commit "The Raven" to memory that I couldn't direct my mind. Sometimes related—but mostly unrelated—thoughts invade my thinking until my mind is far afield and I don't know how I got there. It worries me when I am asked a question and I prepare to answer and suddenly I find my mind miles away and someone waiting for an answer with a puzzled look on his face. Sometimes I am talking to someone and I forget the point I want to make or even what I am talking about. Even when trying to read, my thoughts so dominate that it is impossible to make any progress. I wonder how I am going to keep up with atom bombs, jet engines, radar, penicillin and all the changes that have taken place in the six years I've been away. I think I'm afraid I can't think well enough or fast enough anymore to compete with people who have changed with the changes.

One of the young-looking soldiers has come through the car passing out questionnaires and finding himself getting bombarded with our own questions: "What's a corporal's pay? What did the Marines do in the war? What happened to Hawaii? How are we getting back? Will there be a quarantine? When do we get some ice cream? What's the GI Bill?" It went on and on as he went from side to side being sure everyone got a questionnaire.

I filled in the answers as the train made its way through the countryside. The lake disappeared behind us. We went from drab countryside to beautiful valley to wooded hillsides to countryside.

I was interrupted in both filling out the form and watching the landscape by a band playing "Happy Days Are Here Again" and a medley of Army, Navy and Marines hymns. Back to the window, then back to the questionnaire: name, rank, serial number, service, where captured, name of last camp, location of last camp, name of Japanese camp commander, age, places of confinement, dates, place of enlistment, date of enlistment, present health, symptoms, comments on treatment . . .

After the questionnaires had been picked up and more of our own questions answered, I started to move around the car and then on to other cars. Ryan caught me by the arm and asked what he had done while drunk. He seemed to enjoy his notoriety. I told him I'd see him in Detroit and went to talk with Harmon. We had bunked next to each other in Chikko and, except for his not trying to control his lice, we got along pretty well.

Harmon had a magnum of sake and a beautiful Japanese picture scroll. He had hit the bottle pretty heavy. He offered me a drink. I took the bottle and held it for a while as he tried to get things in focus. Then I said I would trade him the sake for the picture scroll. He thought it over for a while, then agreed. I took the scroll and put it with my bundle. Before I could give it back to him, it was stolen. I felt bad but didn't have any way to replace it. I finally went back to my seat and went to sleep.

SEPTEMBER 11: I awoke about 3 a.m. and shaded my eyes against the interior lights to look out the window at the occasional light and the hills against the southern night sky. There was no moon.

As the light increased I saw there were many towns along the track and that most have been firebombed. Kyoto was spared, probably because of its shrines. So was Notogawa, an agricultural town. But the residential areas of Osaka and the industrial areas of Kobe are a desert. Now I saw that even the small towns have not been spared, because of their cottage industry. Numerous pieces of industrial equipment such as lathes and band saws pierce upward through the ashes of homes or small shops. Japan has taken an incredible beating since early spring. Now they know what it was like on Bataan and Corregidor.

Somehow I don't associate the bombings with large numbers of casualties. We heard in Osaka that many of those who didn't contribute to the war effort were moved to the countryside. There seemed to be a tremendous number of children at Takurazuka in relation to the number of dwellings, but I saw that town only after Osaka had been bombed.

As the train went through Nagoya I could see a number of large buildings that survived, but the rest of the city looked like it was spared nothing at all. I have now seen much of southern Honshu and, if it is a fair example, Japan has little war or peacetime industry left. They probably never can rebuild.

At 3 p.m. the train glided to a halt. A Japanese conductor came to the front of the car and, with everyone quietly listening, said "Yokohama" in a low voice. As I reached for my bundle of possessions, I and everyone else in the car stopped and listened until the last notes of "San Francisco" faded away. I felt a pressure in my chest that made it impossible to talk or even to breathe or think. It doesn't look like we will be ostracized for surrendering. I'm sure there were very few who didn't get the same message.

Along the platform, four or five paces apart, fully armed soldiers stood at a ready position protecting this raggedy-assed marine, whose only piece of military uniform was a field scarf containing everything he owned except what he wore.

We stopped in front of the band, staring at the serviceman-musicians until the last trombone slid to a close and the musicians, many with tears in their eyes, stood at ease. As we passed down the platform, the prisoners in front of us bunched up until they were forced on by us, who were forced on by those behind us. In a moment I saw the reason for the slowing in the line—a tall, red-lipped, curvaceous, 100 percent American girl. A tall, very thin prisoner walked over to her in disbelief. He reached out with his right hand and squeezed her elbow. Then he turned away, his shoulders and chest convulsing. Her lips quivered and tears started down her cheeks as she tried to maintain her composure. I turned away. Oh, God, how can anyone stand this much emotion?

By the time the last of the line made it through the turnstiles, the band was reassembled at one side of a large paved area. A guard of honor stood on the other side. As we walked between rifles at present arms with the band playing another medley of "Anchors Aweigh," the Army's caisson song and "The Marines Hymn," I felt caught in a vice of emotion—music on the one side and a splendid group of our peers on the other saying in their separate ways: "It's all right; it's over; we have redeemed the captive, we have avenged a violence; it's a time for healing; we are sorry it took so long." Few sleeves were dry among that group of 301 men.

Trucks waited for those of us who could get in them, ambulances for those who could not. Then, as the band played "Aloha-o-ee," a group of Navy nurses, young and healthy and clear-eyed, appeared around the ambulances and, as the trucks began to pull away, waved and threw kisses to men who were in rags, poorly shaven, long in need of haircuts and averaging 50 or 60 pounds underweight.

The four soldiers who had accompanied us from Notogawa betrayed no emotion. From what I heard, none of them ever talked about themselves. There never was a moment that they failed to exhibit absolute control. They did their job well.

Arriving at a wharf, we were asked to discard every scrap we could do without. I discarded nothing. I had a pair of Japanese cloth and rubber shoes with the separated big toe, a pair of Japanese soldier fatigue trousers, a Philippine Army denim jacket, no socks, no underwear, no headware. Few had much more than I and few less.

A dockside warehouse had been converted, with the help of canvas partitions, into a receiving station. It was almost dark when we arrived. I realized I had not seen a Japanese since the conductor announced our arrival at Yokohama. We are indeed part of America again. Permeating the area was a clincher: the overwhelming aroma of bacon.

I went to the edge of the pier and saw an array of ships of all sizes. There goes my chance of flying back to America. I wonder which one I will go back on. I'm not happy about either the length of the voyage or the seasickness—inevitable for me.

We were escorted into the source of the bacon smell, a make-shift mess hall, clean as a whistle, with cloth on the tables and huge platters of hotcakes, bacon and eggs, toast, butter and jam, and aluminum pots full of coffee. The meal was glorious and completely American in its menu and its abundance.

Those finished first were asked to start processing immediately. "Through this door. Strip. Leave your bundle here to be sterilized, into that bath first." It smelled like the disinfectants we used to clean barracks floors. After a few minutes, it was into a hot soapy bath where I stayed for long, long minutes, ducking my head under repeatedly and combing out my long and dense hair to remove lice or bedbugs and their eggs.

Then into a hospital gown. Through another door. "Cough—no hernia." Another door. "Lungs okay." Another door. "Heart okay." Dress. "Go through that door"—actually a flap of canvas. What I dressed in was a Navy seaman's clothing used enough so that the buttons fastened easily, and big enough that I didn't have to struggle to get the blouse over my head. White socks and black Navy shoes. I felt I had lost an identity and didn't understand my new one. How does a seaman act, think, walk, talk?

Dressed, I was directed into an aisle with open offices on either side. Someone was in the first three. As I went by the fourth, a nurse called me in. "Here, soldier, sailor or marine," she called. "Which?"

"Marine."

"Name?"

I gave it in full.

"How are you doing, Bob?"

I gasped and said, "Okay."

"Rank?"

"Corporal. You'll hear this many times, but you are the first American girl I've talked to in six years."

"Whatever have you been doing away from civilization so long?"

"Waiting, mostly."

"I'll bet. Age?"

"Twenty-four to you; 25 to the War Department."

"See what lying will get you! Where did you enlist? Serial number? Where captured? Where interned? Don't chew on this thermometer. Pulse, please. Why that odd look?"

"Your touch, I guess; it's been a long, long time."

She smiled. "Disappointed?"

"No. Relieved. I didn't know how I would act."

"How do the girls you've seen so far impress you?"

"I don't know. Too loud, I guess. Maybe they're as nervous as we are."

She held out her hand and said: "Goodbye, Corporal. Thank you. God bless you. Don't take up with the first pretty girl you meet."

I murmured something and left quickly. It was when she said "Thank you" and I knew she wasn't referring to the interview that I realized sympathy is going to be tremendously difficult to cope with. If I don't keep my guard up against it, it will rob me of my strength and will.

Back to the mess hall. The tables were empty of everything except coffee. Prisoners came out of the medical section one by one and mingled with the Navy personnel, including nurses. I found a seat against the wall where I could sit with my back against a post and watch as the Notogawa group came through the canvas flap in sailors' clothing. I tried to recognize them as they gathered around the Navy personnel, especially the nurses. There was little laughing; smiles developed, then quickly dissipated. The nurses and the sailors were bombarded with questions, but I didn't know what to ask first, so I listened and watched.

After an hour or two, when preliminary examinations were complete, all Navy and Marines personnel were assembled on dockside. We were given simple instructions—stay near, we would be boarding a landing craft and taken to a ship for the night.

After a short wait, we boarded the landing craft and spent a chilly and damp hour going to our destination, the battleship Colorado. It was a long way up the gangplank to the deck. My hips and shoulders ached from the ride and the climb. It was just after midnight when I saluted the colors and the officer of the deck and stepped aboard. Seats were provided immediately and the OD went down the line and welcomed us to the Colorado.

A few minutes later, a bos'n's mate took six of us below decks to a cafeteria where he told us he would do everything he could to make us comfortable. We got egg salad sandwiches, ice cream and coffee. I ate half a sandwich and a second dish of ice cream. As it did in my childhood, the cold gave me great pain over my left eye. No sooner would the pain leave than I would take another spoonful and it would return and I would put my palm over my left eye and sip coffee to warm the roof of my mouth. We didn't know what to say to the bos'n's mate and he didn't know what to say to us, so we talked about the Colorado. Then we were taken to sleeping quarters where six men already had given up their bunks to us and were sleeping on cots. Fresh air steamed in through a duct.

I covered myself with a thick Navy wool blanket and went to sleep trying to remember all that happened this day, one of the fullest and most meaningful—and most bewildering—of my life.

15

"I'm not the Same"

SEPTEMBER 12: We are known to everyone—if not by the way we wear our clothes or by our constant look of amazement or our inability to negotiate a ladder or a compartment closure, then by our hair. If we don't go to the front of a line, the line goes behind us. None of us has any money, and none is needed. Ship's stores belong to the prisoners. Anything we want is ours. I took razor blades, a shaving cup, a brush and a comb. The only use I had for cigarettes in captivity was to trade my way off clean-up details, so I declined when they were offered here. I forgot to get any hair oil, but I've still got the bottle of Vaseline hair oil I carried throughout prison life. I could also use more paper, pencils and envelopes, but I didn't want to go to the head of the line again.

No sailor will take a seat in a mess formation if he thinks a prisoner has not yet found a place to sit. The ship's daily ration of ice cream goes first to the prisoners, then to the crew. One prisoner walked into a mess hall and found himself face to face with his brother, who was a member of the crew.

We've begun to loosen up a bit and ask and answer questions. We are eager to learn how the war was won, and the crew is eager to hear our story of captivity. Usually it ends up with one prisoner talking for all of us and one member of the crew speaking for all of them, while a large number of crew and some prisoners crowd around listening and occasionally volunteering a remark. We've learned a fair amount of World War II jargon and names of weapons and equipment we've never seen.

We are amazed at how few have any intention of making the Navy a career. What looks like a great life to us is a prison life to them. Some are going to join the 52–20 club ($20 a week unemployment payments for a year). Others are going to school on a government-paid program. Still others are going to jobs they left or hope to get. Others just plan to get "out—way out."

Magazines are available everywhere. I see in every one numerous articles I want to read. Which magazine to start with is a major choice, followed by which article to read.

This is a newer and better Navy than the pre-war Navy I knew. There is an identification with home and civilian culture that was lacking in the professional Navy. Most of the pin-ups are wives and sweethearts rather than Petty and Varga girls. The enlisted men are much more interested in, and better informed on, politics and economics and social matters than those I knew early in my enlistment. Many are homesick. I never knew a homesick marine after boot camp. I can't make up my mind whether it's better for the country to have a professional military or one that has strong ties to civilian life. I lean toward the civilian, especially in the lower ranks. I think I've had enough of the military.

This is the first time since pre-war Mariveles that I have had three meals at a table in one day. I now weigh 122 pounds and feel heavier and stronger with each day that passes. The abundance and variety are unbelievable. The preparation is equal to restaurants I've known.

This evening we were each personally invited by the duty petty officer to a special movie for prisoners. They escorted us to deck chairs, front row center, where a large area was reserved for the repatriated. The picture was the first look we've had yet at life in America. It left us filled with hope for what lies ahead but sick with thoughts of recent years. I stayed on the bow after the movie trying to sort out my thoughts. For some reason, I fear boredom after such a long time of continuous struggle. I can see behind but not ahead. I have no idea what I will be doing in one, five or 10 years, and the void I look into frightens me. It will have to be exciting, whatever it is.

I headed back to my bunk determined to burn the bridge that service life has represented to me. I had to ask the officer of the deck to find my bunk for me after lights out. (And I expect to find my way around as a civilian!)

The biggest pleasure in sleeping was not having to turn over every few minutes to give a hip or a shoulder relief from a bamboo strip or a tatami mat. At three or four o'clock I had all the rest I needed, but there was no place to go and nothing to do. I lay there in the semi-dark trying to direct my thoughts along a given path, but no matter how hard I tried, I could not maintain a train of thought. I tried to trace my thinking, and found I could not do that, either. It frightens me.

SEPTEMBER 13: The captain decreed that a mid-day victory dinner would be celebrated for prisoners of war. It was magnificent. Again we were served the choicest of everything. I could hardly believe so much flavor could be contained in each mouthful of steak. What a contrast with the rice and eggplant or radish soup. The steak was accompanied by eggs, the prisoners' choice of great meals. Somebody must have told the captain. We also had french fries, olives, pickles and pie, each a first since our release. We were seated so there was a prisoner or two at every table, making each of us a center of attention. The crew was incredibly thoughtful of me, as I'm sure they were of the others. Their main interest was the kind and amount of food we got in the camps. They marveled that so many survived.

Not long after the victory dinner word was passed for the prisoners to stand by for transport to another location. It has to mean we're headed home.

About 2 p.m. we mustered on the quarterdeck for pictures, handshaking and well wishes. There are about 70 of us, all sailors and marines. We thanked everyone for their hospitality and, except for one prisoner thought to have appendicitis, we made a tour of Tokyo Bay that lasted more than two hours. We saw an array of ships that staggered our imaginations and our understanding. How could so much be done in such a short time after Pearl Harbor? We slowly went past the battleship Wisconsin and boarded the USS Hyde at dusk. The Hyde appears to be a supply ship of some sort. It does not have much armament and has a large open space on the fantail.

We had another great meal, but I found myself having difficulty eating more than a small portion of a serving. Throwing away what I took but couldn't eat troubled my conscience greatly.

There was a special showing of a comedy for the prisoners, preceded by a newsreel of a Big Three meeting. Roosevelt looked to us to be already dying when the reel was made. The picture was good, but the seats were hard. I stood and watched for 10 or 15 minutes, then looked across the bay at movies on other ships in the distance for a few minutes and went to my bed, which was assigned soon after we boarded the ship. I tripped over a Japanese sword in the dark at the movie. Prisoners keep them nearby, even in the shower. Some MPs were reported trying to confiscate some swords and were told they would have to fight for them. The crews have an incredible interest in souvenirs. When told it is illegal to take the swords, their owners say, "Court-martial me."

There has been almost no talk of money except by ships' crews, who marvel over how much pay we must have accumulated. The prisoners' conversations run: "I stayed in the shower two hours last night ... What about those clean sheets ... Roast beef and gravy ... I'll probably get married to the first cat I sleep with ... I've used half a tube of toothpaste in two days ... How would you like that on your burned rice?"

SEPTEMBER 14: I still haven't seen Fujiyama. It's been too cloudy or overcast. Lines for chow take 45 minutes to two hours. I wait until the line is down. There seems to be increased talk of retribution among prisoners and crew. I guess we could kill some of their leaders, but there isn't much left of the country. Some men who left for air transport to Guam were returned to the Hyde because of bad weather. I started to tell a story about my imprisonment today and forgot what I was talking about. I still can't recall what I was trying to say. A good movie is scheduled tonight, and we've been told to be ready to leave early in the morning for air transport to Guam.

SEPTEMBER 15: Reveille at 4:00. Mess call at 4:30. I waited for the end of the mess line. The sky at 4:00 was very clear and transparent. The stars showed almost no scintillation, indicating essentially no wind at any level. The background was almost pure black—no dust or moisture at any level. Cassiopeia was near the zenith and Orion was visible in the east. I had slept well and was fully rested and awake. I was excited by the prospect of my first flight in an airplane.

The sky lightened in the east. All but first- and second-magnitude stars faded out as the sky turned to violet and then to blue, first in the east and then in the zenith and the west. Then the sun's rays reached the altitude where clouds were forming, and suddenly I knew the origin of the mystique of Japan. A fleet of white boats appeared to populate the sky, now a light blue in the east and a deeper blue above. The clouds were oriented east and west with their ends upturned and the upper freeboard of these magical craft were splashed with gold. Each color—white, gold and blue—was the purest possible. The sky ships faded in the east and appeared ever farther in the west as the sun rose in the east.

The progression of gold across the sky turned me from east to west and, as the sun broke over the horizon, the sacred mountain, a perfect cone, snow-covered at the top, purple at the bottom, appeared as if by magic over the new desert of Yokohama. The entire episode could not have lasted more than 10 minutes. A window to the realm of the gods had been opened inadvertently for a profane eye to glimpse what is forbidden to mortal men. That such beauty should be reserved for a cruel and unfeeling people is beyond my comprehension.

Cereal for breakfast. You cut the side of a small, wax-lined box and pour in milk and sugar. First I ate Rice Crispies, then corn flakes, then more Rice Crispies. The grapefruit juice tasted tinny, but I drank it anyway.

We were placed aboard a landing ship medium (LSM) about 6:15 a.m. and headed down the bay. Fujiyama now had a stratum of clouds about halfway from the ground to the snow line and a pile of billowy clouds at its base. They faded as clouds developed to obscure the sun, but the morning star shone brilliant and alone in the eastern sky. Then it, too, the last particle of light, disappeared into the day, and a day like most other days began.

We were out from the ship less than an hour when a series of signals passed between the LSM and the shore. We returned to the Hyde. Later in the day, one-third of the prisoners were called out by name, taken aboard the LSM, left, and did not return. The rest of us rested, ate, read magazines and saw another movie. Except for the comedies, movies appear transparent to me. The acting seems stylized and artificial. I watched for a while and went to my bunk.

SEPTEMBER 16: Up at 4:00. Breakfast at 4:30. Boarded LSM at 6:00. At airport at 8 a.m. after again touring Tokyo Bay and reviewing the fleet. I missed the first plane when my name was mispronounced and they called someone else. When I was the last one waiting to board and my name still had not been called, I took a look at the list, spotted my name, and said: "No D!" They had been calling Bob "Handy." I got a seat near the rear of a C-46 at 11:13, my last moment on Japanese soil. It was an end without a beginning that I could identify. I could only let it happen; I was out of control. I felt the same way when I boarded the train at Notogawa. The sailor who supervised our departure commented as we were waiting to take off: "Isn't anyone excited?" I said: "We all are." Even at this point, we would believe it only after it happened.

The plane left the ground at 11:37. I asked the coordinator for the time. It was the beginning of a 1,600-mile trip over water.

Unlike those on the Colorado, the sailors I talked with on the Hyde had no idea of the geography or topography of Japan and weren't much interested. They don't know if they qualify for bonuses. They don't seem to understand the GI Bill and aren't much interested in understanding it. They don't have an opinion about Truman or know his credentials. They don't have an opinion on Russia or Communism. They complain about things we don't think twice about. They seem awfully spoiled. I'm afraid of softness for myself and for America. How can I fault the people who have so recently liberated me? Who are the enemy? Softness invites enemies.

I'm invited in turn to the co-pilot's chair. For the 20th time on this flight the pilot explains things I don't have background enough to frame as questions. Aircraft skins are 50 one-thousandths of an inch thick; speed is 186 air miles per hour; wind is 20 miles per hour at 90 degrees on the port side. Radar sends out a beam and its reflection is analyzed to provide information. That speck we are approaching at 9,000 feet is Iwo Jima, Marines took it at great cost so that our planes could fly unmolested from Guam, Saipan, Tinian and the rest of the Marianas to bomb Japan. Mt. Surabaya approached and disappeared behind us.

Lunch of tomato and pineapple juices to drink and turkey sandwich to eat, all first-time-since-release experiences. We ate it all and ended up eating dry bread, which was itself a treat. On leaving Japan, the pilot had considerately climbed quickly to 6,000 feet so we could have a last look at Fuji. Two-thirds of it protruded through a sea of white, billowy clouds. Now he was giving us a look at another pile of rock, Iwo, that was famous for another reason.

We passed three planes close enough to identify—two C-54Bs and one craft, belonging, by its colors, to the Marine Corps.

At a few minutes to eight we landed on a Guam that bears no resemblance to the one I spent part of two days on in 1939. A tropical isle has become an arsenal.

The plane taxied within 100 feet of a waiting room. We got out, stretched and were greeted with coffee, candy and cigarettes by fair-haired American girls. It's their height that strikes us most. Also, they are intimidating by their openness and their ability to handle the situation. The contrast with Japanese girls, who practice a servile deference to their men, could not be greater.

Our names were called as we passed through a gate to a bus. It was a great ride. The road was smooth and the tropical wind blew soft and fresh and full of odors through the open windows.

We came to a lighted area—lighted barracks, lighted homes, lighted streets, everywhere signs of civilization as I once knew it. Entering our assigned barracks we saw the order and cleanliness we were denied so long. Tables, benches, foot lockers, mosquito bars lined up, inviting and convenient. Magazines and newspapers aligned on racks. Everything for our comfort.

I didn't pay attention and failed to accompany my group to the sick bay. A Navy doctor came looking for me and saw that I joined them for a quick examination. From the sick bay we went to the mess hall for steak, reconstituted potatoes, carrots, peaches and huge squares of butter near everyone. I ate like I was hungry.

SEPTEMBER 17: Complete physical exams—eyes, ears, nose, throat, lung X-rays, blood. Electrocardiogram showed no present heart problem. Evidence of beriberi discounted. Two cavities after nearly four years without dental care—it must have been the diet.

At night we were shown a film of naval firepower as used against Iwo Jima. It was impossible to absorb. Salvo after salvo poured onto the island from dozens of ships. The contrast with what we were able to mount against the Japs in the Philippines—World War II fought with World War I weapons— was striking.

SEPTEMBER 18: Payday! First since Cavite. Fifty-dollar advance until pay records are obtained.

After most of an hour in the canteen without buying anything, I returned to lie down for a while. I don't know values and I'm afraid to spend money that I earned at a dollar a day on something that costs several or many days' pay. Two weeks of rice and radish soup, 12 days of work, lice, fleas, bedbugs and worms in exchange for a camera or a watch or a gold-filled pen and pencil set. Everything I saw is incredibly expensive. I'm keeping my 50 days' certificate in my pocket.

I got another jolt in the afternoon. We were called to the quartermaster Quonset hut to come up to regulation in our clothes. Suddenly I realized I never want to get in a uniform again, never line up in formation, never salute or "Sir" someone. I can't believe the resentment and revulsion that welled up. Somehow I haven't associated being repatriated with rejoining the military. I'm 3½ years beyond my enlistment.

I must have thought freedom meant becoming an instant civilian. I'm willing to return to the States in my Navy fatigues, especially the shoes, which are the best footwear I can remember. But now I have to go regulation.

Once I got into my new clothes it wasn't so bad. The underwear is a forgotten luxury. The trousers are loose and bunched at the belt. The shirt is stiff and smells of whatever they put on new clothes. I still don't have headwear, so I don't have to salute. And I don't have any chevrons or emblems; I was supposed to buy them at the PX. I look five years younger than I am. I feel like a recruit and I'm sure I look like one. It has its good points.

SEPTEMBER 19: WACs come through the hut frequently, always with magazines, writing paper, candy, gum and a number of other things. Many prisoners are showing interest in re-enlisting. All have nearly eight years in and some 10 or 12. I notice there are no older POWs in our Quonset hut. The oldest might be 30. We've spent all our late youth and early manhood in the service. We don't know anything else. Any other life is a big blank. I know how they feel, but I won't spend an extra day in the service.

I'm having difficulty with food. Greasy or oily food almost nauseates me. A year ago I could drink a cup of oil. I eat cereal for breakfast and vegetables and fruit for the other two meals. Meat and gravy looks good and smells great but I can only eat a bite or two. I got vitamins on the Hyde, but one of them, the littlest pill, sets my skin on fire. The large capsule I can taste for hours. Sometimes I take them, sometimes I don't. My stomach always feels full. I haven't had any chocolate in days, but I have ice cream every day, usually at the same time. I walk quite a bit but don't have the energy to exercise or go for a swim.

Once in a while the music is good and I hear a new song I like, but most of it bothers me and some of it irritates me. It seems like I've missed something. Some songs seem frivolous. They're all too fast. I used to be able to learn a song after hearing it a few times. Not anymore. I guess I'm not the same as I was before the war. Somebody said: "If you're happy you're free, why aren't you smiling?" I said something like: "I thought I was."

I stood in line a long time for a beer this afternoon. They ran out and I complained to the duty officer. We were allowed only one can. I ended up with three cans after I complained to the officer of the day and he had the beer line reopened for the prisoners. I had two other POWs stand in line for me. I spent my first money on beer, Sick's Select, made in Seattle.

Tonight we had an open-air stage show, but I couldn't hear well and didn't find out who the performers were. A large number of marines and sailors came early and got seats up front. I didn't feel comfortable with a lot of people behind me, so I sat in the back where I couldn't hear much. I left during the stage show but came back for the film, "Fighting Lady," which I also left because I was tired. I wanted to see Guam, especially at night, but there was no provision for sightseeing. I also wanted to see Agana, the capital and only large community on the island when I was here six years ago, but I didn't try very hard.

I went to the executive officer today to see how I would find out about my older brother, Ray, who also was in the Marine Corps before the war. I was sent to the Red Cross, but they told me they couldn't learn anything for several weeks and I would be gone by then. I don't know what service my younger brother, Dick, is in, if any.

SEPTEMBER 20: Some POWs left for the States today by airplane.

SEPTEMBER 21: I've been thinking about finishing high school and maybe going to college in January. I still have a semester and a half to go in high school.

There are a lot of amusing stories and jokes. I enjoy them but I rarely laugh. Most of the POWs have another to pal around with. I find myself resisting friendships. I want to be left alone.

There are few insects on the island. The air under the mosquito net always feels used, so at first I slept with my head out and then didn't put the net down at all after getting tangled in it several times. It rains about every day here, but no one seems bothered by it. If you get wet, you soon dry off.

I saw "A Medal for Benny" tonight. It gave me an understanding of America and the effect of the war on its people. I really got lost in the picture. It was followed by a comedy with Ida Lupino that I would like to have seen, but I was too uncomfortable and went to bed hoping there would be no call to board the airplane tonight.

SEPTEMBER 22: Awakened at 6:00 to the news we will be leaving the island at 8:30. I won't be finding out here whether my brothers are alive or dead. Breakfast was served at the ward galley. I packed a small bag. It holds everything but my Navy shoes. They offered scrambled eggs and toast, but I had cereal and coffee.

I've had the feeling that the hospital staff has had enough of us. It may be that they don't know how to please us or that we don't know how to show appreciation. We don't know whether what they do is standard practice or we're being given special treatment. Increasingly I feel that everything I do or say is artificial or stage acting. I'm sure that's the way it looks to the ward staff. I wish they were men. I wouldn't have to worry so much about how to act or talk. It's very difficult to talk. We've had a life that's hard for us to talk about and have almost nothing else to say. I wonder how there always seemed to be something to talk about in high school and even in China. Now I measure every word. Also, I wonder what is behind what people say rather than what they say. I wonder if they know that we want to be warm and friendly but don't know how. It seems easier to make small talk now that we are leaving. I wish there were some way to get pictures of the nurses and aides.

I expected we would be seeing reporters, photographers and chaplains but we haven't. The chaplains sent word that they are available. We haven't seen any of the Navy or Marines brass, either, but several lower officers have inquired about officers they knew that were in China or the Philippines.

At 8:30 we were on a super-smooth highway headed toward the airfield. This was dense jungle when I was last here. Now the road is lined with trucks, earth movers and quonset huts. At the evacuation center we ran into a group that was supposed to leave at 8:00. Their plane was delayed until 10:30; ours is delayed until 11:00.

At 11:00, word was received that we would be delayed until 2 p.m.

At 11:30 an American Red Cross girl asked how I was holding up with the delay. We both held a cup of coffee while she found out I was from Michigan and I found out she was from Iowa and Missouri. Her name was Loretta. I forgot her last name as soon as I heard it. She talked about her two younger brothers and her married sister and how drab life is in farm towns. I told her that kind of life sounded awfully good to me. She was signaled by another Red Cross girl and said she had to go to lunch; she had been up since 5:30 and had duty from six until noon, but said she would be back after eating. I was afraid the call would come to board the plane, but at 12:45 she was back, and no call had come for any of the three groups that were waiting to leave. She wanted me to talk and after a while it came without hesitation. Mostly I talked about my intent to get "way out" of the military, but the more I talked the more I convinced myself I didn't know what I was talking about.

For some reason I couldn't stop talking and the more I talked the more detached from reality I became. Two of the three groups departed. We watched together as they disappeared in the east, then talked some more. All the disconnected thoughts I ever had were voiced by five o'clock. I think she realized how ignorant and shallow I felt because she took over the conversation and tried to reassure me about how I had survived, how I had learned something of four languages and three cultures, and how I would put it all together in college and build a fine life.

Shortly after 6:00 my group was told to get our belongings and stand by. As we waited for the call to board, I asked her for her address. She said no, that I would meet some nice girl in the States and wouldn't even remember her name. I had the feeling she emphasized the word "nice." I thanked her for spending so much time with me. When the call came, she held my hand until nearly all passengers had gone through the door, then turned and left through the door on the other side of the waiting room.

I felt a pressure in my chest until the plane leveled out, then a deep feeling of incompleteness, that I had bared a shallow soul and had been gently rejected. I promised myself I wouldn't let that happen again.

I worried for a while about the ferry pilot being able to find the next speck in the ocean where we were to refuel, and how the navigator compensated for drift. The noise pretty much isolates you from everyone aboard, so I got a blanket and eventually went to sleep puzzling over why I'm feeling increasingly trapped rather than increasingly free as I approach the United States.

16

Stateside at Last

SEPTEMBER 23: I awoke with a strong pressure in my ears. We were losing altitude fast. A flight attendant was securing bundles and blankets that scattered while I slept. It was becoming light in the east. The clouds that had been below were now above, and there was another layer below. They came together to the east and south and faded into the darkness behind us.

Suddenly we were in the lower clouds, then below them. An occasional whitecap showed that the gray underneath was ocean. The flaps were lowered, the ocean came up and the wheels touched dry land on Kwajalein before I even saw the island.

It was a long taxi to the waiting room. We were told to freshen up and eat something and not to wander away from earshot of the plane. The ground crew was told to check the magneto on one of the engines, and the flight crew disappeared into another building.

Rather than being laid out geometrically, the tent area of the enlisted men is a confusion of areas chosen to minimize the work required to obtain a level shelf of coral. Many tent-dwellers have propellers attached to a single-throw crankshaft that lifts and then thrusts a plumber's friend into a bucket filled with seawater and clothes. A ring of salt formed a circle around the buckets and a rivulet of white marked the runoff.

The inhabitants of these tents are the most indifferent and unfriendly I have yet met. I tried to inquire about life on the island from three or four of them and, getting only terse words or blank stares, went back to the waiting room. The enlisted men who were stirring were washing in helmets or tending to their wind-driven washing machines. The building used as the waiting room or transfer station was constructed of wood and appeared very vulnerable to the tropical elements.

We wanted to wash and brush our teeth but found there was fresh water only for cooking and drinking. We ended up stripped to our shorts but still in our shoes rinsing off in the ocean. For the first few minutes afterward we felt as though we had been painted with a thin coat of powder. But the feeling soon went away and we felt somewhat refreshed from the long flight.

The latrines are built on large concrete foundations well above ground. I've never figured out how they handle the long-range sewage problem of any island, but there was neither odor nor flies.

As the sun rose, its rays became more penetrating than any I can remember, but on the shady side of any structure the wind was cool and it was easy to stay comfortable.

I could eat little of the pasty oatmeal and limp hotcakes we were served for breakfast and went back to the boarding area, where I read the Kwajalein Hour Glass and leafed through the comic books that everyone looked at so avidly.

Our pilots appeared with another group of four and we were ordered aboard. The former crew were now passengers as the new crew taxied the plane to the downwind end of the runway. We watched three or four B-29s take off on their ferry flight back to the States. The new pilot revved up the engines, then taxied back to the waiting area, offloaded all of us and taxied over to the service area. I had begun to sweat profusely in the poorly ventilated passenger compartment and welcomed the fresh air again. I walked over to the Red Cross shack, where a radio played a station that alternately faded out and came in strong. They also had a phonograph, coffee, milk, ice cream and doughnuts, all of which looked good but which I was finding increasingly difficult to eat.

The Chaumont carried untold thousands of troops back and forth across the pre-war Pacific. Here it is being loaded to remove the last significant American presence from North China in 1941.

WESTERN UNION

1220

A. N. WILLIAMS
PRESIDENT

NEWCOMB CARLTON
CHAIRMAN OF THE BOARD

J. C. WILLEVER
FIRST VICE-PRESIDENT

The filing time shown in the date line on telegrams and day letters is STANDARD TIME at point of origin. Time of receipt is STANDARD TIME at point of destination

ZAE150 126 GOVT 5 EXTRA=WASHINGTON DC 10 216P

MR & MRS RAYMOND C HANEY (PARENTS)=

R F D #2 BV= 1057 University

THE COMMANDANT US MARINE CORPS REGRETS TO ADVISE YOU THAT
ACCORDING TO THE RECORDS OF THIS HEADQUARTERS YOUR SON
CORPORAL ROBERT E HANEY US MARINE CORPS WAS PERFORMING HIS
DUTY IN THE SERVICE OF HIS COUNTRY IN THE MANILA BAY AREA
WHEN THAT STATION CAPITULATED X HE WILL BE CARRIED ON THE
RECORDS OF THE MARINE CORPS AS MISSING PENDING FURTHER
INFORMATION X NO REPORT OF HIS DEATH HAS BEEN RECEIVED AND
HE MAY BE A PRISONER OF WAR X IT WILL PROBABLY BE SEVERAL
MONTHS BEFORE DEFINITE OFFICIAL INFORMATION CAN BE EXPECTED
CONCERNING HIS STATUS X SINCERE SYMPATHY IS EXTENDED TO
YOU IN YOUR ANXIETY AND YOU ARE ASSURED THAT ANY REPORT
RECEIVED WILL BE COMMUNICATED TO YOU PROMPTLY X=
    T HOLCOMB LIEUTANANT GENERAL USMC
    THE COMMANDANT US MARINE CORPPS.

By the time I was liberated, my few possessions easily fit into this Marine Corps field scarf. Four decades later, I stumbled upon it, stored away and nearly forgotten. In it were my prison journal and several wartime mementos — including the two telegrams reproduced here.

WESTERN UNION

1201

A. N. WILLIAMS
PRESIDENT

(37).

The filing time shown in the date line on telegrams and day letters is STANDARD TIME at point of origin. Time of receipt is STANDARD TIME at point of destination

.Z33 40 GOVT=WASHINGTON DC 20 904P

MR AND MRS RAYMOND C HENEY=

RFD #4 BV=

PLEASED TO INFORM YOU OF THE LIBERATION FROM JAPANESE
CUSTODY OF YOUR SON CORPORAL ROBERT E HANEY USMC. HE
ARRIVED AT GUAM ON 15 SEPTEMBER 1945 ENROUTE TO THE UNITED
STATES. FURTHER DETAILS WILL BE FUNRISHED YOU PROMPTLY WHEN
RECEIVED=

A A VANDEGRIFT GENERAL USMC COMMANDANT OF THE MARINE

CORP.

15 1945

THE COMPANY WILL APPRECIATE SUGGESTIONS FROM ITS PATRONS CONCERNING ITS SERVICE

A high school graduate at last — spring 1946. Some of the service ribbons are incorrect. I was sold the wrong items at the PX.

Time passed quickly, and at 10:30 we again boarded and soon were in the air. It cooled down quickly. As we came around, I looked down and saw that Kwajalein is a small part of a submerged reef that somehow has risen a few feet above high tide and dried out. Kwajalein isn't much as a tropical isle, but as a stepping stone to the Far East it must have been intensely important. I am amazed that in the five or six hours I passed there I failed to have a single conversation and found out nothing about it.

We headed east-northeast looking for Johnson Island. The nurse assigned to the flight was cool and efficient. She announced that if we wanted anything we should ask. Most asked for something to read and passed comic books around. I read a few, wrote in my journal, stared at the ocean and the sky, dozed and wondered what lies ahead.

It was thoroughly dark when the plane arrived at Johnson Island. We had moved east two time zones from Kwajalein, shortening daylight by nearly two hours. As we taxied to the waiting room, only a few lights were visible on the island, almost all on the starboard side of the plane. There was no evidence that a world existed beyond the lights. There was little evidence of the island itself except for a small circle under the lights. The lights in the distance shed no light on the ground and seemed suspended in air, too bright to be mistaken for stars. A bus with weak, almost amber lights took us to the mess hall. We were warned to be back in 45 minutes.

There was fresh water for washing, warm from the pipes that lay on the still-warm island surface. Breaded pork chops were served along with mashed potatoes, gravy and applesauce. It was my first fresh pork since well before the war, maybe since the trip on the Henderson in 1939. I ate the meat and applesauce and a spoonful of potatoes. I finished eating ahead of most of the prisoners and waited outside the mess hall, where I talked about the trip and Johnson Island life with an airman. When I left for the bus he gave me his copy of the Moaning News, and said he was sorry it took so long to free us.

Roll was called as we boarded the plane. The door swung shut and the hasp was closed. In a few minutes we were off the ground and headed for Oahu, 400 miles away.

SEPTEMBER 24: The bus taking us from the plane arrived at Area Heights Hospital on Oahu, Territory of Hawaii, at 4:30 a.m. We were given breakfast about 6:00 and the opportunity to requisition partial pay and clothes and were assigned to beds in a ward reserved for POWs. I slept until noon after taking a long, hot shower and shaving. It's hard to believe that a little more than a day ago I was on Guam in the Western Pacific.

The word was passed that a small group of us would be leaving at 4:30 in the afternoon on a PBY-2 amphibian. Red Cross girls invaded the ward and were so animated I didn't have any idea what was going on. At the airfield I ran into a number of marines I knew in North China. They were taken as prisoners to Shanghai, where they worked for a year and a half on a monument to the Japanese dead. Then they were transferred to northern Honshu, where they worked in a mine. Only one had died until two were killed by a food drop toward the end of August.

At 1800 hours a half-dozen of us boarded the PBY bound for Alameda, California. The plane taxied to sea for about 20 minutes, then took off in a cloud of spray. One final bounce and slap and the water fell away. I looked back as we made a great arc to the left and saw where our wake had stopped in the water. White-uniformed sailors watched from docks and decks as we swept to the east and leveled out. I saw two slow-winged birds, white as snow, fall behind as they, too, headed east. A submarine showed its full length as its conning tower broke the surface.

Diamond Head was fully lighted by the evening sun, standing watch over Waikiki Beach. A string of palms formed a green fringe along the shore. I counted almost 50 craft in a perfect echelon plowing through the water leaving fans that faded in the rear as they formed behind the ships of the flotilla. In a beautiful sunset, the clouds ran from gold in the west to red alongside and purple ahead. As we gained altitude, a cloud bank appeared behind over the island, pink on the bottom, spread out across the horizon from south to north and purple on top. Then as we climbed above the layer, the top layer's colors turned the same as they had appeared from below, and the sun set a second time as we left the islands behind us. As the sun touched the horizon, the bottom of the clouds again turned pink and then faded to gray.

I turned my attention to the east, where I could see the stars above but nothing below. I was given a Navy hospital blanket, lay down and slept well, the noise of the plane shutting out all activity.

SEPTEMBER 25: I awoke about midnight and found the nurse-flight attendant serving a meal of soup, crackers, ham, potatoes, peas, bread, butter and coffee. Fully awake, I sat up from 1 a.m. until 4 a.m. watching seas and rivers of clouds appear under the wings in the moonlight as the plane rose and fell like a chip on the water below. Occasionally we entered a cloud bank and for a few moments the wings would disappear from the tips to the engines.

At 6:00 we were served juice, rolls, coffee, bacon and eggs. I made a sandwich of the bacon, eggs and roll and took it with a cup of coffee to my seat. I still had some of it at 8:30 when we were told there would be no more smoking because of a fuel leak. At 10:00 the word passed that land was in view, but it turned out to be a bank of coastal fog. Twenty minutes later, a line of waves breaking on the beach could be seen, and a few minutes later the beach itself. The word came to strap on our belts, and we began to lose altitude. An odd excitement came over me, mostly a wondering at how it would be to set foot on American soil after so many years and so much doubt that it would ever happen. It became increasingly hard to breathe. I didn't know for sure whether it was caused by loss of altitude or nervous anticipation.

Beach homes appeared, roads began to take shape, fields like postcards formed patterns on the hillsides. Down to about 2,000 feet, we circled a ship-studded bay once and landed off Alameda. The plane was slowly pulled up a concrete ramp and I stepped out on a wide concrete area populated by a variety of aircraft.

We were taken to a building nearby where we were questioned at some length by intelligence officers. They must have marveled at how little we knew. At noon we were fed an indifferent lunch and assigned to a ward in Oak Knoll Navy Hospital. I weighed in at 127 pounds, and went through my third fairly extensive physical examination. I'm finding there is almost no interest in nutritional deficiency diseases.

I skipped dinner and was in bed asleep well before lights out.

SEPTEMBER 26: Again I was offered a chance to draw a pay advance. About 9 a.m. I was ordered to go to radiology for additional X-rays—there were "clouds on my lungs in two places." At noon I attended my first general mess in America.

Someone came up and shouted in my ear: "Hey, China marine!" It was Edward Duggan from Santa Monica, California— the same Edward Duggan I searched for, and didn't find, in the confusion after the bombing at Sangley Point—the first marine I sought out whenever I wanted a game of tennis in North China. He had lost 30 or 35 of his 160 pounds and looked 20 years old rather than 25, but said he was well. Only the last 10 or 12 months of captivity were bad for him, and he avoided the deficiency diseases that felled so many. We exchanged addresses, ate our meal together, said goodbye, and went our separate ways.

I wandered around most of the day, always worrying a little about being able to find my way back to my ward and wondering whether I could remember the wing name and area number.

At mid-afternoon I saw a large number of sailors and marines boarding a bus. When I found out it was headed for San Francisco, I got on, too. I decided I was going to look for Angelo Manzano. I traced him to Merchant Marine Hospital in the Bay area by going through a welfare office on Brush Street. The woman there made innumerable calls before she found out he had been an outpatient at the hospital.

I then went to the Bank of America to withdraw the money I've been depositing there since 1939 through an allotment against the day I get out of the service. They were closed. I gave up and went to a movie. It was 3 a.m. when I got back to the hospital. I slept until nine o'clock, worrying off and on about the X-ray.

SEPTEMBER 27: Half of San Francisco is in uniform. The girls seem awfully hard. I guess they have to be, with so many outsiders roaming around.

SEPTEMBER 28: I left for San Francisco at 11 a.m. Buses run every few minutes. I can't understand my lack of interest in anything, except maybe finding out what happened to the Spaniard. I told Angelo I would sponsor him, or my family would, if he wanted to become a citizen. His prison camp time might count as residence, since he served on a U.S. merchant vessel.

I visited the Harbor Branch of the Bank of America, on referral from another branch. My account was stopped on June 5, 1942, when the War Department announced I was missing and presumed dead. They gave me a cashier's check for $497, which included four percent interest. All I had to do was give them my Marine identification card.

Welfare had no further trace of Angelo and directed me to the Red Cross, which directed me to Oak Knoll, where I was a patient. Oak Knoll had a record of his arrival—and transfer to the Merchant Marine Hospital. I was going to call Immigration, but decided to call Merchant Marine Hospital a second time and give them the information that Oak Knoll had given me. They again identified Angelo as an outpatient, but told me they had no address for him and no appointment scheduled. I left a message and my Michigan address. I left the next step up to him.

I went to two movies that evening and left both about two-thirds through. The acting seemed transparent. I seemed to see through the plots. The language seemed artificial and forced. Even the music reminded me of the way they used music in the old westerns. I looked for a wristwatch between movies and ended up buying an Ingersoll for a dollar. I traded a day in prison for a watch! Some others I looked at would have cost almost three weeks. A Waltham would have cost almost a month.

I got in bed at 2:30. The watch made a lot of noise, so I wrapped it in a sock and stuffed it in a shoe.

SEPTEMBER 29: I slept very late. I got up, shaved, bathed and went to the mess hall, which smelled greasy and steamy. I ate a little creamed chipped beef and drank nearly two glasses of milk and took a large vanilla cookie with me when I left. Coffee is beginning to eat away at my stomach, so I usually have it now only at breakfast.

I've been trying not to think of my family. I didn't plan to contact them for another week or so when my feet are back on the ground. I've feared their questions, and especially their sympathy. But when I got back from lunch the nurse had a telegram waiting for me. The War Department notified my parents that I was back the day I arrived. I had to call.

I waited until 5:10. I felt tight and at a loss for words at first, but they seemed to know that it was difficult for me. They told me my brother Ray is a first lieutenant in the Marine Corps and my brother Dick is a captain in the Army Air Corps, both very much alive. My brother-in-law is still in the Navy and getting out soon. I talked to my youngest brother, Bill, who is nine now, and my youngest sister, Mary, who is 10. I told everybody I'm fine, but need to gain some weight and strength and get accustomed to civilization for a little while. They didn't complain that I didn't call sooner. I felt like a heel. I told them I don't have any plans and will spend my three-month recuperation leave with them. I promised to write and call. It was most strange talking to my father. He told me I'll be welcome, and that my being a prisoner has been very hard on my mother.

It was easier than I thought it would be. I'm glad it's over.

I went to the recreation area, had a couple of beers and went to bed greatly relieved. It has been seven years and five months since I called Michigan from Seattle and asked permission to enlist.

My second set of lung X-rays turned out negative.

SEPTEMBER 30: I woke early and went to mass in the theater. I helped prepare the altar but claimed I had forgotten my Latin and couldn't serve. My thoughts are increasingly wild and uncontrollable. I went to offer a mass of thanksgiving but found myself reviewing incidents of the past three years and thinking what I could have done and what I would do now if I had the chance. At the elevation I suddenly realized what was going on in my mind and that I had heard no mass at all. Then my thoughts wandered off again. I hate myself for not being able to control my thoughts—and I hate myself for hating. I offered the mass and my hardships in thanksgiving for my safe return and the safety of my brothers and made a dedication of the rest of my life to His service; but even as I did it, I felt the resentment and hatred trying to break through. Oh God, is there another sinner such as I? Why do the strongest memories surface at a time of quiet and reflection on the life of the Prince of Peace? The road ahead will not be an easy one.

I spent most of the day in the recreation room shooting pool, mostly by myself. I can concentrate with a cue in my hand, but not in church.

OCTOBER 1: A doctor gave me a going-over today for not helping myself more. I asked him what anyone was doing for me that I could do myself and how he knew what I was doing or wasn't doing. He saw me clench my fists when he came and stood about a foot and a half in front of me. Then he backed off. He was about six-foot-five and towered over me.

I later felt he was testing me. But he showed me something in myself I have to be very careful to guard against— self-pity. He may have been the best of the doctors I have seen.

Part III
AFTERMATH

If life goes on after a momentous
happening, especially if it is a traumatic
one, there is a second harvest. It can be
either positive or negative, and is likely
to be both.

17

An Uneasy Truce

Steel wheels slapped steel rails and the passenger car swayed gently. I should have been lulled to sleep, or to lazy sightseeing. But—just as I did when yet-unseen Japanese were closing in near Manila—I fantasized slipping away and into the countryside to fight another day. My anxiety seemed almost as great as it had been on Luzon. Hard to believe, for now it was Detroit, my home, my very beginnings that were closing in. It had been nearly eight years.

The power of will had brought me this far; it would take me farther. I rode into the high-ceilinged old depot on Detroit's west side, three blocks from Briggs Stadium where just months earlier, in October 1945, Newhouser and the Tigers had won the final war-years baseball championship. I got off with my seabag and boarded a bus for the 16-mile ride north to Big Beaver.

I was nearly 25 and looked too young to buy a glass of beer. Anyone who saw me would logically assume I had come of draft age just in time to don a uniform and miss the war. In fact, I was an old China marine, had been there before it started, and had spent the entire war concentrating on living one more day. The rest of my life would be shaped by that experience; but now it seemed just the other day that I last had touched this ground, a confident 16-year-old off on some vague adventure. Much had happened—almost more than mind and body could handle. At the same time, many things had not happened at all. Time had passed. Horrible, incredible events had happened before my eyes. But while I encountered and survived an apocalyptic rite of passage, the normal events of a young man's experience were bypassed. It was as if I had been island-hopping through my young adulthood, missing the social and educational landfalls that connect teenaged currents with life's mainstream. This old China marine was in many ways still 16 years old. My confidence, however, was a casualty of the Pacific.

As the bus neared the crossroads, I stood and dragged my seabag to the fare box, reached into my pocket and said: "Next street."

The driver put his hand over the box and said: "Servicemen free."

I got off, nodded to the driver and looked around.

Most of Big Beaver was visible from the intersection—two gasoline stations, a variety store, a meat market, the Kroger grocery, the pool hall and the barber shop. A few yards to the north was the creek where I dropped buckshot to frogs as they hid a foot or so under the surface until they got so heavy they could scarcely move, then picked them out of the water, shook out the shot, let the frog leap back into the water, and looked for another victim. To the north was the house of the two sisters who had the two electric automobiles and behind them the Methodist church with the little gym and only one basketball hoop. Across from the church was Black's house with its magnificent beech tree and the barn where we shot each other with peashooters as we sneaked through the stalls and lofts. Behind me was the boarded-up door of the little second-hand store where I had bought books for a nickel and traded them back two-for-one. Things were as they had been—stagnant, haphazard, rural. And home.

I dragged my seabag a few steps north and looked around the closed auto repair shop and up the dirt road to the school I attended and the house where I lived two doors away. The figure hurrying toward me was my mother. If we said anything, I don't remember what it was. I left the seabag at the corner and hurried over the bridge to meet her. We went back for it. I threw it over my left shoulder and put my right arm around her as we walked.

I put my seabag on the porch and we entered the $600 house that had produced a Marine Corps lieutenant for the war in the Pacific, an Army Air Corps captain for the bombing of Africa, Romania and Germany, and a Marine Corps corporal for the defense of a few acres of the Philippines. It was good to be home and it was difficult to be home.

We sat in facing chairs and looked at each other. No one else was there. It had been a hard eight years on my mother. It showed not so much on her face as in her clothes. The colors ranged from gray to black and the style made me think of my grandmothers. But she was healthy enough, and little by little the family news was revealed.

My oldest brother was married and would be coming home soon. My younger brother was stationed nearby at Selfridge Field and would come at her call. My married sister had an apartment in a Detroit suburb and expected her husband to be released from the Navy at any time. My youngest sister and brother would be home from grade school soon. And my father would soon be home from his job.

And that is how it happened. One by one, or in pairs, they all came home. They saw the seabag on the porch. Most of them opened the door a few inches and peeked in. What they said varied, but what they felt was largely the same. None pried. They all knew it had been hard for me to make this trip that had taken so long. It was January 1946.

* * *

I came back from the Pacific in better mental and physical health than most of the ex-POWs I have met. That is a telling fact, because my mental and physical—and social—health were a genuine mess.

The colitis, which first appeared at Cabanatuan, remained a problem for years. I came home hungry, but could not eat when a meal was set before me. My strength and stamina were low. I was moody and depressed, confused and had trouble sleeping.

I dreamed the same basic dream nearly every night and sometimes several times a night: I was in a large excavation; Japanese soldiers were searching for me; I ran through caves and into crevices and around outcroppings with soldiers on my heels. They knew generally where I was, but when they got near they looked through me without seeing me. I was never quite sure they didn't see me, so I kept looking for a better place to hide. As the soldiers approached me toward the end of the dream, I would wake up—often in a cold sweat.

How different from the formless terror of childhood nightmares. I remember, for example, the incomprehensible fright that accompanied a dream about a coin rolling along a smooth surface. By an act of will I had to keep the coin rolling; but inevitably it would slow down, stop rolling, and through a complicated process seem to be going backward while it was fluttering on its side but still going forward. It was that process of precession that held the terror. I never knew why. Sometimes I ponder how the formless fears of childhood can attach themselves to realities that hold no fear in themselves, while the violent and anxiety-laden realities of a war experience produce dreams that do not distort reality. Bombs beget fear of bombs and hunger begets fear of hunger. What begets fear of a coin vibrating to rest on a table top?

At Oak Knoll Naval Hospital, preparing for re-entry into a post-war society that was more foreign to me than China or Japan, there was no provision for dealing with confusion and lack of confidence, much less for pondering the significance of dreams. What we worked on was the colitis and the food problem, first at Oak Knoll and then—after a month—at the naval hospital in St. Albans, Long Island. We got my weight to hover around 135 pounds on my 5-foot-10 frame.

Nothing that happened at St. Albans, however, indicated progress toward my being able to go out and stake a claim to my piece of the boom years. On one intensely bewildering day, I stood before a clothes rack in the mess hall with a decision to make: on which peg to hang my cap. I could not decide, and I rushed from the mess hall. The panic, first over which peg to choose, and then over not being able to choose, was indescribable. I quickly asked for a leave and a transfer to Great Lakes Naval Training Station north of Chicago. It was to be my first and only leave during my time in the Marine Corps. I went to the hospital at Great Lakes. Then, a week later, I made the melancholy trip to Detroit.

The word got around, and within a few days I had seen many friends from my school days, boys and girls, now young men and young women. They had been easy pre-war friendships, not deep but comfortable, and without reservations other than the conventions of the times. When I returned, contacts were made but friendships were not really renewed. I was merely hanging out in the company of faces I could name.

I dated occasionally, but with no one regularly. I was not good company. My shoulders would sag, and the colitis was a hard problem to deal with. I could talk sports or trips or cars with the fellows, but had almost nothing to talk about with the girls. Mostly we went to movies, which avoided the need for talk. The pictures were often hard to get involved in, but I could become absorbed in mysteries and spy stories—a preference that has stayed with me in the era of television. I was really comfortable with only one girl, who made up in beauty of soul what she lacked in beauty of face and form. She was the sister of a sister-in-law. She died a few months after I went away to college.

I felt I was a fraud, playing a part I did not know well. I tried to be one of a group I did not understand. None of their well-meaning advice—get a job, get a girlfriend, look up some of your prisoner friends around Detroit—was possible for me.

There was the occasional party, and far too often I spent long hours in taverns, drinking more than at any time except the China days. It was difficult getting to sleep and staying asleep. The beer—and sometimes hard liquor—helped. My weight rose to 140 pounds—about 30 pounds below my average service weight before capture.

For some reason—perhaps for dental work—I returned to Great Lakes and visited the hospital to see who was still there. A marine named Appenzeller was the only patient I knew. He was missing a lung and was to be transferred to a sanitarium in Arizona. Appenzeller had a 1939 Lincoln Zephyr, a 12-cylinder job, and he wanted me to sell it for him. No one else had the $700 he wanted. I bought it myself.

The Zephyr gave me a great measure of freedom. At first I took short trips into the farmland and wooded countryside of southern Michigan, then I made longer trips to look over colleges I thought I might like to attend. One such venture took me to Big Rapids, in the center of the state's Lower Peninsula, home of Ferris College. Big Rapids was very much a small town and very rural, the kind of place the Red Cross girl on Guam had been so happy to escape. From my vantage point, it looked like a very decent place to be.

I needed just two courses for a high-school diploma: civics and Michigan history. Big Beaver school gave me credit for the semester in which I had left late in March 1938, and my service time was credited toward other courses. All I had to do was study at home and take two final exams. This simple regimen was to be my first non-military task, and it was a disaster. I could not read a paragraph and sometimes not a sentence without being plagued by intrusive thoughts. Sometimes I would sit for hours, with my mind darting off to the other side of the world and a war that was supposed to be over, before completing a few pages. The school was generous to a fault in giving me the credit I needed. The prospect of performing to college standards was not bright.

I visited my father one day at his work to meet a young Japanese who had been removed from California when the Japanese population there was interned in concentration camps. I knew almost nothing of that, and learned little during my lunch with the young man. He wanted acceptance and I gave it to him. I remembered Tani, who had been impressed into the Japanese military, another injustice, but I also remembered the Japanese in Manila and Davao who after long years as Philippine citizens became instant Japanese with the bombing of Pearl Harbor. This young man had been hurt enough; I said nothing except about Tani. But for his clear and precise English and his rare use of idiom, he was as American as I was. I wondered about his parents.

My father tried. I tried. But except for a warm reception when I first returned, our relationship remained as chilly as ever. When I left in '38, I had told him I would return when I was 21. "Don't bother," he had said. Now the same son was in his house and in a morbid frame of mind, for which he had little patience. Father had taken a beating as a marine at Belleau Wood and Chateau Thierry in World War I, and in my childhood I had seen tears on his face as the flag passed during a Fourth of July parade. You can't exactly say we had nothing in common. Yet we didn't.

Two or three weeks after my return to Michigan I went to Hamtramck to visit Jim Barna's mother. Barna and I had made a mutual promise to make such a trip if only one of us returned. Of all the things I was unprepared for, this turned out to be perhaps the biggest shock of all.

Barna's mother had known of Jim's death for several months. That is, she had been informed of it. Accepting it as fact was another matter. She lived in a run-down house on a run-down street and was in very poor health. Her greatly swollen feet supported a body that was far too heavy.

Mrs. Barna was bowing her head at a faster rate than the movement of the rocker in which she sat. Tears streamed down her face and the face of Barna's 15- or 16-year-old cousin who was attending her aunt. I told them how I had known Jim and some of what we went through together. Then I told them how he had died—executed after being caught stealing from the Japanese in Luguna Province. She asked no questions, but quietly repeated, "No," over and over again from deep in her chest. When I ran out of things to say, I rose and went to the door, followed by the girl, who asked in a low voice: "Why did you take that from her?" I was thankful, as I left, that I had been unable to find Ditt's family in Chicago.

It was another wartime friend who chanced back into my life

and, indirectly but profoundly, changed it. Maybe things would have turned out all right if Hez Bussey hadn't come along. I might have gone to Big Rapids, collected a degree and gone on to some kind of success, but that is questionable. And I would not have met Sue Motsenbocker, who was to become my wife, lifetime friend, mother of my children and companion through decades haunted by events I never revealed to her.

Hez Bussey was a handsome, brilliant, furious half-Cherokee from Oklahoma. He was an Army soldier when I met him soon after leaving Kanaoka Hospital for Chikko Camp. Even reduced to 130 pounds, you could see the potential athleticism on his six-foot frame. The potential would never be tested, because malnutrition had done permanent damage to the receptors in both of his eyes, leaving him with only peripheral vision. He would constantly battle to see by averting his gaze, and you could tell he was partially blind.

The call came from the Connecticut School for the Blind one afternoon, just after I had returned from my scouting trip to Big Rapids. Would I be interested in picking up the blind soldier, taking him to Norman, Oklahoma, and enrolling him in the university there? They would pay expenses. I accepted immediately and received the written agreement a few days later.

On April 1, 1946, I had been paid out of the service with $1,700. At Great Lakes, another prisoner I had known in Japan was paid out with an almost identical amount. He headed straight for a jewelry store and bought a $1,700 wristwatch—then borrowed money from me to get home to Marquette, Wisconsin. He had traded three years in a prison camp for a watch with a gold face and three slivers of emerald set into it. I couldn't believe it. Much later, I would realize that my fellow POW's flippant purchase demonstrated a confidence in the future, and his place in it, that I did not possess.

What I did with my $1,700 one fine day was hide it over the glove box of the Lincoln Zephyr. My clothes were in the back seat. I drove into Detroit, then across the Ambassador Bridge to Windsor, Ontario, the only place where you travel south to Can-

ada from the United States. I was on my way to pick up Hez
Bussey. I was still "hanging out," this time on the road, but at
least I had a modest goal, one I thought I could handle. And I
could use the trip.

Two days later, after stops in London and Hamilton, I found
myself on the Canadian side of Niagara Falls. There were few
visitors, some families but mostly couples, young and old. I was
the only visitor who was alone.

At the border, customs officers stopped me, gave the car a
good going-over and questioned me closely. The officers marveled over the Zephyr's 12-cylinder flathead engine, inquired
about the school for the blind and advised me to visit the Finger
Lakes. I stayed that night in Seneca Falls in a cubbyhole under
a staircase that was used all night by vacationers and students
from nearby colleges.

About 12:30 a girl of college age wandered into the little room,
expecting to find someone else. She talked in a torrent for five
or 10 minutes, sitting barely on the edge of the bed while I
searched for words. She got up suddenly, banging her head
lightly on the stairs, leaned over, patted me on the head, and
left. I felt like a child.

In Rome, New York, I tried to call an Army Air Corps flight
attendant who had talked to me for much of the trip from Oak
Knoll to St. Albans. I had been able to talk more easily with her
than anyone else since my return to the States. Her sister answered. Betty Raul was in Japan.

Outside Rome, I picked up two college girls hitchhiking. Both
had just completed a summer session at Cornell. They talked
endlessly about books they had read, making me feel increasingly stupid with each title and author I did not recognize. I told
them I had been overseas for six years, and there weren't many
books there. I left them off at Kingston and headed east into
Connecticut, not much bolstered in my sense of social or literary
prowess. Late that afternoon I arrived at the school for the blind
at Avon, west of Hartford.

A little girl named Sullivan, a kitchen worker filling in at the school office, did not stand on ceremony when I walked in and identified myself. She took me in tow, and we went off in search of Hez Bussey.

Hez recognized me with his averted vision when I was within six or eight feet. He was clearly the center of attention in a knot of blind students. I was introduced around to totally and partially blind service personnel who were learning to cope with their condition. Hez had that day received a braille pocket watch from the school and a letter of encouragement from Helen Keller.

The school put me up for the night, which was easy because it was between semesters. A local college was hosting a dance for the blind students, and we went. Volunteers from Hez's school were there, some of them with their daughters. So was the Sullivan girl. One of the mothers, whose daughter Judy was with her, had taken special note of my Army friend, who besides his charisma had an IQ in the top percentile and a stout refusal to be limited by his handicap.

Hez was scheduled to leave on Monday, giving us the opportunity to accept an invitation to spend the weekend with Judy's family in Waterbury. We drove down early the next afternoon. Judy was a student at Middlebury College. She paired with Hez. Judy called a friend of hers, Justine, a beautiful girl of French extraction who was a junior at the University of Connecticut. It was a perfect weekend.

We picnicked, toured a factory owned by Judy's father, and went to dinner and danced both evenings. Judy and Justine were refined, almost elegant, without being prudish. The ex-marine from Michigan and the Indian from Oklahoma felt in the presence of royalty.

Late on Sunday night, I took Justine to her door and searched for words that would show my appreciation for her company. Instead I mumbled and shrugged and shook her hand and hurried to the car as she held up a hand to her mouth while she closed the door. It was a long trip back to Avon Monday morning.

The Zephyr then headed westward through country I had never seen and Hez never would, except in whatever recognizable flashes his eyes allowed. We followed the valleys of the Appalachians through Pennsylvania and into West Virginia, through Kentucky and into Arkansas and on to northeastern Oklahoma. We visited Hez's relatives there, then made a dash for our objective, Norman and the university.

I found the Veteran's Administration office and the VA representative who had been notified that Hez was on his way. I found out what would be required, and learned we were about a week early.

We knocked around for the week, Hez spending much of his time with the son of a woman family friend he had known before the war, and with an older graduate student who was a distant relative. I played several rounds of golf with rented clubs on the sun-baked college course and spent considerable time on the campus.

Enrollment was opened in the middle of August, and I was staying to see that my friend was settled in before heading back to Michigan. The mileage and per diem allowed by the Connecticut school were more than enough to cover expenses. We had an appointment early on a Monday morning with a professor named Couch, dean of the University College and acting dean of admissions. Within 15 minutes, he had both of us enrolling and me signing up to be Hez's reader. By noon, we were moving into Cleveland House, a dormitory. The Zephyr sported a rare on-campus parking sticker.

The next day I was interviewed by language department professors and given credit for Spanish 1 and 2 and Italian 1— I had 15 units toward graduation before attending a class. Hez and I took most of the basic courses together, which was like me getting paid for studying.

My father had finished only grade school and my mother had left school after the 10th grade. For me, the university was a new world. Two of my English professors were members of the Royal Academy; my philosophy professor was highly published and he read papers at symposia all over the world; my geology professor was a distinguished scholar from Switzerland; my language professors were from Peru and Italy; I read Greek and

Latin in translation under professors who between them could speak most of the languages of Europe and the Middle East. Best of all, and to my surprise, I found that I could reason along with them and, later, contribute something to an advanced class or seminar. But mostly I sat in the back and kept quiet.

I had some advantages. I was considerably older than most, although a good number of returning veterans were enrolled. I was still not strong and had digestive problems, but that only helped keep me out of action and near my books. I was strongly motivated by my doubts that I was of college caliber. I had an obsession with making up for lost time. I had a childhood background of reading and a love of books, something not unusual for poor and even uneducated people of the time—an advantage now lost to television and paid for by society with unending remediation programs. And for two years, I had a duty to read for Hez.

I did not enter the university with a clear objective of becoming a writer, but it was always in the back of my mind. Before long, I realized that literary criticism was my major interest. I was never able to put my own writing to a test in a novel or scholarly work, other than a master's thesis, but I developed a considerable ability to identify and apply the criteria upon which other persons' work could be analyzed or evaluated. This proved highly useful at the university and later in industry. I learned to think in my first class in literary criticism—that what is asserted must be considered fully and unemotionally, must be based upon all available information, and must be well-reasoned. I looked first to the premises, then to the logic. It gave me confidence in scholarly argument, and even in the give-and-take of a high-pressure industry.

Just before Thanksgiving 1946, I took a bus to Shawnee, Oklahoma, to spend the holiday with Hez and his family. The bus was crowded with students on their way home for the holiday. One was Sue Motsenbocker, a girl with the softest voice I had ever heard. Before long, I was going to a little town near Shawnee to see Sue and her parents rather than to see Hez's family in Shawnee. We would be married on the day after

Christmas a year later. By 1951 we would be the parents of two little girls.

Meanwhile, by taking heavy class schedules, I earned a bachelor's degree in 2½ years and was admitted to a doctoral program. By now I had designs on making an audacious transition: from raggedy-assed marine, to confused civilian with no education, to college English professor. About halfway through the classwork for a Ph.D, I took a position as instructor in an English course tailored for service personnel. This would be the first step, a traditional one for language and literature scholars aiming for a professor's chair. My hopes were high, but not for long.

The instructorship was painful to an incredible degree. The university experience had opened my mind, honed it and made me ready for some kind of achievement. But here I was teaching a relatively simple class—and finding myself easily confused, uncertain of things I knew perfectly well, disorganized in handling homework and tests. I stuck with it for 11 months. It was a major disappointment and required a complete shift of direction.

Early in 1951 I resigned the instructorship, withdrew from a class I was enrolled in, submitted what was to have been my dissertation as a master's thesis and stood for the oral examination. Then Sue and I loaded everything into a rented trailer, hooked it to a 1940 Dodge and headed for Los Angeles, avoiding the snow on Route 66 by taking the southern route through El Paso and Phoenix. Looking in the rear-view mirror with the wisdom of retrospect, I can see a long shadow cast by events in the Pacific.

18

The Silence Begins

Each of us who survived brought home his own unique shadow, but there are patterns. Alcoholism was common. I suspect wife and child abuse, physical and mental, was also common, though it has not been studied, to my knowledge. Young men who left home with a swagger came back with an excruciating tentativeness; living without confidence of seeing another day had left them with little confidence for building a new life. Suicide—which, oddly, was rare while men were struggling to stay alive (no, I never once considered it)—was all too common once the prisoners returned to civilization. A panoply of physical symptoms, many a result of nutrition deficiencies, have been lasting wounds for thousands. And the vast majority of us used—and still use—silence as a salve to avoid sharp, specific, vivid, chronic, memory-born pain—not the *memory* of pain, but *pain* whose stimuli were stored permanently, subject to involuntary recall.

In Oklahoma, early in my own four decades of silence, I told Sue I had been a prisoner. In marriage, I thought, the whole story would come out. Incredibly, it did not. Even with life's partner I could not talk about the experience. The certainty of pain—one of the few things I was certain of—blocked the words, and they were not spoken. Chikko and Cabanatuan and the Inferno in the hold of a Japanese cargo ship would remain unknown to her, and to our children.

I intended to write, and specifically I intended to write about the war. I was engrossed in my studies and my academic career, and that was a serious impediment. But already it was becoming clear that, even in the privacy of a writer's cocoon, expressing what I had seen was inextricably linked to pain and hurt. Until this manuscript I did not write a word about the Philippines or about Japan—ignoring more raw material than any aspiring writer could imagine.

For two years I spent hours almost every day reading for Hez Bussey, a man who had been there with me, who would not have needed a reader if the Japanese had not starved him blind. I never once talked about the war with Hez. And he never once talked about it with me.

Hez, with whom I spent more time than anyone but my wife, was disappearing into that rear-view mirror. I did not stay in touch with him. Insularity went hand in glove with silence. Hez—with his charisma and indomitable will—went on to be a successful, politically active lawyer. I heard that he became a justice on the Oklahoma criminal court of appeals. Many who applauded his achievement had no idea just how great it was.

Down the road I would retain no links with any of the faculty or students. Somewhere unused in my belongings were all those names and addresses I had gathered in Japan as the war came to its nominal end. I exchanged letters for a short time with the two Englishmen I was with in the Japanese military hospital and the Aussie who had been "executed" by the Japanese.

A lifetime pattern of silence on the single most formative experience of my life, and a reluctance to forge lasting friendships, had emerged. I was "aloof," as I heard more than once. It was true. What my colleagues did not know was that the aloofness, like the silence, helped keep the past at bay. I was not denying it; I was controlling it. It was an exercise of will, the same will that carried me through the Philippines and Japan.

My master's thesis was accepted. I suppose it might still be on file in some musty alcove in Norman, Oklahoma. It is titled: "The Problem of Isolation in the Works of Eugene O'Neill."

I know there is value for me in putting these words on paper;

I hope there is some value for others. The story of POWs in general, and those of Bataan and Corregidor in particular, has been told neither often enough nor well enough. But as important as it is to me to tell the story, it is important that the tale not be perceived as a whine. That it is not meant to be. I paid what some would see as an inordinate price for life and freedom. But freedom is not free, and many paid a far greater price.

We are organic creatures, beginning as colorless things and taking on the marks of experience in our personalities and our characters. If it had not been for the war, I would be a far different person today. Much that is positive has derived from the experience. I feel I almost certainly would have been somewhat more "successful," by standard measures, had I not gone to war. But I also feel I would have been somewhat more shallow and lacking in dimension. I don't think I would have liked myself very much. And I don't think I would have accomplished much that is now important to me.

Difficulties notwithstanding, the war and the prison camps were intensely interesting. I was alive then in a sense I had not known before. I have found little growth when life was easy. No matter how narrow the civilian lives of ex-POWs I have encountered, they often have reflected a depth and a wisdom that is not typical of persons who have lived more placid lives. Survival is in itself a success, but survival to which one has contributed is a matter of great satisfaction, not as a practical thing to be applied to a career path, but as a matter of integrity in which one sees himself as having fulfilled a potential for which he was destined by nature and spirit. It is a good feeling.

Put another way: As absurd as it is to suggest than anyone would choose to undergo the horrors of the Japanese camps, the experience became a measure for judging life afterward—and few having such a measure would easily give it up. In a way, we are a privileged few. We know what hunger really is. We know cold. We know fatigue, we know illness, brutality, slavery, insipid monotony. Values were established that are not easily relinquished. Where before it was goals that were important, now it is the path to the goal or even the path to nowhere. It is the living that becomes important, not the attaining. There was more pleasure to the POW in Japan in a hot cup of green tea or a sheltered spot in the winter sun than there is to the affluent in many of the fruits of his affluent society. We can be slaves to more than a military enemy. I suspect many ex-prisoners have learned that lesson. Wants, no matter how urgent, do not always have to be satisfied.

My war included no heroics in battle. And self-doubt is inevitable in the aftermath of a Fort Hughes. Within the tortuously circumscribed possibilities of the Japanese camps, however, I made my own little assaults. The garden I planted in Cabanatuan's Camp 3, for example, might seem meaningless. It was not. In Japan, testing the honshos' limits proved there was more than a faint pulse in the living dead. And finding a soft spot in the slavemaster's culture—fear of his superiors—was a successful probing action. We had few weapons, and they were puny. But many of us deployed them.

My childhood and youth helped prepare me for the war years. The university ultimately gave form, structure, understanding and perspective to the experience. Contrary to what I expected, it did not come from psychology courses—which tended to cast me in the role of victim rather than as the agent of my own survival. It came first in courses that taught me how to think, and then in courses that were food for thought. But it was the war that was the major formative event in my life and the foundation upon which the remainder of my life was to be laid. The war remains the source I look to almost exclusively for lessons on which to make decisions and base judgments.

I fled Oklahoma, then, trailed by a long shadow from across the Pacific. By revealing that long shadow here as best I can, perhaps I can help make the shadows shorter for future POWs. Knowledge and understanding beget positive action. Few understand just how far the shadows can reach.

I know there is value for me in putting these words on paper; I hope there is some value for others. The story of POWs in general, and those of Bataan and Corregidor in particular, has been told neither often enough nor well enough. But as important as it is to me to tell the story, it is important that the tale not be perceived as a whine. That it is not meant to be. I paid what some would see as an inordinate price for life and freedom. But freedom is not free, and many paid a far greater price.

We are organic creatures, beginning as colorless things and taking on the marks of experience in our personalities and our characters. If it had not been for the war, I would be a far different person today. Much that is positive has derived from the experience. I feel I almost certainly would have been somewhat more "successful," by standard measures, had I not gone to war. But I also feel I would have been somewhat more shallow and lacking in dimension. I don't think I would have liked myself very much. And I don't think I would have accomplished much that is now important to me.

Difficulties notwithstanding, the war and the prison camps were intensely interesting. I was alive then in a sense I had not known before. I have found little growth when life was easy. No matter how narrow the civilian lives of ex-POWs I have encountered, they often have reflected a depth and a wisdom that is not typical of persons who have lived more placid lives. Survival is in itself a success, but survival to which one has contributed is a matter of great satisfaction, not as a practical thing to be applied to a career path, but as a matter of integrity in which one sees himself as having fulfilled a potential for which he was destined by nature and spirit. It is a good feeling.

Put another way: As absurd as it is to suggest than anyone would choose to undergo the horrors of the Japanese camps, the experience became a measure for judging life afterward—and few having such a measure would easily give it up. In a way, we are a privileged few. We know what hunger really is. We know cold. We know fatigue, we know illness, brutality, slavery, insipid monotony. Values were established that are not easily relinquished. Where before it was goals that were important, now it is the path to the goal or even the path to nowhere. It is the living that becomes important, not the attaining. There was more pleasure to the POW in Japan in a hot cup of green tea or a sheltered spot in the winter sun than there is to the affluent in many of the fruits of his affluent society. We can be slaves to more than a military enemy. I suspect many ex-prisoners have learned that lesson. Wants, no matter how urgent, do not always have to be satisfied.

My war included no heroics in battle. And self-doubt is inevitable in the aftermath of a Fort Hughes. Within the tortuously circumscribed possibilities of the Japanese camps, however, I made my own little assaults. The garden I planted in Cabanatuan's Camp 3, for example, might seem meaningless. It was not. In Japan, testing the honshos' limits proved there was more than a faint pulse in the living dead. And finding a soft spot in the slavemaster's culture—fear of his superiors—was a successful probing action. We had few weapons, and they were puny. But many of us deployed them.

My childhood and youth helped prepare me for the war years. The university ultimately gave form, structure, understanding and perspective to the experience. Contrary to what I expected, it did not come from psychology courses—which tended to cast me in the role of victim rather than as the agent of my own survival. It came first in courses that taught me how to think, and then in courses that were food for thought. But it was the war that was the major formative event in my life and the foundation upon which the remainder of my life was to be laid. The war remains the source I look to almost exclusively for lessons on which to make decisions and base judgments.

I fled Oklahoma, then, trailed by a long shadow from across the Pacific. By revealing that long shadow here as best I can, perhaps I can help make the shadows shorter for future POWs. Knowledge and understanding beget positive action. Few understand just how far the shadows can reach.

19

Finding a Niche

What awaited in Los Angeles was a good place to hide. My brother-in-law was an executive with Phillips Petroleum Co.'s construction division, and he found me a job chasing parts in a pump factory. It was well-suited to my emotional capability.

I had begun taking Librium in 1948 on the prescription of a psychiatrist. It got me over some rough edges of anxiety, and I used it only on occasion. For long periods, however, I felt exceedingly threatened by people behind me, close in front of me, or in authority over me. I had an overwhelming urge to strike out when confronted or cornered. Cars following close behind caused the hair on my neck to bristle. I became panicky at the slightest hint of entrapment. Even clothing that was tight around the neck raised fears—and I recalled how grateful I had been to be issued loose-fitting sailor's clothes for the trip home from Japan. I often awoke from dreams in desperation. If I heard of someone trapped in a well or cave-in, it bothered me for days or weeks. It still does.

Whenever possible I had arrived early for classes so I could get the seat I wanted. Frequently I had a pain in my chest when subjected to stress and many times fought the urge to run from a stressful or crisis situation. I could handle intellectual discussion without too much of a problem, but when the discussion was emotional, my instinct sometimes said "fight" or "run." I ran from my family in Michigan. I ran from a teaching career.

But after four years in the pump factory, moving up twice into management jobs, I had a chance to run *to* something for the first time.

It was a job offer that would change my life, an environment where at last I could find some success as a civilian, and make use of my education. The Rocketdyne division of North American Aviation needed a writer and editor in a department that prepared major management reports and technical manuals. Recipients of these documents were dissatisfied with what they were getting. The corporate office needed information to make proper management decisions and to communicate with the board of directors and stockholders. Internal management needed to know what was going on without being drowned in paperwork. Manuals and handbooks had to be written. Change was so rapid that no one really knew what was needed; everyone felt he was flying partially blind.

The early '50s were a time of immense urgency nationally and worldwide in the aerospace community. The Soviet Union had captured a large number of Germany's rocket scientists and technicians. The United States had landed some of the most valuable German personnel, and a great store of information on the V-2 rocket and its engine. Much of what the U.S. got was through the efforts and foresight of Deiter Huzel, a German engineer who, on the collapse of the Reich, loaded engines and documentation onto trucks and headed west from Peenemunde—away from the advancing Russians and toward the advancing Americans. Keeping the convoy out of Russian hands was touch and go. I learned the details from Huzel, now an American citizen, when eventually he asked me to critique the manuscript of his book, *Peenemunde to Canaveral.*

Before I arrived, Rocketdyne had, based upon the V-2, built a rocket engine with twice the thrust and half the weight. It was a stunning accomplishment and put the United States ahead in what was to become a magnificent competition. In work or on the drawing boards were engines for the Navaho, Jupiter, Thor and Atlas missiles and several experimental engines. The Thor and Jupiter and later the Atlas engines have powered the lion's share of America's early satellites and all of the U.S. manned vehicle launches.

This might not have been the kind of writing I originally had in mind. But it was heady stuff in which to find a niche after a disturbing and disappointing post-war decade. And, as it turned out, it was an environment for solid writing that could produce tangible results. I would never write a best-seller. On the other hand, no novelist or historical writer ever helped bring a multi-million-dollar project into space on time and successfully.

In these early rocket programs, success did not come easily. Nearly every test involved new or modified hardware and was an attempt to advance the state of the art. Failure preceded success by months or even years. The major topic of discussion in Rocketdyne's weekly chief engineering meeting, which I attended, was not to announce success but to explain failure. When the Thor engine finally achieved full thrust and full duration, Bob Morin, the program manager, said dryly: "After a series of random failures, a random success."

I set up a news bulletin communication system soon after arriving at Rocketdyne. All engineering managers were required to report major milestones or major problems or failures as soon as they happened. I reviewed them and distributed the information by written message or by phone to those who had a need to know. I also distributed a weekly engineering report, and I inherited the responsibility for various reports to our corporate offices. Later I wrote reports that justified division budgets, reports for government and corporate monitoring agencies, and a book entitled *An Introduction to Rocket Missile Propulsion* for the training and public relations departments.

Technology gave way almost daily to new technology. New materials were developed for applications never known to man. New instrumentations, controls and test devices were developed to handle pressures, flows and switching at temperatures of hundreds of degrees below zero and thousands of degrees above. The contrast with what I could have imagined during the war years was inconceivable. That I would be involved was even more inconceivable.

By 1960, confidence was high. Scientific and technical objectives within the company were being met and exceeded. Skeptics in solid-propellant circles, who pointed to the tens of thousands of parts and components in a liquid rocket engine, from the lowest levels in industry to their strongest proponents in Congress, were silenced by our success and the specific impulse available in liquids. New research projects were undertaken to support the initial deep space flight conceptual studies and nuclear weapon applications. It was four years that changed the world. For the first time, man could fight a war halfway around the world without going there.

It was exciting. I was contributing. I lost myself in the significance of the moment. Things went well. Nonetheless, the long shadow loomed.

I had bought an old one-bedroom house near Rocketdyne in the San Fernando Valley. It had huge and numerous trees on an acre of land completely surrounded by a six-foot chainlink fence. With a hammer and a carpentry book, I soon added three bedrooms. It was an oasis. We had three children when we moved to the acre, with its climbing trees, its tree house, its orange, lemon, grapefruit, loquat, apricot, persimmon, pomegranate and shade trees, over a hundred in all. While there we added four children, a goat, several dogs and cats and a handful of chickens that roosted in lower branches. It had a large circular driveway and a large parking area that yielded to basketball and tetherball. It was the best place I ever lived.

Neighboring houses could scarcely be seen and neighbors and traffic were seldom heard. We became an insular family. We belonged to a church but limited our involvement to attendance at religious services. In all the time we lived there, some eight years, we probably did not entertain more than a dozen times, almost always something involving our children. We rarely accepted invitations to attend school, church or acquaintances' social functions. We dropped our children off at their friends' homes, or their parents did the same at ours. We said hello and goodbye at the gate.

Neither during the four years at the pump company nor the

four I spent at Rocketdyne did I hear from or about any other prisoners of war. At neither job did I tell anyone of my war background. I never made a conscious effort to recall the experience, but there never was a day that I did not encounter numerous reminders. Cripples, burn victims and pictures of emaciated people brought back the old days. There were many other triggers, most so subtle I scarcely recognized them as sources for the intruding thoughts.

I set up barriers against them, but they constantly got through, leaving me distant and depressed. It inevitably had an effect upon my family, who did not associate my moods with the war. Time does not heal all wounds; it buries them in very shallow graves.

20

An Island in the Hills

As often as the dark side of the past intruded on the present, I continued to function with my share of success as a communicator in the fascinating world of aerospace. In a 26-year career, I fulfilled scores of assignments that typically involved scouting out a communications problem, defining who would benefit most from being linked to which information, and determining how best to get the data to them in a timely fashion.

Unlike the machine-gun positions I set up on Caballo, these efforts were tested under fire. The vast majority of them produced good results. I like to think my carefully thought-out gun positions would have produced good results, too. The initiative and practical analysis I was able to muster as an uneducated 20-year-old might have foretold an affinity for the kind of tasks I tackled for Rocketdyne and, later, for North American's Space Division and for McDonnell-Douglas. Likewise, my wartime experience with leadership—my own and that of others—foretold the downside of my aerospace days.

When my hastily assembled squad of men abandoned the Old Wall at Cavite, leaving just Jim Barna to fire a futile shot at enemy planes and me to ponder the powder keg below us, I acquired a lifelong skepticism of my qualities as a leader. When Lieutenant Leone played cards while a corporal planned and executed the Caballo beach defense, it left a bad taste in my mouth for line responsibility. My comfort zone with those in authority over me was not helped by the fact that our tiny piece of the Philippines action was part of a major disaster precipitated by some of the worst generalship in American military history. Neither is the picture enhanced by the obsequiousness, incompetence and limp spirit of our putative leaders in prison camp. By the time I found my niche in industry, I found I could fly high as long as I had firm backing and a free hand. Other chemistries were a problem.

One of my final assignments at Rocketdyne was of the good-chemistry variety, and showed how well it could work. We had a problem in measuring the specific impulse ("bounce per ounce of fuel") of the sustainer engine for the Atlas missile. The customer was getting a different reading on the test range than we were on our Neosho, Missouri, test stands. Someone had failed to react to a customer memo on the subject, and the customer came back at us through the corporate office. After sitting in on a heated two-hour finger-pointing session, I stopped by the chief engineer's office and said I'd like to discuss a way of preventing any more non-responsiveness on our part. Without discussion, he said: "Do it."

From then on, I pulled all major problem items out of the communication system and the engineering meetings and made them agenda items for the weekly engineering meeting. Each agenda item named the person responsible for action, and the scheduled resolution date. I worked with Mitch Henry, senior engineering staff member, in determining responsibility and schedule. Then I called the responsible parties as schedules approached. It worked almost to perfection.

One day, Mitch Henry came to me and said he had been offered a vice-presidency of the space division at Downey, California, where production of the F-100 was just winding down and the Hound Dog missile was in the flight-test phase. The Hound Dog was a nuclear-warhead weapon launched from a B-52. Its mission was to penetrate enemy territory at very low levels by means of celestial navigation and an innovative terrain-clearance capability, a cruise missile decades ahead of its first use in war. The space division also had a number of research contracts, including one concerned with aerodynamic heating and re-entry that proved to be one of the most scientifically and technically productive contracts the division ever had. It qualified them to build the Apollo manned space module that would take a man to the moon.

Mitch wanted me to come with him and design a complete management information system for Harrison Storms, the space division chief, whose resume included development of the highly successful X-15 experimental rocket plane that set record after record for altitude and speed at the fringes of space.

It was a difficult decision. I had reduced the anxiety I experienced at Rocketdyne to a manageable levels and rarely took tranquilizers my last two years there. I had strong professional relationships that did not intrude on my private life, and I was reluctant to give them up. But in 1961, I accepted the position I had been offered, bought several new suits and began commuting 25 miles across Los Angeles.

Still more heady times awaited in my new environment. We won the contract for the second stage of the Saturn C-5 launch vehicle, and NASA chose us over McDonnell Co.—which had produced the Mercury and Gemini space systems—to produce the Apollo command module. In less than three years, our work force grew from 5,500 to 31,000. The programs were exciting. The pace was fast. The work went well. I soon had a management information and communication system in place that was an improvement over that of Rocketdyne's by the addition of an executive chart room and closed-circuit television.

After several years of commuting, Sue and I bought a home 20 miles east of the space division and rented out the old home I was so fond of, with its many trees and chainlink fence. It was in this new home against the Chino Hills in a rural area noted for its avocado groves that our last two boys were born, our eighth and ninth children. It was a fine large tri-level house on one-third of an acre with a grapestake fence on a cul-de-sac with good separation between homes. I thought I was ready to undertake the conventional suburban life, but that was not the case. Since entering the industrial world, I had not yet invited any of my colleagues to a social evening in my home, nor had we accepted invitations to be entertained in the homes of others. This had been the case for more than 12 years. In another 20, the situation would not change.

The main reason I stayed in staff positions was the buffer it placed between myself and any substantial opposition, which I frequently misinterpreted. Mitch Henry was exactly what I needed in this regard. If I felt something needed doing in my area of responsibility or expertise, I presented the idea to Mitch, who either approved it or ran interference. He knew me pretty well. When he transferred to another job, things were never quite the same.

One sequence of events at North American shows that when you are involved in something as innovative and exciting as man's early ventures into space, the lows can be as gut-wrenching as the highs are exhilarating.

We all had seen astronauts Grissom, White and Chaffey many times, and we felt we were part of the same Apollo team. When all three died in the Apollo 204 launchpad fire at Cape Canaveral, it was an even more emotional blow for us than it was for the country at large. We had recommended an outward-opening hatch, and had been turned down. We had requested permission to test the command module in a pure oxygen atmosphere, and had been turned down on that, too. We had warned about taking untested materials into a pure oxygen environment, to no avail. Materials that will not sustain combustion at normal oxygen concentrations burn almost explosively in pure oxygen—and that is what happened to Apollo 204. Success has a thousand fathers; failure is a bastard. Responsibility for the incident was studied into obscurity.

In the wake of the tragedy, division vice-president Sherm Ellis appointed me as interface with our legal representative in New York. I was to develop whatever information I could that would free the division of responsibility and was to respond without reservation to any requests from our legal staff or the corporate legal staff. I had about 20 persons available, mostly from a department involved in long-range planning, which had a superior research capability.

For a month we developed data that showed the testing that had been done in the Mercury and Gemini programs and the studies that had a bearing on the Apollo 204 disaster. Looking back on it, it was an exercise in futility. No contractor ever implicates the source of its future programs.

One day Sherm asked to see all of the files. I showed them to him, and he asked me to take everything into his office. When we got there, he said: "We've agreed to compensate the astronauts' families." He had me gather up all data and stop any work that was under way. He closed the account to which we were charging the work. It was the last job I ever did for a rare man who was a superior industry executive.

In 1969, I moved on to Douglas Aircraft Co. There was a 20 percent raise—and a management system that exhibited major deficiencies. My buffer was to be the executive who hired me. He was fired six weeks after I started work.

Aside from that little setback, I was handicapped by a lack of knowledge about the company, its people, its politics and its systems. I began to put excessive work into assignments to reduce the possibility of error. Where at North American I had been assertive, at Douglas I began to be defensive. I was becoming weary of the battle. The old pressure in the chest returned with greater frequency. I began to take Librium again as the feeling of being trapped increased in intensity both on the job and in private life.

Nonetheless, I sustained a 12-year career at Douglas that included some major assignments—among them development of a quality assurance program in the wake of the DC-10 crash at Orly, France; a series of security manuals, and a manual for first-line production supervision. Douglas was good *to* me, but with its closed-shop management system it was not good *for* me. The world had begun closing in soon after I arrived at the Douglas plant in Long Beach.

Several years before I finally left the aerospace industry in

1981, it became clear that my days in it were numbered. It was becoming increasingly difficult to maintain a train of thought. Resentments rose in numbers and magnitude. Intrusive thoughts, no longer exclusively related to the war, were a constant annoyance and sometimes a serious obstacle to my work. It was time to prepare for the day when I could no longer perform to the standards of the company.

Away from the job, Southern California was an adventureland to me. Surrounded by ocean, mountains and desert, little imagination was required to fill a day, a weekend, or a vacation with the stuff of which memories are made.

At North American I joined an astronomy group and later became its president. Our workshop had equipment on which we made several hundred telescope mirrors and optical flats. One mirror had a 32-inch diameter. Few satisfactions in life equal taking a raw piece of glass, grinding and polishing it to a perfect spherical surface, then deepening it a few millionths of an inch to a parabola, installing it in a tube, and first focusing a field of stars to pinpoints of light.

We had world-class lecturers. But the field trips were the high point. Palomar was 100 miles south. Mt. Pinos, at just under 9,000 feet, was 100 miles to the north. Within 100 miles were Mt. Wilson Observatory, the Smithsonian at Wrightwood, the site of speed-of-light experiments at Idyllwild on Mt. San Jacinto, excellent viewing sites on Mt. San Gogonio and unsurpassed viewing sites on both the high and low deserts to the northeast and east of Los Angeles. We used them all.

Our family outings were even more enjoyable than the excursions with the club. The private trips allowed us to combine our astronomy interests with the exploration of Southern California's deserts and mountains.

One trip took us to Mt. Whitney, where we drove to the parking lot at 8,000 feet late one afternoon. The next morning we set out to climb as high as we could. The family stopped at the base of the switchbacks at 10,000 or 11,000 feet. I decided I would try to make the summit. About halfway up the switchbacks, possibly at 12,500 feet, unable to get my pulse under 180 a minute, lightheaded but not too much so, I started back, resting every few hundred feet and looking to the east across the White Mountain and Panamint ranges to Death Valley. I arrived back at camp after dark, having been "rescued" by a 73-year-old, 100-pound backpacker who did the John Muir Trail from Yosemite to Mt. Whitney every year. His wife was waiting at a spot they had agreed to several weeks before.

We may have been an insular family, but we were hardly an immobile one. Sometimes we went north along the coast past Santa Barbara as far as Pismo Beach, then back through the San Joaquin Valley and up past Fort Tejon, where the camel corps route from Texas ended prior to the Civil War. Sometimes we roamed south past Tijuana and Ensenada, where Robert Louis Stevenson is said to have written *Treasure Island,* to the beaches of Baja California.

At other times we went as far as St. John's Indian School in Laveen, Arizona, to help with their annual fiesta which raised money to help with the education of Pima, Papago, Navaho, Hopi and Apache children and those of a dozen other tribes.

We made numerous trips up the Owens Valley past Mt. Whitney to Bishop, to Mammoth, to Virginia City, to Reno, to Pyramid Lake in northwest Nevada, over Tioga Pass into Yosemite Park.

Reviewing destinations in my mind's eye shocks memory with the number of interesting places we were able to visit from our Los Angeles cocoon: the low desert, the Salton Sea, the Colorado River, the backroads east of the San Bernardino range, the Grand Canyon and Barringer meteor crater in Arizona, the Carlsbad Caverns in New Mexico.

We had to rank among the highest-mileage families in America. It was fun, it was enlightening. If a full life could not be had by a travel-minded family in Southern California, it could not be had anywhere.

For Sue and the kids, the trips always included one exasperation that—unknown to them—stemmed from the short rice ra-

tions and grim uncertainties of the camps. I would always prepare for a day trip as if we were driving to Tierra del Fuego. I
still do.

Sue probably first noticed it back in Oklahoma, shortly after
the birth of our first child. I so loaded the car on a trip to visit
my parents that I had to pay double on a ferry. We never un-
packed the car top carrier. When our teenaged children made a
drive across the country, I made an itinerary for them that
charted their course day by day, point by point. On a 200-mile
drive, I take enough food and water to survive for several days,
and tools for emergencies. Uncertainty, uncertainty. (I still eat
rice, by the way, all the time. I love rice—possibly because at
one time I could never get enough of it.)

Several of our family forays took us into the great central
valley of California. It was sparsely populated and incredibly
productive, an island of calm in a stormy sea. A few years before
leaving Douglas, I began to realize that here I had found an
avenue of escape from the corporate world where I had func-
tioned and survived, but not prospered.

On one of these central valley trips, I investigated almond
orchards as an investment. And then, when a piece of family
property had matured, I looked for other property I could trade
it for to avoid immediate payment of capital gains taxes. By
chance, I found that piece of property 300 miles north of Los
Angeles, almost in the exact center of California. It was an almond ranch, owned by a gentleman of 86 who homesteaded the
property in 1920. It had not been profitable for more than a
decade, but it had excellent soil, good access and was flood-irri-
gated with water from the Sierras in the area of Yosemite. We
bought it having in mind a complete renovation of its 40 acres
of orchard and using it as a source of income for my retirement.

For several years I left for the farm late on Friday afternoons,
drove six hours, arrived around midnight, worked the orchard
all day Saturday and Sunday, and drove another six hours, arriving back in Southern California late Sunday evening. The
ranch probably extended my time in the work force by three or

four years. It was a complete change of pace and occupied most of my thoughts during the drive and while doing farmwork.

One thing you learn in the aerospace industry is to identify the experts and rely almost blindly on their advice and instruction. I put this practice to good use on the almond ranch. I soon found trades people I could rely on for the whole range of orchard requirements, following their advice without second-guessing.

We stripped the farm of its trees, my oldest son doing most of the chain-saw work; sold about 400 cords of wood; installed a first-class sprinkler system; planted three varieties of mutually pollinating trees, and established an orchard that, when mature, should produce about 60,000 pounds of highly nutritious, high-protein almonds a year.

Thirty years earlier, I had retreated from Michigan to Oklahoma, then to a secluded acre in the San Fernando Valley, then to a home against the Chino Hills. And now, just as on that foreboding night at Fort Hughes, I knew that this was where I would make my final stand. The house sat on a knoll overlooking the Merced River basin. The nearest neighbor was a half-mile away; the nearest town was a distance of 12 miles. There were several villages within three or four miles. The house and barns dated from the early '20s. It took 45 years, but I had gone full circle.

21

Pain and Progress

One evening on the farm in 1986, a Corregidor prisoner was interviewed on a local television news show I was watching. He had participated in a POW/MIA event at a VA hospital. It was an odd experience. Corregidor happened yesterday for those of us who were there. It is ancient, almost forgotten history for most. Television itself was merely a flickering concept when we were captured. Now here was one of my comrades being interviewed on a news show. After 45 years, another survivor was in my house for the first time, talking about the war.

A few weeks later I stood face to face at a church meeting with the man I saw on TV.

"Are you the one I saw who was a prisoner on Corregidor?"

"Yes."

He was Calvin Swanson. I took him aside and told him I had been there, too.

Cal told me that a group of ex-POWs met regularly at the VA hospital in Fresno. After four or five months, I ran out of excuses and agreed to attend a meeting with him. A sliver of confidence bred by several years on the farm, a nascent desire to confront the issue in the semi-open—I'm not sure what it was that motivated me. But I went. And I went again. And again. The group discussions were a litany of problems and hurts. I did not participate. Months went by—perhaps 10 months—and I did not say a word. No one pressed.

I learned much about POWs, their problems and their solutions. I learned, for one surprising example, that well more than half of my Philippines comrades at those meetings have been in the food industry in one form or another—and that several own California almond ranches. The idea of a non-perishable, highly nutritious crop—as close to certainty as exists in the agricultural crapshoot—became a magnet for those who had been processed through Bataan, Corregidor and Japan. Perhaps. I observed the others. I listened. I remained silent.

The Bataan/Corregidor prisoners were repatriated at a time when hundreds of thousands of servicemen were returning to the United States. We were lost among them. Serious mistakes were made in the medical-scientific bureaucracy. As a result, the full effect of the prisoner experience will never be known. A survey of the health of those who stayed in the service would have provided a reasonable basis for projecting health-care requirements by the VA. It was never done.

The long-term effects of pellagra, scurvy, beriberi, dysentery, colitis, malnutrition, cold, lack of emotional and intellectual stimulation and delayed or foregone social adaptation could have—and should have—been the grist for a number of medical research mills. The opportunities, however, were totally lost.

At a minimum, such studies would have indicated the incidence of medical problems in relation to those POWs who stayed in the service, the non-POW service population, and the general population. Because of this lack of information, each POW, without medical records, had to prove service connection for any lingering problem, which even after a few years was an impossible task. Perhaps we deserved better.

Many of us turned our backs on the military and the VA. I am one of many who declined for years to associate with other POWs. Some made the first steps toward coming in from the cold before me. Some are still out there.

Today, I am sure, our return would be different. We would probably be greeted by one social worker, one psychologist and one medical recordkeeper for every Navy cook plying us with steak and eggs and ice cream. Information would be taken, placed in computers, and then tracked and analyzed in every way that a relational database can function. That is progress.

The meetings I sat through in silence were conducted by a psychological social worker named Barbara Winslow. One evening she finally drew me aside and asked why I didn't speak. I told her it just hurt too much, and I couldn't.

This remarkable woman asked to see me privately, and for some reason I was able to talk with her. She found out I had been a writer, and she told me to put my story on paper.

"But I can't write about this and retain a train of thought," I said.

"Okay. Tape record it," she said.

And so it began, pain and progress.

I filled four tapes, an old corporal talking to himself and being bombarded by intrusive thoughts—as he had since 1945— and dodging some of them and grasping hold of others and making them the substance of his task.

Meanwhile, Barbara Winslow was transferred to a new job in another city. I sent the tapes to my brother Bill, the one who was born the year I ate bananas to make weight for the Marine Corps. Like my other siblings who emerged from the $600 house, humble beginnings did not deter him. He is a marketing executive, writer, editor, publisher and world traveler. Bill, for whom that camphor chest of China souvenirs was a childhood wonder, had been urging me for years to write my story—or that part of the story of the Philippines and Japan that had passed before my eyes.

He had the tapes transcribed. It was months before I could bring myself to read the pile of paper that came back to me. When I did, I found it embarrassing—disgusting, I thought. The pages were filled with acrimony, vitriol, emotion and far more commentary than fact about what I had seen. My disappointment was great.

"Just get the *story* down," Bill said. And I started over, not throwing the first version away but setting it well aside. I made it a practice to keep a notebook with me at all times, forging paragraphs and pages from memories and from the intrusive thoughts themselves as I cultivated, pruned, fertilized and groomed the orchard on tractor and on foot.

I learned years ago to avoid pain by controlling my memories, and, to some extent, the imaginings that were based upon them. When I found myself thinking thoughts that conflicted with my concept of charity or that produced discomfort—whether they were associated with the war or not—I managed by an act of will to redirect my thinking. Success was mixed. Memories prompting the most mean-spirited emotions were the most difficult to handle.

Now—writing down the events and emotions of war and imprisonment—I was not banishing these thoughts but exploring them fully. I sorted them out. Sometimes I had to abandon the task for weeks at a time, but I "got the story down." It took four painful years, from tapes to notebooks to this manuscript.

Writing of the book began with my attendance of meetings of the Fresno chapter of the American Ex-Prisoners of War, held at the Veterans Administration Hospital. Midway through the project, I joined the Disabled American Veterans. More recently I joined the American Defenders of Bataan and Corregidor. These are not, for me, places to tell war tales over a beer. I do not think yarn-spinning about the prison experience is likely for me. But the memberships are something that would not have been possible for me just a few years ago. I still do not converse about my own experience, though I finally have been able to comment briefly to my family about isolated incidents. I expect publication of this book will, of necessity, require an interview or two; they will be difficult but no longer impossible. In the final stages of the publishing process, my editor asked blunt questions that I might not have been able to handle in the past. I responded to them with difficulty at first but then with increasing facility and relief. He is the only one other than Barbara Winslow with whom I have been candid to date. The change holds much promise.

I look forward, after my children read these pages for the first time, to sitting down with them and answering questions they must have wanted to ask for many years. We have been a close family, and I hated to see them having to share my problems. I'm sure they found me cold and distant when they encountered a wall between us. I am proud of them and the strong marriages they have made. I hope they may read these pages and discover the roots of many confusing, unexplained characteristics. Perhaps they will gain insight into why their father has an obsessive concern for the cleanliness and availability of food, for example, and why he plans against so many uncertainties.

As for Sue, I hope she does not read these pages. It is late in the day, and she has seen enough of the long shadow. She does not need to see what cast it.

Perhaps some of my comrades in arms, American and Filipino, will read these pages. If so, I send you greetings; I am proud to have been one of you. Your stories deserve to be told; it is an injury to history that they have not been.

As for me, it is time for a rest. Then I will go on a bit farther, a raggedy-assed marine in a dwindling parade.

Unfinished Business

I never did report Leone or Saunders. I told the American occupation forces about the mysterious cache the Japanese officer made at war's end, and about the metal dumped into Lake Biwa. I answered the appropriate questions about mistreatment in the camps. But I never put any of our own on report.

Leone and Hagan were cogs in an entire military establishment that was not ready for the Japanese. Saunders and his ilk in the camps were frequently detestable, but with liberation came an urge—unrealistic, as it turned out—to truly put the entire experience behind me. What lay ahead in August 1945 was frightening enough to consume all thought. In 1991, however, it seems historically useful to petition for an accounting at a much higher level than I contemplated as a corporal on Caballo and at Notogawa.

The American and Philippine army units on Bataan did their jobs well. Malnourished, diseased, underequipped, victimized by a vacillating government at home and by a command in the islands that was more political in its planning than it was military, without hope of relief, having lost their air arm through folly and having lost their food and medical reserves through equal folly, with no hope of retreat to the island fortress they were protecting, 12,000 American service personnel and perhaps 55,000 Philippine Army scouts, regulars and reservists on Bataan fought a gallant fight to the limit of human endurance.

The fortified islands—Corregidor, Caballo, Fraile, Carabao—for an additional month absorbed one of the most intensive bombardments in the history of warfare before they, too, were forced to yield. It took the Japanese five months to open Manila Bay to their shipping—this at a time when the Imperial invaders were conquering other allied outposts in the Pacific almost at will.

Given the best of planning and execution with the resources available at the outset of the war, it is doubtful that the defense of Bataan and Corregidor could have lasted more than a year. It is pointless to debate what those seven extra months would have meant. History demands, however, a clear understanding of how the time—and the men—were lost.

The multiplicity of errors at Pearl Harbor have resulted in no less than nine congressional investigations. Even the historically ignorant are generally aware of our unpreparedness and inept defense there. By the time Corregidor was under siege four short but disastrous months later, what was desperately needed was not another litany of failures but a symbol of military prowess and valor—a hero. And the record shows that MacArthur received the Congressional Medal of Honor for his defense of the Philippines. The home front got its hero, and historical accuracy got a black eye.

Had MacArthur's economy in the expenditure of personnel in the offensive part of the American war in the Pacific not been in some measure his redemption, his loss of more than 100,000 troops in the Philippines might have marked him as the worst general in the history of U.S. warfare. As it was, because of factors including public and military morale and the shared guilt of the War Department, the cabinet and the president himself for failing to correctly assess the threat and either fortify the Philippines or withdraw vulnerable military units from them, the tragedy and humiliation were disguised as a sacrifice made necessary by a greater enemy in Europe.

MacArthur and the United States were extremely lucky that General Homma did not pursue our retreating forces into the Bataan Peninsula when he reached San Fernando in the Province of Pampanga late in December. Instead, Homma elected to take Manila, the symbol of the Philippines in Tokyo minds. If he had possessed the decision-making flexibility of any other country's field generals, there would have been no effective resistance on Bataan beyond the middle of January 1942, and essentially no defense of Corregidor. On such does the fate of armies and nations depend.

The fruits of MacArthur's public-relations campaign have endured for decades. History—and public perception, which was all-important to MacArthur—requires something better. Therefore, I have proposed that the American Defenders of Bataan and Corregidor Inc. take the first steps toward securing a congressional investigation into MacArthur's conduct as leader of the islands' defense. My proposal suggests several areas of inquiry, including:

● The extent of MacArthur's participation in the abandonment of War Plan Orange in favor of Rainbow Five.

● The reason that MacArthur delayed notifying Admiral King of Pearl Harbor's destruction.

● The reason that most of Clark Field's aircraft were destroyed without having taken to the air.

● The reason that the aircraft at Nichols Field were destroyed on the ground.

● The reason that MacArthur did not recall personnel, arms and supplies from Batangas, Ligazpe and Nueva Ecija provinces and Manila and direct them to Bataan and Corregidor immediately after the destruction of Clark and Nichols fields.

● The reason or reasons that MacArthur's estimates of enemy strength communicated to the War Department were so much greater than actual.

● The reason that MacArthur intimated in a communique that he had visited the Bataan front when he had not done so, and the reason or reasons that he failed to visit those troops.

● The reason that MacArthur did not separate Luzon and southern Philippines forces into separate commands to avoid the necessity of surrendering all forces when Corregidor was surrendered.

• The reason no military action was taken by MacArthur from the bombing of Pearl Harbor until he abandoned Rainbow Five shortly before Christmas 1941.

• The reason MacArthur did not battle-harden the 4th Marines prior to the fall of Bataan.

• The reason MacArthur denied the award of the Medal of Honor to General Jonathan Wainwright.

• The reason that after five years as field marshal of the Philippine Army, that army was not an effective fighting force.

• The extent to which the destruction of the Army Air Corps in the Philippines contributed to the early fall of Indochina, the Malay Peninsula and the Dutch East Indies.

Dispassionate and in-depth consideration of these issues is due my American and Filipino comrades. They endured much and fought well. Too many made the ultimate sacrifice. Only when the conduct of war which resulted in the premature fall of the Philippines is fully investigated and reported by a competent national, non-military authority will those who for long years questioned the perception of their value in the eyes of their countrymen rest secure in their service and their place in military history.

Acknowledgments

First, Tom Ferguson. Seldom at age 70 does one find a perfect partner. That happened to me when Tom Ferguson was assigned to edit this manuscript. To put into words the debt I owe him would take a writer of the talent of, well, Tom Ferguson. I thank all of those generous persons who have helped me complete this book. Especially I thank: Barbara Winslow, VA social psychologist, who knew me better than I knew myself; my brother Bill—editor, author and public relations and advertising executive—for his advice, confidence, encouragement and persuasion; Mark Haney, Bill's son, who so diligently converted scrawl into type on his word processor; Mary Lynn Wilkins, who converted my interminable tape cassettes into type; Sue White, Jonathan Haney and his wife, Patricia Weltjens Haney, for help in manuscript preparation; Leo and Patrice Fitzpatrick, for their friendship and encouragement; Christie Torres, for her encouragement and youthful wisdom; and my family, who endured the long silence in love, patience and understanding.